SELFHOOD

A Key to the Recovery of Emotional Wellbeing, Mental

Health and the Prevention of Mental Health Problems

or

A Psychology Self Help Book for Effective Living

and Handling Stress

Dr Terry Lynch

Mental Health Publishing

Published by Mental Health Publishing,
56 Culcranagh, Dooradoyle Road, Limerick, Ireland
353.61.319747
www.mentalhealthpublishing.com
info@mentalhealthpublishing.com

ISBN 978-1-908561-00-8

Distributed and printed by Lightning Source, UK and USA.

Lightning Source UK Ltd,
Chapter House, Pitfield, Kiln Farm,
Milton Keynes, MK11 3LW, United Kingdom.
enquiries@lightningsource.co.uk.
Tel +44 (0)845 121 4555 or +44 (0)1908 829525
Fax +44 (0)845 121 4594

Lightning Source Inc. (US),
1246 Heil Quaker Blvd., La Vergne, TN, USA 37086
inquiry@lightningsource.com
Tel (615) 213 -5815
Fax (615) 213-4725

Cover and illustrations by Paul Morrissey, Edgewater Graphics, Limerick.
Design and typesetting by Red Barn Publishing, Skeagh, Skibbereen.

A CIP catalogue record for this book is available from the British Library.

Contents

Acknowledgements

A very big thank you to the people who have attended me over the years. It has been a privilege to work with you. Your stories have provided the background for this book. Thank you also to those of you who wrote your own personal contributions to this book.

To my partner Marianne, thank you for your love, encouragement and ideas, and very practical help including proofreading and editing. Thank you to our children, Gary, David and Ciara, for your love, enthusiasm, support and patience.

Thank you to Patrick C. Coughlan from Carrigaline, Co. Cork for your great friendship, support and encouragement.

Thanks also to Brenda O'Hanlon for your help with editing in the early stages of this book, and to literary agent Jonathan Williams for your help over the years.

Thanks to Paul Morrissey of Edgewater Graphics for the diagrams and the cover illustration and to Red Barn for the typesetting.

Important: author's note regarding medication

The contents of this book should in no way be seen or interpreted as advising individuals to reduce or stop their medication. Reducing or stopping medication, particularly when done inappropriately and without medical supervision, can have major consequences, including the need for hospital admission. Medication should not be reduced or stopped without individual professional medical advice.

INTRODUCTION

Why I wrote this book

For the past twenty years, I have been working with people experiencing emotional distress and mental health problems, the first ten years as a General Practitioner. While working as a GP, I began to realise that the medical model was insufficient when applied to people suffering with mental and emotional distress, including those diagnosed with a mental illness. My experience with the people who attended me alerted me to the very real emotional distress underlying mental health issues. I became increasingly aware of the inadequacy of my medical training to enable me to understand and make sense of their distress and to effectively help them to recover. I expressed my concerns in my first book, *Beyond Prozac*.

Motivated by a desire to understand the core issues involved in emotional distress and mental health problems, I retrained as a psychotherapist. For the last ten years, I have provided a recovery-focused mental health service in Limerick city, Ireland. I work with people across a range of general counselling and mental health problems including depression, bipolar disorder, obsessive-compulsive disorder, eating disorders, and schizophrenia.

While working as a General Practitioner, I became increasingly aware that mental health services seemed to overlook key issues. Over the past fifteen years, I have worked hard to formulate clearly just what is at the root of emotional distress and mental health problems. In this regard, the self, and its relevance to mental health problems, has received little attention in recent decades, particularly since the notion that mental health problems are biological in origin took hold within psychiatry and subsequently within the broader community. What I feel is often overlooked is the human being themselves, their life history and experiences, their ways of perceiving and dealing with those experiences, themselves, others, and the world around them. These important issues shape how an individual processes and integrates the often challenging and difficult emotional and psychological aspects of being human. As the title suggests, my focus in this book is on the self, the person and their experience of themselves and of life, and on both the loss of and the recovery of one's sense of selfhood. I believe, and I have seen this occur in many people with whom I have worked, that recovery of one's sense of selfhood is a key factor in the process of recovery of mental wellness, including the process of recovery from mental illness.

I can only work with a limited number of people. I wrote this book so that a wider audience might benefit from the understanding, insights and methods I bring to my work with people.

Life inevitably involves the experiencing of loss, grief, fear, disappointment and pain. However, this does not mean that we inevitably become damaged or debilitated by our experiences. Limiting the impact of hurt on us, and minimising the risk that our painful experiences will have an ongoing debilitating affect on us involves (a) enhancing our sense of self and dealing effectively with the world, so that we experience hurt far less frequently, and (b) ensuring that we process emotions, hurt and trauma as fully as possible, minimising the risk of long-term effects. Both are recurring themes throughout this book. Having a solid sense of selfhood, we can experience, process and integrate our painful experiences, moving forward with personal growth and learning.

What is selfhood?

Words containing the suffix 'hood' encapsulate the characteristics of the experience of the term to which it is attached. Childhood is an umbrella term used to encompass all aspects of being a child. Manhood refers to the global experience of being a man, similarly with womanhood, motherhood, and so on. I use the term 'selfhood' to refer to all that applies to being a person, including the inner, private world we each continuously experience. When I speak of an individual's sense of selfhood, I am referring to their experience of and sense of themselves, and their overall sense of self in relation to the world around them. I am referring to their overall sense of selfhood, which is an aggregate of the individual's sense of each of the components of selfhood, as depicted in Diagram 1.

The more developed and balanced these characteristics are, the greater our sense of selfhood. People with a solid sense of selfhood contain the components of selfhood within their boundary, in their own personal space (more on this later), as depicted in the diagram.

Our level of selfhood is directly linked to our level of mental wellness, our experience of emotional distress and mental health problems. Living with a high sense of selfhood means generally feeling safe, in control, empowered, self-centred and self-confident. It means believing in yourself, and dealing effectively with your emotions, with challenges and taking risks, and managing to get the majority of your needs met. Having a high level of selfhood therefore greatly reduces your risk of experiencing ongoing emotional distress and developing serious mental health

COMPONENTS OF SELFHOOD

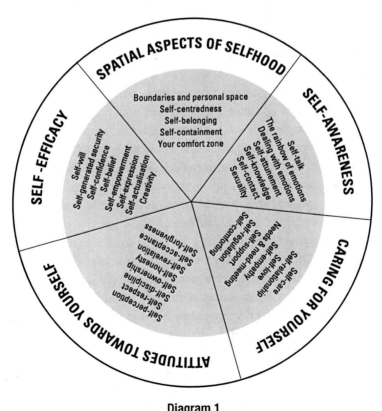

Diagram 1

problems. In contrast, having a low sense of selfhood means almost constantly feeling unsafe, feeling disempowered, having little sense of control in your life, consumed with self-doubt. It means having little or no self-confidence or self-belief, you and your emotions in virtually constant turmoil and you feeling all over the place, resulting in few of your needs being met. This ongoing state considerably increases your risk of developing enduring emotional distress and mental health problems. The individual components each contribute significantly to your overall sense of selfhood.

Developing the components of selfhood leads to an enhancement of these qualities within you, and has a positive impact on your overall sense of selfhood.

In my work with clients, I have repeatedly observed how central selfhood is to people's level of mental wellness or illness. The components of selfhood are consistently present, or more accurately, absent, in my dealings with clients over a ten-year period. I discuss selfhood further in sections one and two. In my experience of more than two decades working with people experiencing emotional distress, including people diagnosed with mental illnesses, selfhood keeps surfacing as a key link to mental wellness and mental illness.

I have seen how, with the right guidance and support, people can recover their sense of selfhood. I have worked with people diagnosed with conditions such as depression, bipolar disorder, schizophrenia, obsessive-compulsive disorder. I have witnessed many such people reach levels of recovery far in excess of what has been achieved within mainstream mental health services, often to the point of full recovery. The recovery of selfhood is an essential part of overcoming emotional distress and recovering from mental health problems.

A strong sense of selfhood is a springboard for a meaningful and happy life, making our journey through life much easier. Some of the components of selfhood may seem so ordinary, so obvious that one might think they need not be mentioned or described. Sometimes it is the ordinary and the obvious that we fail to see, that escalate when repeatedly left unattended, often creating havoc in many aspects of our lives. Generally, when a person's level of selfhood is low, each of the components of selfhood is correspondingly low. When an individual's level of selfhood is high, all of the components of selfhood are generally solid and strong within the person.

It is my hope that this book can be a tool that supports people in their journey toward a whole and balanced sense of selfhood and thus a more complete and contented life.

Who is this book for?

In my work with clients, I seek to develop and recover those aspects of selfhood that may be absent or overlooked. In doing so, the person can more fully engage with life and with experiences they find challenging or difficult. The contents of this book closely mirror how I work with people who attend me in person.

If you are unhappy, unfulfilled, and stuck, if you experience a lot of overwhelm, anxiety, fear and insecurity, if you have little sense of inner power, self-confidence, self-belief or if you feel that your life seems beyond your control, this may be the book for you. This book will help you to understand yourself better. If you or people who matter to you have been diagnosed as suffering from anxiety, depression, bipolar disorder, obsessive compulsive disorder, eating disorders, schizophrenia or addiction problems, or have felt suicidal at times, you will find much here that will make sense to you and help you.

This book is for people of all ages, since the issue of selfhood is relevant, no matter what age we are, and can be fostered at any stage of life. You can raise your sense of selfhood and your level of mental wellness by implementing the advice and actions set out within these pages. This book is relevant to anyone involved in mental health care, including psychiatrists, general practitioners, the professions of nursing, psychology, psychotherapy, counselling and social work, and those involved in the implementation and administration of mental health services. I have personally encountered several hundred users of the mental health services whose major loss of selfhood went largely unnoticed by their health carers. This pivotal issue rarely seems to appear on the medical radar. It may better serve people if professionals working in this area organised their understanding and their interventions around the true nature of the individual's difficulties. In this context, low selfhood is a core issue for people diagnosed with mental health problems.

This book will be of considerable interest to parents. Parents who have a strong sense of selfhood are better positioned to foster a strong sense of selfhood within their children. The topics discussed in this book apply both to parents and others who have a significant input into and impact upon young people. Many parents work with their children on issues relating to selfhood and effective dealing with the world as a natural part of parenting. By increasing their understanding of mental wellness as discussed in this book, parents can make changes to their patterns of interacting with their children. The effect of these changes may seem almost imperceptible at first. Over time, these changes will have considerable potential to foster the child's sense of selfhood and enhance the effectiveness of how they deal with their world.

If the topics covered in this book were taught in schools, many young people would understand themselves far better and would become empowered to live more contented lives and deal more effectively with the world. I believe that recognition of the key importance of selfhood would result in much happier societies, far fewer people being diagnosed as suffering from mental illness, and in far better outcomes for those who are so diagnosed.

A plausible hypothesis

As explored in detail in my book *Beyond Prozac*, it is far from established that mental health problems are biological in origin. Although researched intensely for decades, this notion remains a hypothesis to this day. In this book, I present a plausible hypothesis: that selfhood is a key factor in our level of mental wellness or mental illness. In addition to helping people to recover their sense of selfhood, I hope that this book will encourage debate and comment, and ultimately contribute to creating an effective recovery-focused mental health service.

The biological hypothesis is never tested in any individual. No person with a mental health problem or diagnosis ever has a biological abnormality confirmed by any test. In contrast, in my professional experience, the aspects of low selfhood that I describe in this book are *always* experienced by the individual concerned and are *always* verifiably present. This adds a level of credibility that has not yet been established for the biological hypothesis, despite decades of investigations involving thousands of research projects aimed at verifying the biological hypothesis as an established fact.

People in mental and emotional distress need help on two fronts.

They want relief from their emotional pain, anxiety, agitation, distress, but they also seek to recover their life. The medical system pays scant attention to the latter, concentrating primarily on the former, the alleviation of symptoms, usually by the use of medication. The alleviation of symptoms is important and has its place, but it is insufficient to promote recovery. The medical approach is not geared toward effectively assisting people to achieve meaning, purpose, fulfilment, and the recovery of their life. This requires a broader focus on all of the aspects of the individual and their needs, as discussed throughout this book. The recovery of selfhood is of key importance in this regard.

According to the World Health Organisation, mental health is more than the absence of mental illness, but it is not sufficient to describe mental wellness in terms of the absence of something. The components of mental wellness itself need to be clearly described. This lack of clarity regarding mental wellness contrasts sharply with the widespread acceptance of the concept of mental illness. Mental wellness remains an elusive, poorly defined concept, yet mental illness is an idea we readily accept within society. These contrasting positions do not sit well with each other. Before we as a society begin to define and describe mental illness, we should be able to describe, understand and clarify mental wellness in great detail. Since mental wellness is pivotal to each of our lives, it is surprising that it is so poorly understood. Having a solid sense of self is of pivotal importance to our level of mental wellness.

A comprehensive understanding and clarification of mental wellness is a requirement for the development of clear strategies of prevention of mental health problems, early effective interventions, and mental health promotion. The potential of mental health promotion, and the treatment and prevention of mental illness is compromised if mental wellness is not clearly understood and described. If mental wellness is clearly understood, then pathways toward attaining, maintaining and regaining mental wellness emerge with greater clarity, direction and purpose. This book is one such pathway.

Throughout the world there are countless traditions, cultures, diets, styles of eating and preparing food for consumption. Irrespective of the person's dietary habits, culture or country of origin, all human beings share similar dietary requirements and needs. Vitamins, minerals, protein, carbohydrates and fats are essential for the healthy functioning of the human body. Similarly, a strong sense of selfhood is a universal component of mental wellness, regardless of where we live and the traditions of our culture.

It is my hope and my intention that this book will clarify aspects of our shared experience of being human, and empower those who read it to live more contently, more effectively, with an enhanced sense of selfhood.

Book contents

Throughout the book, I include experiences from the lives of people who have attended me for professional help. In section one, I discuss the principles and concepts that underpin this book. Section two consists of a detailed consideration of the process of recovery of selfhood. This section begins with an exploration of some important themes relating to the recovery of selfhood. The components of selfhood are discussed in detail. A list of actions are included for each component, designed to cultivate each component of selfhood. At the end of each of the five categories of selfhood, I include two case histories. I had originally intended to include a case history for each component of selfhood, but reduced it to two per category due to limitations of space. Names and personal details have been changed to maintain privacy and confidentiality. I include the case histories to demonstrate how the components of selfhood manifest in people's lives, and to give a sense of how I work with people. The book concludes with a brief exploration of the peace dividend, the experience of inner calm that is the product of effective recovery of selfhood. Five personal testimonies of this inner peace are included, written in each person's own words.

How to use this book

This is a practical, self-help book. The potential benefit of any book parallels the work you put into making the contents real in your life. You would not expect to learn to play golf or become accomplished at horse-riding in a week, simply by reading a book. Enhancing your level of selfhood requires you to work at it.

I recommend that you work through the book in sequence. Once you have grasped the book's ideas and concepts, you can dip in and out, reading and working on the areas of particular relevance to you. You can work through this on your own, which for many people will be the most practical way. Small groups could use this book as a workbook, meeting weekly or two-weekly to discuss and explore their experiences.

I recommend devoting time every day to this work. Thirty to sixty minutes a day would be ideal. That would be enough time for you to work steadily through the actions in the book. As you go about your day, bear in mind what you have been reading and working on. You should find the material surprisingly relevant to the feelings, thoughts, interactions and situations you experience. As you become more familiar with the contents and style of the book, you will create your own individual way of working with it. If you have any comments or feedback about the book, I would be happy to receive them. You can email me with your comments at *terry@mentalhealthpublishing.com*.

The Mental Wellness Book Series

This is the first in a series of books I am writing about mental health. Books about schizophrenia, bipolar disorder, depression, anxiety, eating disorders and suicide will follow. The purpose of this series of books is to expand our current understanding of mental health and mental health problems. Describing and explaining the often subtle yet key emotional and psychological aspects of mental health and mental health problems will be a recurring goal and theme of the Mental Wellness Book Series.

There are other aspects of life that are relevant to an individual's mental health and wellbeing, such as genetics and biology. My intention in the Mental Wellness Book Series is to focus on aspects of life about which effective action can currently be taken to improve and maintain mental health and wellbeing. The study of genetics and biology as they apply to mental health and wellness as yet offers little practical and meaningful scope for improving mental health and wellbeing or preventing mental health problems. Whether or not they will do so in the future remains to be seen.

Mental healthcare systems are generally based on a model of mental illness, rather than mental wellness. Within many mental health services worldwide, mental health problems tend to be dealt with largely in isolation from the individual's life, experiences, needs, struggles, world-view, their sense of self and how they deal with the world. Many mental health services do not sufficiently appreciate how intimately a person's experience and perception of themselves and their dealings with the world are related to their level of mental wellness or illness. The Mental Wellness Book Series is my attempt to rectify this situation.

Section One

BASIC PRINCIPLES AND CONCEPTS

What is a human being, and how do we live?
The term 'self' is often used in everyday language. As we end conversations with others, we frequently say 'mind yourself', or 'look after yourself'. People who are nervous before stressful situations are often advised to 'just be yourself'. What is this 'self' we speak of so frequently? This question has been the focus of many books and countless debates down through the centuries. A detailed discussion of this topic is beyond the remit of this book. For practical purposes as I see it, the self refers to our awareness of who we are and how we experience ourselves within our world. A core aspect of the self is our inner, private world, the ever-present flow of our thoughts, feelings and senses within our own personal experience of human existence.

There are many aspects to who we are and to our experience of ourselves and the world. We have a physical aspect: our body, the vehicle through which we experience life and make contact with others and the world. We have an emotional aspect: we continually experience a wide range of emotions as we journey through life. A psychological aspect: we have ongoing streams of thoughts. We have social and relational aspects: we seek contact both within relationships and within a range of social contacts, networks and interests. Relationships tend to be extremely important to us. We have a sexual aspect: sexuality is a core element of being human. Many people believe that we have a spiritual aspect. People vary on this but, for many, it is an essential aspect of being a person.

In my experience, human beings function best when all of these aspects are in a state of healthy activity and flow, when our needs as they apply to all of these aspects are generally being met. I often use the analogy of a multi-lane highway to explain this to clients, as depicted in Diagram 2. On a busy, seven-lane highway, drivers can switch from lane to lane as appropriate to their needs. We human beings need to be in a position to access all aspects of our being as appropriate. On a major seven-lane highway, each lane is open and in regular use by many drivers. If some lanes are closed to public use, then the enormous volume of traffic that previously had seven lanes to work with now must be channelled through the remaining lanes.

Similarly, many of us invest enormous amounts of energy on one or two of these aspects, leaving others unattended to. Some of us place major

FREE FLOWING

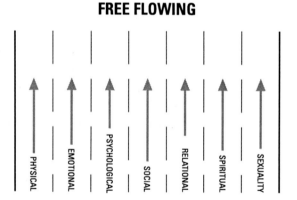

CONGESTED

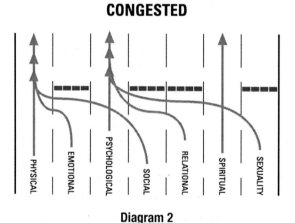

Diagram 2

emphasis on our physical aspect, such as our appearance or our level of physical fitness, whilst paying little attention to the emotional aspect of ourselves, our inner feeling states. Others devote themselves and the bulk of their attention to their spiritual aspect, sometimes forgetting to tend to their other aspects. In my experience, there can sometimes be a convenient avoidance process going on here. Many people choose to focus on the aspects of themselves with which they feel most comfortable. They may therefore be avoiding important aspects of their being, around which they have considerable fear and insecurity, often their emotional, relational, social or sexual aspects.

Unwittingly, we may focus solely on the aspects with which we are comfortable, in order to avoid the aspects we are less comfortable with and the consequent challenges they pose. This applies to many people who live mostly in their heads, in their psychological aspect. They often find that their thoughts are racing. Some of their other channels of experience and expression such as their emotional, relational, sexual and spiritual aspects are often not open and flowing. Their energy gets channelled through the few lanes that remain open, frequently including the psychological aspect (thoughts), which is then in a state of almost constant over-activity and overload.

Balance – such a key theme – is important here. Later in the book, I write about the rainbow of emotions. The rainbow analogy applies here also. We humans function best when all of our aspects are alive and in balance, like the rainbow, where all the colours are equally represented in their full glory and in perfect balance with each other.

From birth through to death, we are continually experiencing ourselves – our thoughts, feelings and sensations. Every interaction we have with people and the world is real to us only insofar as we experience it from within our being, within our personal, individual and private world. People's reactions to external events vary considerably. As we will see, our level of selfhood plays a major part in our personal reactions to life.

We spend much of our time meeting the various needs that surface with us. As the strength of a particular need builds up, we become increasingly intent on satisfying that need, on being freed from the pain or other unpleasant sensation arising from the as-yet unmet need. We want to bring the situation to a satisfactory conclusion. Our need to go to the toilet is an example of how our needs can escalate if not attended to. Until that need is met, everything else pales into insignificance, but not all of our needs are as pressing as our need to go to the toilet. For example, while we may experience a great deal of loneliness, we may decide to defer our relationship needs out of fear of exposing ourselves to the risks involved in close relationships, including the risk of rejection. We may attempt to compensate for this loss by increasing our focus on other aspects of ourselves such as our physical or psychological aspects. Beginning the process of cultivating the components of selfhood may highlight that we have many needs that we may have deferred, sometimes for decades. There is always a price to be paid for doing so, the loss of selfhood and the losses we endure as a result of having low selfhood and not living a full life, great losses indeed.

The key importance of selfhood

According to the World Health Organisation, two key aspects of a person's quality of life are their perceptions of themselves, and their experience of their interactions with the world in which they live. Selfhood is a core aspect of both. Our level of happiness parallels the level of satisfaction we obtain from our interactions with the world and the degree to which we experience our needs being met. Our level of selfhood is central to the degree to which we experience our needs being met, and therefore mirrors the degree of happiness we experience. This illustrates how important selfhood is for each of us.

The following analogy may help to illustrate the difference between these two ways of living – with and without a solid sense of selfhood. Picture two houses adjacent to each other. It is wintertime. The icy winter weather causes the pipes connected to the water storage tank in the attic to burst. Both houses are similarly affected. The contents of the water tank flood each house. The occupants immediately set out to tackle the problem, although in very different ways. Realising that burst pipes in the attic were the cause of the flooding, John calls a plumber, who duly replaces the pipes. Problem solved, no more leakage. John then sets about cleaning up the mess. This takes several days, but at least he knows that the problem is now repaired.

Faced with precisely the same problem, John's neighbour, Jim, opts for a different approach. According to Jim's logic, the solution is to keep the tank full. He therefore arranges a system of filling the tank at a rate that surpassed the speed at which the water drains from the tank. He organises pumps and hoses from the main water supply on the street in through an upstairs window, into the attic and ending up in the water tank. Because the water quickly drains from the tank, John sets the flow of water to the maximum level as he tries frantically to keep the tank filled with enough water to meet the needs of his home.

The importance of fixing the source of the haemorrhage of water does not strike Jim. Instead, he is fixated on maintaining an adequate water level in the attic tank. Water is cascading everywhere. Jim, his wife and children spend their time running around the house with buckets and mops in a frantic but inevitably unsuccessful attempt to keep the house somewhat dry, organised and functional.

A week later, John has almost forgotten about the burst pipes, his attic tank is working properly, and the mess caused by the leaking water has been cleared up. John and his family are free to carry on with their everyday lives. Jim's house is a different story. Water is still flowing everywhere, throughout the house, into the gardens and onto the street. Jim and his family have to give this ongoing situation their full attention. All other activities, with the exception of the essentials, such as eating and using the bathroom, have to be dispensed with. Jim and his family are still battling with their ongoing crisis, becoming increasingly worn out and overwhelmed. They cannot take much more of this, but with no other solution in sight, they have to keep up this enormous effort indefinitely.

You might understandably feel that this is an incredible story. No one would deal with burst pipes in the manner in which Jim approached the problem. Yet there are parallels between this tale and how many of us live. This is precisely how a person with a low sense of selfhood seeks to replenish the components of selfhood. They frantically look *outside of themselves*, to other people, roles or activities, for the characteristics and experiences that only they can provide for themselves in the form of the components of selfhood.

When they do receive what they are frantically seeking from others, approval, esteem, praise, acceptance, for example, often far less frequently than they had hoped given their enormous efforts, they are initially delighted. However, the benefits are always short-lived, rarely lasting longer than a few minutes. As with Jim's water tank, there is a chronic leakage problem. The sense of wellbeing they experience as a result of the external approval rapidly vanishes, like Jim's water disappearing through the burst pipes. Having no *self-generated* sense of these qualities, they cannot hold on to, internalise and retain them when they are received from others, so they disappear without trace within minutes, often within seconds.

They search constantly for approval, esteem, acceptance, and all the other components of selfhood from outside of themselves. They do not turn their attention to the one solution that *will* work: repairing the haemorrhage of their own provision of these qualities by raising their own level of selfhood. Once they deal with this problem, the equivalent of repairing the burst pipes in the above story, like John they find that they do not need to constantly keep filling their tank up from outside sources. They now provide these qualities for themselves.

The greater our sense of selfhood, the greater our ability to deal effectively with change, challenge, growth, uncertainty, the unknown, loss and the unexpected. A well-developed sense of selfhood greatly enhances our ability to create healthy relationships, healthy boundaries, to interact effectively with others, and to carve out a meaningful life. The need for a strong sense of selfhood, for contentment and wellbeing is a key aspect of being human. At the core of each of us lies a uniqueness and individuality that we long to experience and express. When we take action in one aspect of selfhood, a ripple effect often follows. We experience beneficial effects within other aspects of our sense of selfhood and how effectively we deal with the world.

Low self-esteem is often described as the kernel of a person's life or mental health problem. Sometimes it is put down to low self-confidence. Other terms are used to describe the nature of the problems that hold people back in their lives. None fully describe the issue in question. Numerous books have been written on self-esteem, as if this is the root of the difficulties which many people experience in their lives. While low self-esteem is certainly one characteristic of people with a low sense of selfhood, their level of self-esteem often exceeds the degree to which they experience other components of selfhood, self-confidence and self-empowerment for example. They are often acutely and painfully aware that they desire a happier, more fulfilled life, that it should not be this way. While it is true that many people do not hold themselves in high esteem, this explanation is insufficient to accurately describe the nature of the difficulty.

The heart of the problem is more broadly based: loss of selfhood lies at the core of the issue. It is no coincidence that people whose sense of selfhood is low are far more likely to struggle in life and to experience mental health problems. The reverse is also the case. People with a strong sense of selfhood tend to be happier, less prone to mental health problems, better able to handle change, loss and uncertainty. Life in the twenty-first century can be pretty challenging. Living without a strong sense of selfhood can be extremely difficult, leading to great emotional pain and distress. Selfhood is a key filter through which we experience life. Therefore, fostering selfhood is vitally important to the cultivation of mental wellness.

I am not aware of any other factor other than low selfhood that is always present in people who experience mental health problems. Take food, for example. Some people feel that a healthy diet is a major contributor to mental wellness. A healthy, balanced diet is to be encouraged for us all, including those of us who experience mental health problems. Eating healthily is an example of good self-care, one of the components of selfhood. The discipline and ritual involved in preparing and eating healthy food often has a beneficial effect on our mental health. Nevertheless, many people who have experienced little or no mental health problems have patterns of eating that fall far short of a healthy balanced diet. Many others who stick to a healthy, balanced diet experience major mental health problems. The link between food and mental health is not nearly as consistent as the link between mental health and selfhood.

I have yet to meet a person diagnosed with schizophrenia, bipolar disorder, major depression, an eating disorder, obsessive-compulsive disorder, or any other major mental health problem, who had a solid and strong sense of selfhood, and whose methods of dealing with the world resulted in their needs being met effectively across the wide range of human needs. Some people have become quite skilled at hiding their loss of selfhood from others and sometimes from themselves. For example, behind arrogance and brashness there frequently lies a loss of selfhood, of which the person may be painfully aware.

A common theme that I have noticed in people with severe mental health problems is that prior to the emergence of these problems, the person's sense of selfhood has tended to be quite fragile. They have already experienced the gradual accumulation of great self-doubt. This loss of selfhood may not be obvious to others, since the person may go to great lengths to disguise it, but it is there. One particular change or a series of changes, losses or challenges (which objectively may not appear to be particularly challenging) can push that person over the edge into overwhelm and turmoil. It is how a person experiences a situation that dictates the significance of the particular situation for them, not how others might experience and interpret that situation.

Far less frequently I have encountered people who have an existing solid sense of selfhood and have nonetheless developed mental health problems. It generally takes a major shock or sudden, profound life change to undermine their sense of selfhood to such an extent that they become prone to serious mental health problems. Having a fragile sense of selfhood greatly increases a person's risk of becoming overwhelmed when confronted with change, loss and challenge.

The ever-increasing generalised anxiety that usually precedes the development of all major mental illnesses can in part be understood as a progressively frantic response to the accumulation of self-doubt. Life seems to slip increasingly beyond the person's control, and they feel utterly powerless to stop the slide that they can see unfolding before their eyes. What an overwhelming and desperate situation in which to find oneself. The greater the loss of selfhood, the more frenetic the person's experiences, and the more frantic their responses and reactions. They feel as if they are drowning all the time, as though they are constantly living in an intense hurricane where their survival as they perceive it is by no means guaranteed.

There is considerable inter-connection between the various components of selfhood and dealing effectively with the world. A person with a low level of selfhood will tend to have most or all components of their selfhood affected to a major degree. There will be a parallel impact on how effective or ineffective they are in dealing with their world, and getting their needs met.

Having a solid sense of selfhood enables us to know who we are, and therefore know who we are not. A recurring feature of people experiencing mental health problems is great self-doubt about both who they are and what they are capable of, and who they are not and what they might do to themselves or others. I have worked with several people who worried that they might harm others, particularly children, often their own children. Having explored this in detail with the person, it generally becomes very clear to me that these people would not hurt a fly. These fears often have their origin in enormous self-doubt. Because the person does not have a solid sense of who they are, they do not have a solid sense of who they are not, or what they might or might not do to others.

The spectrum of selfhood ranges from those who have a high, solid sense of selfhood right through to people who have virtually no sense of selfhood at all, and all levels in between. The level of disruption created by loss of selfhood mirrors the degree of loss of selfhood. The greater the loss of selfhood, the more likely it is that a major mental health problem may emerge at some stage in the person's life.

The characteristics of loss of selfhood

When our sense of selfhood is low, we experience and manifest this in many important aspects of our lives and in diverse ways. Characteristic manifestations are frequently defensive reactions, designed to prevent further exposure to hurt, exercises in further damage limitation.

Hyper-vigilance and chronic anxiety are common manifestations of loss of selfhood. Another cause of chronic, non-specific anxiety is unexpressed and unresolved emotion, including hurt, sadness, anger and fear. Recurring anxiety is commonly experienced by young children, adolescents and adults who have lost their sense of selfhood, for whom day-to-day living has become an extremely challenging experience. The person's anxiety levels are often chronically raised. Everything is an enormous challenge, survival often being an ever-present preoccupation.

Loss of selfhood is the process of losing touch with aspects of ourselves, of who we are, a protective reaction to real or perceived threats that we encounter in our lives. The reduction in their sense of selfhood is frequently the child's reaction to what they experience as a hostile, threatening environment. Children protect themselves from what they experience as an unsafe environment by lowering their sense of self, thereby reducing the risks they take. For example, they reduce their exposure to observation, criticism, judgement, risk, and failure. They compromise who they are in order to maximise their chances of getting by, attempting to have their needs met as best they feel they can in the circumstances, usually not to a high degree.

Having developed major doubts about ourselves and our ability to deal effectively with the world, many of us literally clip our own wings.

For example, many of us choose to lose touch with the experience and the ability to feel certain emotions, such as anger or sadness, when feeling these emotions fully has become too frightening for us. Similarly, we lose touch with components of selfhood when we reach a point of self-doubt and insecurity where having these components and living them fully feels impossible. For example, if I have developed major doubts about myself, then living with self-confidence appears beyond me. Having self-confidence and living accordingly has now become way outside my comfort zone. I therefore convince myself that I have no self-confidence, I come to believe this, and this becomes my reason for withdrawing into my narrow comfort zone and staying there. The same is true for other components of selfhood. If I have developed major doubts about myself, I will find it next to impossible to feel self-empowered, self-centred, to belong, to believe in myself, to accept myself, or to generate my own sense of security. It becomes easier to believe that I possess none of these qualities and live accordingly, progressively withdrawing into an ever-contracting comfort zone. Risking to believe that I have these qualities and living accordingly feels impossible, since I am convinced that living the life of a confident person involves regularly taking risks which I am convinced I not able for. Many of the ways in which the erosion of selfhood manifest themselves reflect this reality.

When our level of selfhood is very low, we experience life changes as extremely challenging. We may consequently avoid change as much as possible. This puts us in a very difficult position, as we are seeking to avoid changes that are often inevitable, that may contain considerable potential for growth and fulfilment. For example, almost all teenagers with a very low sense of selfhood dread growing up and having to cope with the adult world because they have little confidence that they can do so. The degree of loss of selfhood mirrors the intensity with which it is experienced. As well as experiencing great pain, a person with a low sense of selfhood may experience major loss of most or all of the qualities of selfhood as set out in the diagram on page 3.

People with a low level of selfhood continually experience major degrees of emotional distress. For them, this is the norm, moments of inner peace and contentment are few and far between. They tend to be very prone to stress, regularly being faced with problems and dilemmas that seem unresolvable. They are vulnerable to bullying and abuse. They experience a great deal of loneliness, hopelessness, and despair. They rarely experience a sense of balance or equilibrium, as they are regularly thrown by various shocks in life and seldom recover fully from them. Like a ship without an anchor, they feel like they are being tossed around, at the mercy of every wave. They often fear success as much as failure, have great difficulty making decisions, and are immensely sensitive to possibilities of rejection and ridicule. They tend to have developed protective but counter-productive habits and patterns in order to survive. They may regularly have suicidal thoughts and feelings. Not living a full, rewarding life where their needs are generally met, their potential fulfilled, where they enjoy a wide range of satisfying experiences, is a common characteristic of loss of selfhood. Hopes and dreams are regularly compromised and unrealised, with considerable difficulty finding purpose, meaning and fulfilment in life.

Daily life is about survival, there is little space for anything else. Many experience a dread of exposure, of humiliation when feeling exposed, of rejection. Consequently, they limit their experience of life in order to minimise the risk of feeling such painful and overwhelming emotions. Generally, they repeatedly seek certainty and predictability, yet they frequently feel unsafe and under threat. They tend to be terrified of and therefore avoid the unknown, missing out on so many possibilities as a result. They usually either limit their expectations greatly, or set them so high that they are rarely attained. Minimising risk and restricting one's existence is therefore a regular characteristic of loss of selfhood.

Many experience great social anxiety and consequently withdraw regularly from social contact. They repeatedly choose various ways of escaping and withdrawing from the difficulties and challenges of life and from the intensity of their own feelings. Frequently the person's efforts to avoid are 'successful', in that the person minimises or eliminates exposure to any situation that might provoke anxiety or insecurity. Reality kicks in intermittently, despite the individual's best efforts to ensure that it does not.

People with a low sense of selfhood frequently experience considerable difficulties within relationships. Attempting to read people's minds and misinterpreting others' words and actions is often the result of loss of selfhood, and itself causes further emotional upheaval. Low selfhood is a recurring characteristic of mental health difficulties, and is generally a key feature of individuals who are diagnosed with a mental illness.

How selfhood is lost

Unless they experience a great deal of trauma at an early age, the majority of babies have a strong, solid sense of selfhood, as epitomised by the 'terrible twos'. This is when the toddler makes their statement of individuality to the world: 'I am here and don't you forget it!' Each child has their own individual innate spirit and characteristics. The two-year-old's most natural state is to shine, to be fully alive, all aspects of themselves in full flow, like a bright star. Painful and difficult life experiences generate fear, hurt and insecurity in children, causing them to compromise themselves in order to survive, to be loved, and to minimise the risk of further hurt.

Children may react to perceived threat by shielding aspects of themselves, having come to the conclusion that it is not safe to fully express the bright star that they are and risk further exposure to hurt. They cover over much of who they are in order to protect their wounded hearts. They do not shine quite so brilliantly, if at all. Frequently, the experience of being hurt is often not the consequence of an intentional attempt by others to injure another, although this sometimes occurs too, unfortunately. Hurt is often the result of the very nature of life, relationships and interactions, with their many challenges, uncertainties and conflicts. Hurt can also result from needs regularly not being met.

When we experience hurt, one of two processes usually follows. We may fully experience the hurt, work through it on our own or with someone we trust, leading to a resolution. Alternatively, we may quickly block the feeling and the impact, storing it away inside ourselves. In time we may forget the incident, but the impact is registered within. As the registered hurts mount over time, our sense of selfhood and how we deal with the world may become increasingly limited and compromised. A client of mine recently told me the following story that illustrates this point. One day, she was in conversation with her six-year-old nephew with whom she has a very good relationship. The boy told her that, when he has a painful feeling or thought, or when something bad happens, he puts it into a box in his brain and locks it away. This is an accurate way of describing the process of blocking the feeling, and how we lock these painful experiences away within us.

The ability to feel and perceive things subjectively is a core feature of being human. From birth and possibly from before birth, babies and children are continually sensing and scanning their environment.

Through feeling, sensing and perceiving, babies and children establish connections with others and the world, driven by the need to be safe and secure and to have their needs met. Their needs include the need to be loved, to be valued, to be safe and secure, to belong, to feel fulfilled and to achieve their potential. In her book *Peoplemaking*, American family therapist Virginia Satir has estimated that by the age of five, a child has had approximately one billion interactions with others. She describes an interaction as being any contact, however brief, such as a glance, a touch, a word or sentence, a smile, a dismissal.

The vast majority of these interactions produce an internal subjective response within the child. The quality of this response depends on children's interpretation of the interaction. Gradually, they build up their own personal internal data bank of their experience of contact with others and with the world. Based on this data bank, they come to their own conclusions regarding their sense of self, who they are, and other key issues. They arrive at conclusions regarding whether they are loved, safe, secure, whether or not they believe their needs will be met, how lovable they are, and how capable they believe themselves to be in dealing with the challenges they encounter. Children have their own inherent characteristics and traits. However, the cumulative effect of their interactions with others can be a powerful influence on their emerging sense of self.

The following glimpses from two adult female clients illustrate how and why children utilise this process of sensing and moulding themselves into whatever shape they feel will work for them. Both had considerably lost their sense of selfhood by the time of these occurrences. Consequently, both had developed considerable self-doubt regarding their lovability and acceptability. One woman described how, when aged about ten, she would regularly be down on her hands and knees, scrubbing the kitchen door, because she received great praise and validation from her mother when she did so. She would even wash her sibling's dinner plates to get approval and recognition. When her parents announced that it was time for bed, she immediately raced up the stairs to bed, eagerly anticipating the praise and acclaim that followed. This praise always came, usually accompanied by strongly vocalised parental frustration to her siblings regarding why they could not be more like her. Having come to the conclusion in her childhood that people-pleasing was a safe way for her to get some of her needs met, she held on to this way of dealing with people throughout her life. Now in her fifties, her life is a testament to the immense losses we suffer when we continually people-please, consequently dishonouring ourselves inevitably and repeatedly.

Another woman described how, as a child, she realised that by being humorous, she could impress her family and receive attention and approval. Now in her sixties, she clearly recalls one seminal moment, which occurred when she was about ten years old. She was having dinner with her parents and siblings. As they dined, they discussed the current severe stormy weather. One of the family said that the weather was so bad, it was like the end of the world. She immediately responded 'and this is the last supper'. This witty comment was met with howls of laughter around the dinner table. Everyone complimented her excellent sense of humour, and she basked in the warmth of this positive attention, something she rarely experienced. She remembered coming to the conclusion that humour was a great way to get positive attention from people. She continued to use humour as one her most prominent forms of interacting with people throughout her life, which served a purpose in that it helped her connect with people. But she also used humour to avoid contact with her own sadness. People saw her as a very happy person, which was not the truth. She had suffered immense sadness in her life, which remained unexpressed and unresolved until she began to go beneath her humour defence, deal with her emotional pain, and reach a point where she could be all of herself, including her humorous self, in her interactions with people.

Home is our first experience of community. Much has been written on the subject of love and parenting and how best to create a home environment within which children can grow, thrive and develop into confident and content adults. An in-depth discussion on this topic is beyond the scope of this book. It is mentioned to underline the importance of love, safety and parenting in the development and maintenance of healthy selfhood and mental wellness in young people.

The issue is whether or not the child feels safe, secure and loved enough to risk staying free to fully express their entire being like a bright star. Children are sensitive to the quality, consistency and continuation of contact they experience with their parents. They assess whether they really matter, based on their interpretation of their parent's eye contact, smile, and other reactions to them, their parents being the people they most look to in this regard. Children need to know they are loved, demonstrated in word, deed and in physical touch, and that love will not be withheld. If the child feels that they are not loved or that love is conditional or frequently withdrawn, this may greatly impact on them, generating much anxiety and considerable reduction of their sense of selfhood. They may withdraw progressively from contact with others and indeed themselves.

If this is a regular experience, children may become preoccupied with avoiding further experiences of withdrawal of love, often compromising their sense of self to avoid provoking such a reaction in their parents. They may reach a point where they feel that leaving their heart open is just too much of a risk to take in case the love is again withdrawn. To varying degrees depending on the circumstances, they shut themselves off to love, shielding and protecting their heart, leaving themselves in a dark, lonely place. They keep this to themselves, rather than risk articulating their truth. They are terrified of feeling the raw intensity of their own painful emotion, and the possibility that the need they express may not be met, resulting in an overwhelming experience of emotional pain. For understandable reasons therefore, many children choose not to wake the sleeping giant of distress that may lie beneath the surface inside them.

Children who live in a home where they feel safe have far less need to create protective responses than children who feel unsafe at home, whether it is fear of aggression including verbal aggression, sudden change in atmospheres, or unpredictability and inconsistency within relationships. Children reared in homes where they do not feel free or safe to communicate all that they experience are likely to develop protectors that lower their level of selfhood. They may become quiet and block the feeling and the expression of many aspects of who they are and what they experience. Usually, there is no intention on the part of parents to hurt or harm their children in this way. The parents may not be aware of the ways and means of communicating effectively with their children. They may genuinely not see the subtle growing signs of distress and loss of selfhood. They may not realise the enormous range of emotions, fear and uncertainty that children can go through, and therefore not see the need to do anything about these.

Relationships between parents and their children are more likely to work well when the parent-child relationship effectively mirrors the topics in this book. For example, as self-relationship is a component of healthy selfhood, it helps if parents have a good relationship with themselves individually, and if the quality of relationships in the home mirror the characteristics described in this book in the section on self-relationship. If we want young people to have full access to the spectrum of emotions, it helps if parents themselves are prepared to experience and express the rainbow of emotions in ways that feel safe for all concerned. If we want our young people to become fully functioning adults, freed of the chains of incessantly comparing themselves to others, then home needs to be a place where young people are not at the receiving end of comparisons. Parents themselves need to remain free of the shackles of comparison, both for the sake of their children and for their own sake. Children often pay more attention to what their parents do than to what they say, particularly if what their parents do is not consistent with what they say.

Many factors during childhood, adolescence and adult life contribute to the erosion of selfhood. Sometimes there is a single, major, obvious cause. Often, the child experiences the gradual accumulation of self-doubt rather than one or two major traumatic events. The erosion of selfhood occurs as a consequence of living, interacting, and the changes that occur as our life unfolds over the years. One might argue that these happenings and changes are an inevitable part of life, and that therefore there is nothing that can be done about them. In fact, there is much that can be done. It is often not what has happened, but whether it is noticed and how it is dealt with, by the individual and by the important people in their lives, that dictates its effect. In the early years of childhood, the home is the child's primary environment. Where there is considerable dysfunction in the home and within relationships in the home, this dysfunction is likely to impact on children. Children respond to this by reducing their sense of self in order to best survive in the situation and get their needs met to whatever compromised degree they feel they can in the circumstances.

If they attend a crèche or a pre-school educational facility, these experiences and their interactions within these facilities are added to the pool, to the data bank of their experiences. As they pass through childhood, the nature and relative importance of a child's interactions change. Contact with the world outside the home increases progressively. Friends and peers become increasingly important, and participation in various activities may become a core part of the child's life. In these interactions, the subtle sensing process is ongoing. Children are constantly self-evaluating, assessing how safe they are and where they stand in relation to others within all of the relationships and interactions they encounter. Much of this is going on at a subtle level within the young person, but it is occurring nonetheless. One only has to closely observe a children's birthday party to see how each of the children present is dealing with the ever-changing situations in which they find themselves, and the efforts they go to in order to fit in, to be seen and heard, to belong and be accepted. At a two-hour birthday party, each child may have experienced several hundred interactions.

The child brings their current sense of selfhood to each interaction with others. Each encounter is experienced and filtered through their current sense of selfhood, their perceived sense of safety, challenge or threat, how lovable, acceptable and capable the child believes they are, and their inner data-bank of previous experiences, before they reach a conclusion regarding that encounter. Much of this occurs subtly and speedily. Generally, only the encounters that are interpreted as significant in their effect are noticed by the child. Each moment of contact and experience has the potential either to confirm the child's current self-perception or to alter their sense of selfhood, positively or negatively, depending on the interaction, its effect, perceived significance and interpretation.

Children may ache to be the centre of attention. However, if their level of selfhood is low, their need to feel safe may over-ride their need to be noticed and involved. They may resort to becoming quiet and shy, retiring into the background and watching others take the limelight. Generally, few people notice the extent of the child's distress at not being noticed and involved.

As they grow up, many young people experience the accumulation of self-doubt. Usually this is a gradual process occurring over many years, often beginning in the early years of life. The accumulation of self-doubt can take place rapidly if situations and events are particularly overwhelming. The more children doubt themselves, their lovability, capability and acceptability, the more likely they are both to mask aspects of themselves and to adopt avoidance strategies. Within the various areas of interaction in a child's life, including home, school, friends, other activities, the child bases their perception and sense of self on the over-riding patterns, content and tone of the interactions. Once-offs rarely cause much problems in this regard, unless they are interpreted as being major. If children's most recurring experience at home is that they are loved, that it is safe to be themselves, safe to express themselves and all of their feelings, then their conclusion about themselves is that they are loved, lovable, safe, and therefore free to express themselves fully. They believe that their needs will in general be met. They will have confidence in their own ability to articulate their needs to themselves and others, and do whatever is appropriate to ensure that their needs are met, particularly the important ones.

If, as Virginia Satir suggests, a child has had around a billion interactions with others by the time they are five, it is reasonable to assume that by the age of twelve the number has risen to more than ten billion. The exact figure does not matter. By the beginning of their second decade, the beginning of the transition from childhood into adolescence, every child has had an enormous number of interactions with other people and activities. Through these interactions, children continue to shape their own evolving perception of themselves that they bring with them on their journey through puberty and adolescence and into adulthood.

Healthy boundaries between children and their parents help children to grow up without excessive ties to their parents, ties that can be akin to chains from which many young people find it difficult to break free. Children reared in homes where healthy boundaries are maintained have a good platform of healthy boundaries to bring with them within relationships for the rest of their lives. Boundaries are discussed in detail in section two.

From a young age, children tend to compare themselves to their siblings, often seeing them as rivals for their parents' love and attention. Even small differences in how children are treated can be magnified by the child and interpreted as rejection, particularly if this child does not have a strong sense of self. Parents, despite their best efforts not to, may intentionally or indeed unintentionally single out qualities or attributes in their children which they like, which reflect well on them or which are socially valued. No words are needed, children are tuned into their parents every look and gesture. They can tell if a sibling is favoured and will internalise this, thus experiencing rejection and devaluing their own attributes.

The same set of conditions may affect two children quite differently. In interpreting the situation, each child refers to past experiences of similar events. They consider what responses and strategies have or have not worked previously for them, assessing how to handle each emerging situation, and how threatened they feel. Much of this process occurs very rapidly, without the child being aware of it. Many parents understandably wonder why one child might be more affected during childhood than other children from the same family who would appear to have experienced precisely the same childhood. The argument is often made that, since all children within the same family have the same experiences during childhood, their emotional and mental health problems must be biological in origin rather than linked to the individual's experience of their life. This approach fails to take into account the reality that, no two children have precisely the same experiences or share precisely the same level of selfhood throughout their childhood.

This truth was illustrated in a recent discussion with the parents of a young woman who attends me. The parents wondered why, out of their three now adult children, two were very confident and successful but the third had major problems, since they felt that each of their children were reared in exactly the same way. We discussed this in detail. The girl in question was a middle child. Her younger sister, a year younger than her, had been a demanding baby, taking up a great deal of their parents' time and attention. Her brother was five years older, and was quite bossy toward her during their childhood.

The girl therefore found herself sandwiched between two siblings, both of whom had become adept at articulating their needs from an early age, who consequently had confidence in their ability to get their needs met. Being five years older than her, her brother was more experienced in the ways of the world. She was never going to come out on top in her interactions with him. Her younger sister ensured that she got her needs met through her crankiness. During our conversation, her parents mentioned how, even as a young child, she would just sit there, looking, observing, not initiating anything. At an early age, the middle child lost confidence in her ability to articulate both her needs and her distress. Although raised in a genuinely loving home, where both parents did what they felt was the best they possibly could, her sense of selfhood was affected from her early childhood, and never recovered. Indeed, her low level of selfhood deteriorated considerably during her teenage years, and was the main reason why she developed emotional and mental health problems in her late teens.

All children choose a response, a way of being and reacting that they feel will best serve their needs as they see them. For example, children may go silent if they feel that expressing themselves or becoming angry is already beyond them or likely to create an unsafe situation for them.

It is erroneous to presume that parents will automatically approach the rearing of each of their children in precisely the same way. Many factors may affect the wellbeing and outlook of one or both parents, and consequently change how one or both parents relate to each other, to parenting and to their children. These factors include their experience with the children they already have, changes in the quality of their relationship with their partner, significant changes within important relationships such as illness or death of their own parents or siblings, the level of support each parent has, stress or illness in the home, and changes in the occupational and financial situation of the parents. Such changes may result in some children within the family having a somewhat different experience of life within the home from that of their siblings.

Major shock at any stage of life can erode selfhood, for example, for a child, the death of a parent. Major and sudden change rapidly catapults people out of their familiar comfort zone and into a new and unexpected set of circumstances they may experience as overwhelming and intolerable. Incomplete resolution of major events increases the likelihood of children being affected by the experience, for example, the experience of parental separation, of deaths of important people in their life not properly worked through and brought to completion.

If children sense major vulnerability in their parents, they frequently adjust to this in ways that seriously compromise the full expression of their selfhood. They are prepared to do this, both to protect themselves from further hurt, and to maintain their key parental relationships as best they can. Children whose mother or father or both are unhappy, irritable or unpredictable are likely to respond to this by becoming hesitant, holding back on their own self-expression, becoming outwardly-directed, focusing predominantly on how their parents are, as they now feel fundamentally unsafe within their home. They may go to the opposite pole, becoming aggressive, intolerant and impatient. It is difficult for such children to attain the middle ground, a balanced position regarding themselves, relationships and relating. Parents who are not tuned into modern living, who do not develop an understanding of the world of their teenage children and the challenges they face, can unintentionally leave their children exposed, vulnerable, unsupported and unprepared for the world.

Children who sense that one of their parents is really struggling may respond by minimising their own needs and becoming a carer for the parent. In doing so, the children protect themselves from the pain of continuing to depend on a parent who seems unable to meet their needs.

By attempting to mind and look after them, many children seek to minimise the alarming possibility of something terrible happening to their parent. It is easier both for them and their parent if they minimise the importance of their own needs, and focus instead on the needs of their parents and other important people.

In the process, many aspects of their selfhood become compromised, suspended and unfulfilled, including self-expression, self-acceptance, self-care, the full and proper handling of emotions, self-identity and self-centredness. These children are caring for themselves as best they feel they can in the situation, but they are not learning their fundamental right to high quality self-care. They see themselves in terms of the roles they have adopted, the carer, the joker, the good child, the quiet child, for example, rather than the totality of who they are. Feeling fundamentally unsafe, the children's primary attention has shifted from within themselves onto others, onto the parent(s) about whom they are worried. No longer living effortlessly within their own space and their own boundary (more on this later), their familiar world becomes one in which their attention is primarily focused outside of themselves. They become focused on the wellbeing of others, on the moods and unpredictability of others and the atmosphere in the home, in a frantic attempt to maintain peace, safety and harmony within their lives. Establishing a pattern of tuning out to their own needs and being excessively focused on the needs of others, they lose touch with themselves, and they dismiss and devalue their own needs and wants. Watchful for every nuance or behaviour that may indicate a change of mood, these young individuals become prone to 'mind-reading'. They are regularly leaving their own space, trying to evaluate what others are thinking, feeling and what others are likely to do, and what others want them to do. The process of ungroundedness within themselves is now well established. To maintain some sense of equilibrium and predictability within this distorted and unsafe situation, they may block many aspects of themselves.

They therefore have lost touch with significant parts of themselves. They may become less self-aware though often hyper-vigilant, with less self-knowledge and reduced self-confidence, experiencing major doubts about themselves, their lovability, capability and acceptability. They hold back on expressing many fundamental needs, emotions and experiences they believe will not be well received, dealt with and resolved. Boundaries are compromised, as the children repeatedly leave their own space and others regularly invade theirs.

Self-revelation is compromised, as the child has learned to censor what they say and reveal about themselves, having experienced many times that much of who they are and many of their needs are not acceptable and will not be met. It is therefore easier not to reveal themselves, their thoughts, feelings, ideas, their distress. In time, having practised non-self-revelation for so long, they may become unaware of many of the aspects of who they are that have remained unrevealed. They become disconnected from much of who they are, often feeling numb, deadened, distressed, anxious or depressed, as they are less and less fully themselves and therefore less fully alive.

Brought up in a home with a lot of tension, shouting, abuse, violence, unpredictability, excess alcohol consumption, in a frantic attempt to come to terms with this hostile environment, children may conclude that they are bad people. They may conclude that if only they were good children, their parents would behave better, love them more, be happier, get on better with each other. These children turn the problem back on themselves, a less painful action than taking on board that their parents either do not love them, or cannot mind them or provide for them, or behave aggressively. They sacrifice their sense of self in order to maintain relationships that are vital to them.

Anything that diminishes the human spirit has the potential to erode selfhood at any stage of life, particularly when there appears to be no possibility of beneficial change, no hope of a satisfactory resolution. Other factors include persistent attempts to control, manipulate, intimidate, terrify, abuse or be cruel, and failing to gradually give children the reins of their own power as they get older. Parents who fear the world are likely to pass this fear on to their children.

Influences from outside the home become increasingly important during adolescence. For the sake of their children, parents need to gently surrender their power, authority and influence over their emerging adult children. This is a gradual process, which begins long before children are even ten years old. Children with a healthy sense of selfhood will instinctively seek out their freedom, independence, growth and learning. It is important for parents to seek to maintain the relationship with their children in the presence of the changes that are going on within the growing young person. Perhaps the most productive approach for parents might be to bend gradually and gently with the child's strike for independence and autonomy. Parents who adopt the oak-tree (strong but inflexible, likely to crack under stress, for example in storms) rather than the willow-tree approach (more flexible, rarely break in storms) may find that their relationship with their children becomes increasingly strained, possibly breaking down in many important facets of communication. It helps if parents give their children the message that they are always available to talk to them about anything under the sun. Children may not always take up the offer, but many appreciate knowing that this option is there for them.

While children entering adolescence with a high level of selfhood are at an advantage over those who do not, it does not always follow that this will see them through the turbulent teenage years. The rapids in the waters of adolescence can be so treacherous that high selfhood can be eroded considerably during these years. Depending on their experience of adolescence and how successful they are at getting their needs met during these years, some children entering adolescence with a low sense of selfhood can experience an enhancement of their selfhood during the adolescent years. As a general rule, however, children whose sense of selfhood is already compromised are likely to experience considerable further difficulties during adolescence.

Many habits and patterns we develop can both arise as the result of having a low sense of selfhood, and contribute to a further lowering of selfhood. For example, procrastination is often both the result of having a low sense of selfhood and the cause of further lowering of selfhood. The same is true of many other issues, such as avoidance, a choice made secondary to the erosion of one's sense of self, which then leads to further avoidance, and therefore to further erosion of one's sense of selfhood. Working to raise your sense of selfhood creates a spiral effect too, a positive one, a win-win situation. People who experience a raising of one component of selfhood will also experience an improvement across other elements of selfhood and the effectiveness with which they deal with their world. This reality is evident in the case histories and personal testimonies described later in this book.

There is a fine line between the amount of freedom given to young people and attempts to control them. Young people need limits and boundaries to help them create structure, routine and a sense of limits, discipline and organisation, qualities and characteristics which they can then carry forward into their adult life. Excessive patterns of parental control can have a considerably negative effect on a young person's mental wellbeing. These patterns of control may not always be overt, often occurring in the form of subtle manipulation. A parent with a low sense of selfhood is much more likely to try to maintain their power and control over the young person in an effort to fulfill their need for validation, company and love. Such patterns of control may undermine the young person's attempts to develop a healthy sense of autonomy and selfhood, key components of mental wellness. It may interrupt their journey into full adulthood, and the development of self-confidence, independence and self-reliance that is an integral part of full adulthood and mental wellness.

Excessive parental control can affect how a young person deals with the world, a key aspect of mental wellness. It can interrupt the developing young person's efforts to create healthy boundaries and to master their world. It may create significant imbalances, including an imbalance in closeness between parent and child, either too much or too little. Children entering the teenage years, who are not supervised or sufficiently cared for, may also run into serious difficulties and develop major behavioural problems.

From a young age, many children pick up, by word, look, or gesture, what is expected of them, at home, in school, with friends, extended family, and in other situations and relationships. Children do need to learn how to integrate within these various social systems, but not at the price of loss of their sense of selfhood. As children get older, especially in the teenage years, they reassess the 'should', 'should not', 'must', 'must not', 'ought to', 'have to' messages that they have learned and internalised.

The re-evaluation by the teenager of these rules and expectations is an important part of becoming an adult. This takes many parents by surprise. The child they previously thought they knew, now questions home rules and regulations. They question beliefs that they previously accepted without argument. This is a healthy and necessary process, through which the young person comes to their own conclusions about their values and principles, a necessary step toward becoming an adult in their own right.

Major excesses at either end of the scale can cause significant problems. The core problem at both extremes is generally a major loss of selfhood. At one extreme, some young people do not go through this process of re-evaluation, but instead continue through and beyond the teenage years into adulthood with the same attitudes, beliefs and principles they internalised as children. They do not have a sufficient sense of selfhood to risk questioning the frameworks around which their life is built and have come to rely on heavily, since they do not believe they can rely on themselves. At the other extreme, other teenagers, who reject all the beliefs and values they were brought up with, may become 'anti' everything. It is often far less clear to others and sometimes to themselves what they are 'for', what they support and believe in. These young people run the risk of walking themselves into dead-end situations and relationships that contribute little positivity to their lives and consequently, to their mental wellness. Rather than face up to the fact that their real issue is major loss of their sense of themselves and all that follows from that, they may instead become entrenched in anti-social attitudes that may give them a sense of purpose and belonging within groups of like-minded people.

We tend not to worry about 'good' children, those who always behave well, do what they are told or what they believe others want them to do. They rarely express or even think an opinion contrary to the prevailing one. These children have internalised to a major degree the 'must/must not, should/should not' messages. They have not learned to think for themselves, usually because, for a variety of reasons, it became too frightening to do so. Their thoughts, actions, and to quite a degree their feelings, are shaped and influenced by other people's views. These children can be more at risk than the young people at school whose behaviour is disruptive. The latter group of children have enough sense of self to express their unhappiness and their distress in roundabout ways, such as disruptive behavioural problems.

A balanced approach might be for parents to understand and accept that a key purpose of parenting is to rear children who will embody healthy selfhood and who deal effectively with the world. This understanding can serve as a template for their dealings with their growing children. A balanced approach might also involve consistently communicating to one's children verbally and non-verbally that they love and believe in them and have confidence in their ability to think and make decisions for themselves. When behaviour needs to be challenged or corrected, it is best to ensure that it is the specific issue that is addressed rather than a general criticism or judgement of the individual. This helps the child to see themselves as distinct from their behaviour, for which they are responsible, but which does not classify them as a good or bad person. This might be expressed as 'I am not my behaviour, though it is my behaviour and I therefore take ownership and responsibility for it'. Of course there will be times when stressed parents can't always maintain this. After such moments, revisit the situation with your child, go through it calmly, and affirm to the child that it is not them but their behaviour with which you have a problem. It helps if parents are prepared to apologise when appropriate to their children, and to acknowledge that they were stressed, that they sometimes make mistakes or over-react. Children appreciate this honesty and accountability, and it helps them to trust and feel closer to their parents, and to develop the qualities of honesty and accountability within themselves. Many parents are uncomfortable with this as they feel it erodes their power and may undermine them, however this is not the case. It teaches children that making mistakes is human and that one can accept responsibility for errors without damaging one's sense of self. Children who experience this from their parents are likely to come to mirror this self-belief and autonomy within themselves. Parents need not feel they have to be perfect, getting everything right, never making a mistake. This would be an impossible and unattainable expectation. We are all human. Being a 'good enough' parent will do just fine.

Many of the factors that affect young people's level of selfhood are increasingly outside parental control as the child gets older. Young people are subjected to many external controls and manipulations within society. They are expected to comply with a wide range of expectations and requirements from many sources. Some of these are unavoidable and indeed beneficial. The various institutions and groups with which young people engage need to balance the rights and needs of all members of the group with a desire to minimise external control on the members of the group. Young people should not be subjected to bullying, ridicule, shaming, embarrassment, ostracisation and other forms of aggressive, belittling or intrusive behaviour. Groups and institutions serve young people best when they encourage them to hold on to their own power and to take responsibility for themselves, to make their own decisions, bearing in mind the wellbeing of others within the group. Respect for the uniqueness of each individual must be a major priority at all times.

The experiences of Chris and Jamie in the case studies below illustrate how private and personal our losses and emotional pain can be. Attending me for help with disabling anxiety, twenty-year-old Chris told me the following story. While he was out and about with a friend of a similar age, his friend's father rang his son, asking if he would mind collecting him from the city. The father told his son that he knew his son had his own things to attend to, that there was no rush, that he would expect him 'in his own time'. Chris was instantly struck by this conversation, probably because it bore little relation to the conversations he frequently had with his parents in similar circumstances. Chris would always be told in no uncertain terms to drop whatever he was doing, no matter how important it was to him, and come to collect his father immediately. The level of respect and understanding demonstrated by that father to his friend really impressed Chris. That father had a good relationship with his son, far closer and more open than Chris had with his parents, who certainly meant well, but were rather out of touch with the times and not amenable to change or trying to understand Chris's world. They spent far more time telling him what to do and giving him advice, despite his repeated requests that they instead start listening to him, and respecting him. He did not feel a fraction of the respect from his parents that his friend's father demonstrated to his friend during that brief conversation.

Now in his late twenties, Jamie's childhood had been characterised by complicated relationships. While still a young child, to survive in a dysfunctional home, he became his mother's carer. His childhood and teenage years were largely spent 'parenting' his mother, who was emotionally far more like a child than an adult woman. Jamie had for several weeks been observing swans in a lake close to his home. His attention was drawn to a swan and her cygnet. He became entranced by the interaction between the two over the period of development of the swan, from cygnet into a young adult swan. In the early stages, the mother walked just ahead of the cygnet, with the cygnet following, just as a young child would do. Later, the mother walked beside her offspring, accompanying now rather than leading. As the cygnet continued to grow, Jamie noticed that the mother gradually stepped back from the cygnet as they walked. She allowed the growing swan to increasingly explore and discover the world on its own and test itself in it, learning gradually to survive without the mother while remaining close in case she was needed.

Recently, Jamie noticed that the mother kept at quite a distance from her offspring, ten yards or so behind, as the now practically adult cygnet was prepared to proceed in life as an adult swan. Fascinated by this unfolding story, Jamie ruefully compared the simplicity and wisdom of this to the complexity and chaos of his own childhood. He reflected on the rightness of this situation, the gradual letting go by the mother swan, compared with the extremely dysfunctional holding on to him that he had experienced from his mother. Jamie thought about how this severely distorted relationship had greatly hampered his ability to break free, to fly the nest as the cygnet was preparing to do, to successfully come into his own space as a confident adult, ready to step into the world.

The experiences of Chris and Jamie are examples of a common theme I notice in my work with clients. I call it 'the presence highlights the absence'. The opposite is also the case, as the absence often highlights the presence. For Chris, the absence of a close, respectful relationship with his father meant that he immediately noticed the presence of such a relationship between his friend and his father. The gradual, appropriate shift from the cygnet being appropriately minded early in life, to the gradual fostering of autonomy, reminded Jamie of how absent such a proper process of appropriate minding and letting go was in his own life.

The 'presence highlighting the absence' is a recurring theme in life. A person whose beloved partner has just died will become aware of couples everywhere. A woman who desperately wants to have children, but is unable to, will be likely to notice babies and pregnant women as she goes about her day more than anything else. Not having parents around me for much of my childhood and teenage years, I was repeatedly stuck by the presence of parents in the lives of my young friends. I was painfully aware of how different their experience of life must have been as a consequence of having parents to protect, love and look after them.

The recovery of selfhood

Life is a series of unfolding journeys. The process of recovering your sense of selfhood is itself a journey. As we travel through life, each destination reached soon becomes the starting point of another experience. People who focus exclusively on the destinations they strive for are frequently left feeling disappointed and deflated upon reaching them. The feeling of great joy they were expecting often does not materialise, certainly not to the level or for the length of time they had hoped.

See the journey of raising your level of selfhood as bringing something new and precious into your life. Most things that are worthwhile take time to come to fruition. The raising and maintaining of healthy selfhood may be the most important journey upon which you will ever embark. Therefore, be gentle with yourself, and give the journey and yourself time. The key factors involved in maintaining your selfhood at a low level include a high degree of fear, self-doubt, having a perception of yourself as being powerless and insecure, and a major dread of taking the necessary steps forward. These fears cannot be overcome overnight. A rushed approach generally results in failure, as it invariably means putting too much pressure on yourself to tackle issues and situations for which you are not yet ready.

Generally, the greatest constraint on the pace of progress is the individual's fear of change and of changing, of letting their guard down and being overwhelmed either by their own feelings or by the world. Some of my clients have been convinced that they were ready to make rapid progress in terms of dealing with their issues and their distress and the raising of their level of selfhood. However, their defence mechanisms, their reactions and often their bodies told a different story. They were too frightened to implement the actions needed to progress their recovery at anything like the rate they believed appropriate for them.

Their level of inner disconnection from aspects of themselves was such that the difficult experiences and emotional pain effectively became compartmentalised, removed from their awareness. The desire and sometimes the need to lock out feelings and, as a consequence, block out painful experiences, is understandable and makes perfect sense. However, the feeling itself may remain frozen within us, and therefore may continue to subversively wreak havoc while its owner remains in a state of not-so-blissful ignorance about the concealed aspects of their psyche. People will often go to great lengths to resist any attempts to uncover these painful aspects, their unfinished emotional business, while apparently being eager to progress.

Crash courses in raising selfhood and effective dealing with the world therefore rarely work, can be counter-productive and sometimes even destructive. If you are prepared to persist, you will grow into a new and enhanced way of experiencing yourself and your world. The aim is to create a life-long solid level of selfhood and effective methods of dealing with the world, which is the greatest protection from mental health problems that I know of. Gentle persistence is the key to turning a potentially profound process of change into a reality. Your investment of time, energy, attention and yourself in this journey has the potential to yield immense results.

Regularly remind yourself to pace yourself on the journey toward recovering your sense of selfhood. Specific activities, such as the actions recommended throughout section two, carried out for short periods every day will over a period of months yield results. Doing too much too quickly may cause you to abandon the project because it rapidly becomes overwhelming, too great a challenge, or because results are not coming as quickly as you would like. Progress that is too rapid may result in you taking risks and actions that are many steps beyond your current capabilities. You risk experiencing major anxiety, a consequence of stepping too far and too quickly beyond your comfort zone, particularly if your level of selfhood is quite low.

The faster we travel, the less we connect with ourselves and with our journey. A car driver travelling at 150 kilometres per hour has to keep totally focused on the road ahead to avoid a major mishap. There is no margin of error at that speed. Unexpected developments like a tyre blow-out or having to swerve suddenly are likely to have disastrous consequences at such speed. At 150 kilometres per hour, the driver will remember little of his journey. A driver at 50 kilometres per hour can experience and enjoy the journey while remaining fully focused. At 50 kilometres an hour, the driver is far more likely to have noticed and therefore remember the atmosphere, landscape, scents and sounds encountered, the conversation just enjoyed or some quality alone-time. Aesop knew what he was doing when he wrote the Tortoise and the Hare fable. The hare may be much faster off the mark, but the tortoise generally wins the race, through pacing and persistence. The hare may win a sprint, but life is far more of a marathon than a sprint.

Ensure that your expectations are realistic. Regard your recovery of selfhood as a medium-term project, perhaps the most important project that you will ever undertake, because virtually all aspects of your life are likely to benefit from this work. The lower your level of selfhood, the slower you will need to take this process. For example, people who lost their sense of self in their early teens, who withdrew from everything in their mid-teens and were diagnosed as having schizophrenia in their teens or early twenties would need to take this work very slowly, especially in the initial stages. For them, baby steps will feel like giant strides. Gradual progress, without any pressure from anyone, yourself included, is the best approach.

Diagram 3 illustrates the process of recovery of selfhood. Very few journeys consist only of straight lines. The journey of recovering one's sense of selfhood is one where there are ups and downs. During this process of recovery of selfhood, you will have 'good' times and 'bad' times. When you slip, and we all slip from time to time, reassure yourself that this is a normal part of the process, it is to be expected, it is not a disaster. When you have 'setbacks', try to resist the temptation to believe that you are right back where you started, because generally you are not. Setbacks happen. Factor them in. When they happen, just keep up the work. If you let your focus go a little, no problem. Gently but firmly get yourself back on track

RECOVERY OF SELFHOOD

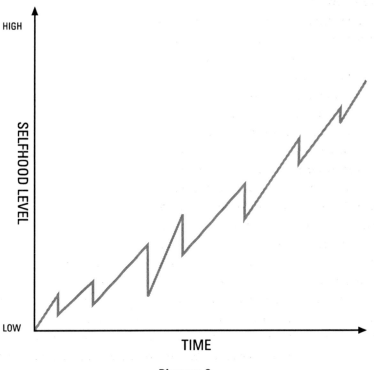

Diagram 3

without undue delay. Roll up your sleeves and start again. The key thing is to get back on track after a slip, the sooner the better, but even if you let it slip for some time, you can still get back on track, even when you do not believe you can. If you continue giving in to the feeling that you are right back where you started, you run the risk of remaining stuck where you currently are. The process of recovery always involves setbacks, which should not be seen as a sign of failure, because they are an inherent part of the process. What might appear to be a step backward is more accurately understood as the person finding themselves out on a limb, outside their comfort zone. They are in a place that is unfamiliar because they have generally avoided taking such steps. This place therefore feels beyond the capacity of their current level of selfhood, and may therefore evoke considerable fear and anxiety. They may therefore temporarily revert to a level that for the time being feels safer and is associated with fewer expectations and fewer risks, and that is perfectly understandable and appropriate at that time. After a period of withdrawal into their comfort zone, their sense of equilibrium is restored and they are more ready to again make choices consistent with raising their level of selfhood, such as the actions that follow in each section on the components of selfhood.

When you are doing well, do not presume it is over just yet, or you will set yourself up for disappointment, as have many clients of mine. Try not to do this, as it is not realistic to do so, because you will feel devastated when slip-ups happen.

On a car journey of two hundred miles, you do not stop the car every five minutes to see how much progress you were making. Doing so would greatly add both to the length of your journey and to your sense of frustration. I therefore generally say to clients that repeated and prolonged analysis of where you are currently is not generally helpful. Rather, I suggest that they focus gently on the work they need to do, and let the results look after themselves.

As illustrated in Diagram 4, the process of recovery of selfhood resembles a long sweeping bend on a road, where the curving nature of the road means that you cannot see beyond what is immediately ahead of you. However, as you travel along the road, gradually, the next section reveals itself to you. Similarly, on the journey toward your recovery of selfhood, it won't be possible for you to get an overview of your entire route. It will only be possible for you to see where you are currently, and what is immediately in front of you. If you stick with the process of recovery and keep doing the work, you will make progress, even though it may not always feel like progress. The road to recovery of selfhood will gradually reveal itself to you as you continue on your journey, and you will soon become aware of possible next steps. Each step you take brings you into slightly new territory, from which the view and horizon has changed, some things left behind, others now brought into sight. You do not have to believe you can do it. Indeed it is far more likely and appropriate for you to doubt that you can do it. This is a natural protective mechanism, by which you guard yourself from disappointment by not investing hope early in the process and risking your hopes being dashed.

Every step matters. When you climb the stairs from one floor to another, each step contributes equally to you managing to reach the next floor. This reality becomes clearer later in the journey, when you look back and see how far you have come. Small successes accumulate over time. The steps you make toward recovering your selfhood add up, provided you are prepared to persist.

ROAD TO RECOVERY OF SELFHOOD

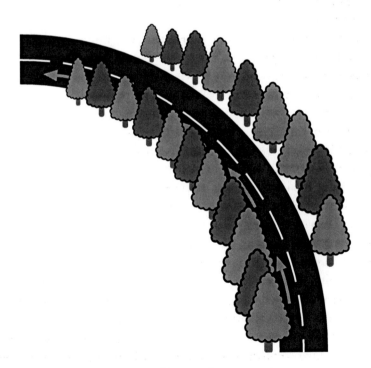

Diagram 4

With any journey, you naturally accept your current position as your starting point. If you were setting out on a two hundred mile car journey today, you know there is little point in wishing you were commencing your journey from a different location. As you begin the journey toward recovery of selfhood, accept that you are where you are, that your current level of selfhood is your starting point. People with a low level of selfhood can be impatient, seeking immediate results. However, this does not work for several reasons. It cannot work, because achieving too much too soon does not respect the key factor that slows the process – your own fears and self-doubt. There is also the risk that you may become disillusioned and therefore become less enthusiastic about future attempts to raise your level of selfhood.

If your sense of selfhood is low, you probably have a tendency to see and to experience life as being extremely complicated and very difficult to handle. If this applies to you, then address each task by breaking it down into a series of small, manageable steps and then tackle each step, one at a time. Whenever doubts, fears, and all the reasons why you cannot possibly do this task flood into your mind, gently and persistently bring your attention back to now, to the specific step you are planning to take. Complete that step, no matter how often your mind wanders, or how much self-doubt engulfs you. There is no failure here. Come back to the step as many times as you have to. Keep trying and you will get through that step. If you do not complete the step, no problem. You also have the choice to try another, different step. When you do get through a step, you will often experience a sense of satisfaction and completion (though in the early stages this can be short-lived) which over time gives you a sense of achievement, and more awareness of your inner power.

Keeping it simple means respecting the way the world is. For example, it takes far less energy to swim downstream than against the current. The law of gravity is so predictable that we fully accept this law without a second thought. I have yet to see any person jumping up and down for hours, attempting to defy the law of gravity by floating in mid-air, scratching their head in wonderment as to why they can't manage it. We all know that such an exercise would be entirely futile, so we would not waste our time on such a pointless endeavour. Just because we cannot see a law with our eyes does not mean it does not exist. We cannot see the law of gravity, but we sure know it is there.

Many of us regularly try to defy other laws of the world, other facts of life that are as absolute and consistent as the law of gravity. For example, many of us repeatedly attempt to live in the future or the past even though the only time we ever truly have is the present. Even when we become preoccupied with either the future or past, it is always in the present that we do this, using up our precious present moments in the process. Many of us insist that life and the world should be the way we want it to be rather than the way it is. Jenny decided in her forties that she would not take responsibility for herself and her life. She lived this way for the following twenty years, but life kept sending her reminders that declining to take responsibility for herself and her happiness simply cannot lead to happiness and fulfilment. Similarly, the only esteem that really registers within us, that we can retain within us, is the esteem we have for ourselves. Yet many of us spend much of our lives swimming upstream on this one, repeatedly seeking esteem and approval from others, which, like trying to defy gravity, simply *cannot* work.

One of my grandmother's favourite sayings was 'look after the pennies and the pounds will look after themselves'. This can be extended to many areas of life. Look after the simple everyday things well, and the big things will generally look after themselves. This principle certainly applies to the recovery and maintenance of selfhood and mental wellness. Sometimes we get preoccupied with the big idea, neglecting to live in the moment and take the simple necessary actions. In the context of mental wellness and the recovery of selfhood, if we look after the little things, with honesty and avoiding the temptation to self-deceive, blame and procrastinate, this helps to get our lives back on track. Be prepared to work for the recovery of your selfhood. Hoping or wishing for recovery will not suffice.

If you have lost your sense of selfhood to a considerable degree, the task of raising your level of selfhood and dealing effectively with the world may seem enormous. When our level of selfhood is low, we tend to become preoccupied with the big picture, seeing only the enormity of particular tasks and challenges, rather than the steps involved in overcoming these challenges. Focusing on the big picture in the early stages, or when things are not going well, tends to result in people losing heart and feeling overwhelmed by the apparent enormity and impossibility of the challenge. Focusing on what needs to be done and the effort to be made now, in the present moment, on a day-to-day basis is a much better approach. Even Mount Everest is climbed one step at a time. According to Chinese philosopher Lao-tzu, a journey of a thousand miles begins with a single step. Foster this way of thinking and behaving in your own life. As Ralph Waldo Emerson once said,

'All great masters are chiefly distinguished by the power of adding a second, a third, and perhaps a fourth step in a continuous line. Many a man had taken the first step. With every additional step you enhance immensely the value of your first.'

The most effective way to live is primarily in the present, coupled with a gentle awareness of the past and the future. People with a low level to selfhood tend to spend the majority of their time focusing on the past or on the future, rather than living consciously and fully in the present. Focusing on either the past or the future can be a tempting diversion from the challenges involved in being fully focused in the present. Worrying about the future can be a way of attempting to prepare ourselves for the future, to be as prepared as we possibly can for what we believe will be a series of disasters. This is understandable but counter-productive on many levels. We place our whole being in a virtually continuous state of high alert for anticipated threats and attacks, the vast majority of which never happen. We pay little attention to the fact that the great majority of our perceived threats do not materialise. Our radar is set to pick up what we perceive as potential threats, and to ignore or dismiss when things go well for us, and when the supposed threats do not come to pass.

Whenever your mind wanders off and you find yourself dwelling on either the future or the past, bring your attention back to the present. This is not a complicated process. All you have to do is concentrate on the time and the place where you are right now, your surroundings, for example, the room, the furniture, the scenery, smells, temperature, your bodily sensations, and whatever activity you are currently engaged in. Describe these to yourself as you do so, out loud if possible, silently to yourself if not. This helps to return you to and ground you in the present moment again. Make this your norm, through repetition but without pressurising or becoming frustrated with yourself, over and over again, until you master it. It takes as long as it takes. Do not put time frames on this.

If your attention is repeatedly drawn to specific times or events in your past, it may help to explore this with a good therapist. You may have unfinished business regarding those times, for example, you may not have grieved fully for and worked through losses or hurts you experienced in your past. A good therapist may help you to work through this and move on with your life.

Most people are aware of the concept, process and importance of physical training, but many are less familiar with the value and the process involved in mental training and emotional health. For example, most of us know that in order to achieve physical fitness, it is safer to do this on a gradual, phased basis. Not only would a crash course in physical fitness be dangerous, it would also be doomed to fail. The same principles that are involved in the process of achieving and maintaining physical fitness also apply to mental fitness, and to emotional and mental wellness.

Becoming mentally fit and emotionally healthy involves implementing the various types of actions described in this book. Having become mentally fit, it requires less effort to remain so, but effort is still required nonetheless. Doing the work involved in building your level of selfhood is akin to placing wafer-thin layers of selfhood, one on top of another. Before long, the layers build up, creating a solid foundation of selfhood, an expanding inner confidence based on an inner knowing and a growing conviction regarding the accumulation of little successes and growth that no one can take from you, because *you made them happen.*

The recovery of selfhood requires close attention if it is to be successful. The outcome is generally directly proportional to the amount of time, energy and attention you are prepared to put into it. Becoming impatient or obsessed with this process does not help. You need to regard the recovery of selfhood as the cultivation of a change in your attitude and your approach to yourself and to life. Changing your habits, patterns, world-view (how you see the world) and your self-perception (how you see yourself) will take time. Selfhood is for life. Incorporate the work involved in raising your selfhood with the patience and perseverance of a marathon runner rather than the sudden and powerful, but short-lived, burst of speed and energy of a sprinter.

Regarding how long it takes to recover your sense of selfhood, there is no single answer to the question that applies to everyone. It takes as long as it takes. The conventional marathon runner is a good metaphor in the context of how you go about beginning and continuing the process of raising your level of selfhood. The marathon runner is not concerned about how many people are ahead of him or her at the end of the first mile. Rather, they concentrate on themselves, on their own race, running at a pace that suits them, always mindful that the race is over twenty-six miles long. No one remembers or cares who was ahead after the first mile. Your recovery of your sense of selfhood is your own personal, private journey. Do not compare yourself to others, or become preoccupied with where others might be in terms of their level of selfhood or their life. That is really none of your business, and is not likely to help you. Maintaining the focus of your attention on yourself and your own personal space is a necessary part of raising your sense of selfhood.

While it may help to have support from other people on this journey, it certainly is possible to do this work on your own. It helps the process if you seek out people or groups who will support you on your journey and in your life generally. If you are confident that you have good support from family or friends you can trust, their support might be better informed if they were to read this book. With the best will in the world, many friends, family and even many members of the caring professions may not understand either the experience of distress or the process of recovery and how it impacts on you personally. These people may give well-intentioned but sometimes counter-productive advice without having fully thought through the impact of their words. They need to bear in mind that a person with a low sense of selfhood, who is in the early stages of their recovery journey, will take the opinions of those close to them very seriously. They do so because they do not yet have a sufficient level of selfhood to trust in their own opinions.

As you will repeatedly see as you work through the book, an essential part of the process of recovery of selfhood is a fundamental shift in the direction of your attention. People with a low level of selfhood have a major imbalance in this area. They tend to be either far too focused outside of themselves and their own personal space, or they excessively cut off from other people and the outside world, locked away in their own thoughts and their own isolated world. A flexible balance between these two poles is generally the outcome of recovering your sense of selfhood.

Balance is such an important aspect of effective living. It is therefore a major aspect of the journey of recovery of selfhood, and surfaces regularly throughout section two. Extremes of anything (far too much or far too little) are generally not conducive to mental wellness, particularly over a protracted period of time. The adage 'moderation in everything, including moderation itself' applies. We need to regularly bring ourselves back to the middle ground, the point of balance and equilibrium. We need to be able to flow as and when appropriate and necessary along the spectrum between both extremes, whilst being largely grounded in the centre, the mid-point of the spectrum.

The process of recovery of selfhood invites us to increase and deepen our understanding of ourselves, how we think, feel, interpret and act. It invites us to consider other, more effective ways of thinking, of dealing with our emotions, of taking more appropriate action, and of relating to ourselves, others and the world. It involves seeing ourselves as the key decision-maker in our own lives, and working toward managing our lives more effectively.

You are your own life manager. You are your own personal decision-maker. You have choices in every situation and you are continually making choices and decisions, whether you realise it or not. Choosing not to choose, deciding not to make decisions, these are choices too. If you feel you are always depending on other people for safety, esteem, approval, acceptance and other aspects of selfhood described throughout this book, this is occurring because of your repeated choice to live in this manner. You have chosen that way of living. You have the right and the ability to make different choices.

We should reflect carefully before deciding against working to raise our level of selfhood. As is clear from the case histories in this book, the stakes can be very high.

Section Two

RAISING YOUR LEVEL OF SELFHOOD

This section begins with a brief discussion of action, reflecting and revisiting, writing and affirmations, important themes in the process of recovering your sense of selfhood. The components of selfhood are then each considered in detail, under five headings: spatial aspects, self-awareness, caring for yourself, attitudes toward yourself, and self-efficacy. Each section contains actions designed to help you raise that component of selfhood.

As you begin, do not become preoccupied about how much time you should put into this work every day, or how long you need to persist with this work. As I said earlier, allocating thirty to sixty minutes a day to reading the book and doing the actions is a good start, in addition to adopting a general attitude of awareness and mindfulness in your life. Use the opportunities that will arise during your day to put the ideas and actions in the book into practice. If you have more time on your hands to give to the work, great, but do not overdo it and totally submerge yourself in the book and the work as you will be putting yourself under too much pressure.

In time, you will integrate the actions within you, and you will carry them out effortlessly and time-efficiently, leaving you more time to work on and integrate other actions. The wide range of actions provides you with an extensive selection to try out and experiment with and find your favourites. I recommend that you do every action several times over a period of several months before deciding which you find most beneficial.

Commit to undertake this important journey in a spirit of gentleness, without judgement or urgency. Work your way through this section of the book, steadily, at a pace that works for you. As you progress, you will regularly be struck by helpful insights and awarenesses. Resist the temptation to assess progress frequently.

Employing the ideas and actions in this section of the book will help you create healthy, life-enhancing routines and structures in your life, with a view to achieving a balanced degree of organisation and order. Commit to noticing and changing your habits and patterns of living through mindfulness, appropriate action, persistence, discipline, and awareness of and reflection on your thinking, actions and choices.

We know the importance of spending a considerable amount of time every day taking care of our bodies, for example, by eating healthy food, exercising, the clothes we choose to wear, and getting sufficient sleep. Our minds, our human spirit and our emotions also need nurturing every day. This section of the book contains many ideas regarding how you might nurture yourself. Working on one aspect of selfhood often will have a beneficial effect on another. For example, by working on your relationship with yourself and on the quality of your self-understanding, you will notice that your self-knowledge also increases. Similarly, you can raise your self-esteem by developing other components of selfhood, such as self-awareness, supportive self-talk, self-care, and committing to valuing and meeting your needs in your life.

Action

Appropriate action is generally required in order to raise our level of the various components of selfhood. Progress is generally made by taking small, incremental steps. Many of us feel that if only we could become motivated, we would get up and take action. In fact, we do not have to feel motivated in order to take action, as the following sentence from the international mental health support group GROW's Blue Book illustrates: 'I can compel my muscles to act rightly in spite of my feelings'. When our level of selfhood is low and we have lost motivation, we must first take action, and keep taking it. Take action on the important things in your life, and motivation will follow. Taking action is akin to starting a car and commencing one's journey. Motivation is like a person on roller-skates behind the car, who grabs on to the car, not when it is stationary, but *as it is moving* and is carried along by the momentum of the moving vehicle.

I generally explain to people who attend me that the recovery of selfhood is action-based. I describe working with me as being just that – work – rather than the cliché 'talk therapy'. Together, the client and I create a plan of action, designed to increase their level of selfhood by addressing aspects of selfhood and of their life that need attention. This book is your plan of action. This section of the book is fundamentally a workbook. See and use it as such.

You may feel confused and unsure regarding what actions you might take. This is very understandable. Focus gently on what the next right thing to do might be. Have a go. Experiment a little. It's not about picking *the* right action. It is about making a decision regarding what appears to be the right thing to do now, given your needs, your current level of selfhood, and the information you have at your disposal at this time. There is no need to engage in a prolonged process of debate inside yourself about what action you might take. Taking action is an important step toward getting your needs met, expanding your comfort zone and enhancing the quality of your life.

Initiate one or two steps ahead of where things are now. Many of the actions suggested throughout section two are this kind of action. Then, be consistent about doing that step, making it part of the norm of how you live. For some, this might mean methodically making plans to create alternate activities between 11 am and 1 pm. For another, who has little faith in their ability to read, it might be to read three pages of a book a day. By sticking with this routine, every day, within 4-6 weeks that person has read a whole book. A forty-five-year-old man, who attends me, had not read a book since leaving school. His school days were not a positive experience for him. He lost his sense of selfhood during those years. He lost faith in his intelligence, including his ability to read, and he avoided reading as much as possible since his school days. Equating reading and learning with pain, criticism and failure, the idea that reading could be a source of pleasure seemed implausible to him. On my recommendation, he brought two books with him on holidays. I had suggested to him that he read three pages a day. He began this way, and soon got into the swing of reading. During those holidays, he read both books cover to cover, and he was delighted with himself. As a result of the action he took, one step at a time, he changed his perception of himself from 'I can't and I won't read', to 'I can and I will read, actually I like reading'. As you will see later, changing your perception of yourself is a very important part of raising your level of selfhood. Taking action involves gently thinking and writing about what first or next steps might be possible for you.

A great deal of research suggests that practice and repetition are generally required to achieve mastery in any walk of life. To those who wish to become writers, Stephen King, well-known American author, recommends writing a thousand words a day, six days a week. People who achieve the pinnacle of success in their chosen area – the Olympics, for example – have generally been practising and partaking in their speciality for up to ten thousand hours, a figure sometimes referred to as being necessary to achieve mastery of our chosen activity. While the recovery of selfhood will certainly not require as much time as winning an Olympic medal, the principle is the same: achieving mastery of a significant goal generally requires action, work and persistence.

When we take action, we channel all of our energy and attention into a harmony of direction. Something shifts within us as our whole being becomes involved and focused on the action we are taking. When we make taking action a fundamental aspect of how we live, our sense of aliveness increases. A balanced approach is important here, so that continuous action is not used to deflect from being in the present, from feeling our feelings, or from taking care of our responsibilities.

Often, our greatest challenge is to get involved in activities, and then, to stick at them. When you don't know where to start, start somewhere. Gently brainstorm and consider the possibilities, without putting yourself under pressure. Creating good routines is an important aspect of action in the early stages. Action designed to meet our needs is very important. In my experience, the following is as predictable and as definite as a scientific formula or a mathematical equation:

Prolonged *inaction* results in stagnation, anxiety, increased fear, agitation, frustration, poor concentration, confusion, isolation, hopelessness, powerlessness, loss of confidence and loss of selfhood, and very poor use of time, rarely being truly in the present, and living in the past and/or the future.

Appropriate action, action that is directed toward raising your sense of selfhood, the kind of actions recommended in this book, results in progress toward recovery of selfhood, social contact, the gradual reduction of fear and anxiety, and the gradual growth of hope, inner peace, empowerment, confidence and clarity.

Your recovery of selfhood depends on you taking action. Only when you begin to take action can your recovery begin. What is to be gained by putting it off? As long as you keep procrastinating, few things change for the better. You still face the same challenge, and your self-confidence continues to diminish.

The following incident illustrates the potential power of action. Craig had been diagnosed as suffering from schizo-affective disorder eight years prior to attending me. Now in his late twenties, Craig's loss of selfhood was immense. The degree of anxiety and distress he experienced was such that he was on a range of medications, taking fourteen tablets a day, each of which was fundamentally tranquillising in its action.

As is frequently the case in people diagnosed with a mental illness, for years Craig lived his life in a state of virtually ever-present fear and terror. Having very little sense of selfhood, Craig had little confidence in his ability to create a fulfilling life for himself, and thus for the previous three years he had retreated from the world, spending his time at home with his parents. With my encouragement, Craig had commenced a return-to-education course six weeks previously. Despite experiencing considerable fear about this course, Craig was making a great effort, not having missed a single lecture during the first six weeks of the course.

One Saturday morning, Craig rang me. He told me that he was feeling overwhelmed, both with emotion and with trepidation regarding the course. He had an assignment to complete for the following Thursday. Craig was convinced that it was totally impossible for him to complete this assignment, which on the face of it seemed doable – to practise taking notes on three pages of text. He had taken extra medication two hours previously, but that had not seemed to help. Craig was very upset. He could see no future, and he asked me if he should go to hospital. Craig had had many psychiatric admissions, often seeing the hospital as an asylum, a place to go to in order to escape from life and its challenges. I suggested to Craig that he take action. Familiar with the importance I place on taking action, Craig suggested that he go for a walk, which I felt was a good idea. I recommended to Craig that, at some stage during the day, he begin to work on the assignment, one bite at a time, for example, taking notes on one paragraph of the assignment. I felt that doing so would give Craig some small sense of achievement, of completion. Also, the very fact of doing this work would likely take him out of his familiar helpless and powerless state, to which he regularly retreated when faced with challenge. I suggested to Craig that he ring or text me later that day.

The following morning, as I had not heard from Craig, I sent a text to him, asking how he was. The following was his reply: 'Improved a lot, sorry Terry forgot to text you last night, got an assignment nearly done for college for Thursday last night and doing another one now so am kept busy but no, things have improved a great deal. Still suffering a bit but at least I can go about my daily and college tasks. Thanks.'

Not only had Craig managed to do one paragraph of the assignment as I suggested, he had virtually completed the whole assignment, and started another. In accordance with my previous suggestions, he approached the assignment one step at a time, and slowly but surely got through it all. His forgetting to text me may have been a reflection of the fact that he felt much better, and therefore his need to be in touch with me had reduced correspondingly. The actions Craig took helped take him out of that powerless and hopeless state, where he was seriously considering admitting himself to a psychiatric hospital, from inertia to momentum and motivation, toward experiencing a hint of power, enough to considerably change how he felt.

Taking action in small steps can often lead to an unexpectedly beneficial sequence of events. Malcolm, a lonely man in his mid-forties, told me that one day, when in the throes of distress and feeling particularly alone, he forced himself to go to MacDonalds with a book for a coffee. Before long, a child's balloon happened to come his way. Malcolm gently tipped the balloon back toward the child, who immediately tapped it back to Malcolm. This balloon ping-pong continued for several minutes, Malcolm and the child smiling at each other throughout. Initially, Malcolm felt somewhat self-conscious and embarrassed, but as the contact continued he noticed how effortless this interaction became for him. Eventually the boy went back to his family. Malcolm felt deeply touched and transformed by this lovely innocent contact with the child. I have heard of many such stories. By taking action, we put ourselves in the way of possibilities that are otherwise not available to us. If Malcolm had not forced himself to leave home that day, this lovely little interaction would never have occurred.

Appropriate action-taking needs to become a way of life. One action on its own will not be enough to change the habits of a lifetime. Balanced action-taking is the best approach. For example, a woman who spends most of her life looking after her family and carrying out household chores does not need to do extra chores. Appropriate actions in her case would be in other, perhaps neglected areas and aspects of herself and her life, such as her needs and her creativity. If you are already a real and perhaps excessive action-taker, to the exclusion of other important things such as silence and rest, then an appropriate action for you might be to be still for ten minutes and tune in to yourself, as described in the section on self-attunement.

Even major projects come about one step at a time. The most complex and beautiful structures in the world such as the pyramids and the Taj Mahal were build one step at a time. Action is a central part of living, learning and experiencing. If you and I were sitting at a table next to a swimming pool, we could debate for hours regarding the temperature of the water. But even if we discussed this topic for four hours, we would be little wiser regarding how warm or cold the water in the pool was, and we would have little sense of how that water felt. One brief entry into the pool would immediately answer all of our questions, and result in us having a felt sense of the water on our bodies. This is an example of an important principle: hours of thinking and talking around a problem or issue often gets us nowhere and frustrates us greatly. We use up great amounts of energy with little return, whereas a fraction of that time spent *doing* often yields real felt change and much quicker results.

The range of possible appropriate actions is extensive, far beyond the scope of this book. Action-taking is relative and personal to the individual. Possible actions may vary, depending on the person, their level of selfhood and their particular current prominent unmet needs. The section on each component of selfhood contains several actions. Some of the possible actions for you will likely be quite simple and fairly obvious, as it was for Vincent, who admitted that his bedroom had for years resembled 'an absolute pig-sty'. Tidying it, in small bites, was one aspect of my recommended work for Vincent, and it helped considerably. Having a tidy room was a new experience for Vincent, one that to his surprise he very much enjoyed. He then proceeded to clear out his garage, thus continuing the action-taking, and reaping the benefits of a bedroom and garage that were now organised and user-friendly. He also had a felt sense of productive change, a new and very welcome sensation for Vincent.

Actions need not involve a major expenditure of energy or time. As with all aspects of the recovery of selfhood, small and frequent steps is the way forward. They are best when made part of a routine. Action effects change, thereby having the potential to change how we feel. Actions can be as ordinary as getting out of bed, having a shower, putting on clean clothes and going for a walk, or making changes that we experience through our senses – hearing, sight, smell, taste, touch. Actions that involve getting your hands dirty or that are 'messy', such as gardening, baking or art, can be particularly energising. Since achieving balance is a key consideration, a person who already does a lot of baking and not a lot else may feel comfortable doing more baking, but it would be more beneficial to experiment with actions with which they are less familiar and perhaps less comfortable.

Possible areas of action include:

> household chores (if you are lacking in motivation, you might consider hoovering one room a day as a good beginning); self-care, tending to yourself and your needs, including your social needs such as having a meaningful social network and your need to belong; a daily treat (at least one!), something you might come to enjoy, like a walk; writing (more on this later); reading; swimming, or learning to swim; 15-30 minutes resting or meditating; attending a mental health support group; yoga; Tai Chi; adult education; going somewhere nice for a coffee, with a good book; aromatic candles and oils around the house; meditation; classes, such as art, cooking, whatever you are attracted to or feel you might be interested in (or in which you might have been interested in past years); treatments, such as massage, aromatherapy; daily exercise; making more and better contact with people; initiating more, for example phoning people rather than leaving it to others to contact you; if you spend a lot of your day in bed, getting up half an hour earlier and doing something definite for fifteen–twenty minutes; listening to a relaxation CD in the morning, and perhaps in the evening also. At least some of your actions should be with the intention of pampering yourself.

Experiment with these and other possible actions you feel might suit you, including the actions listed throughout this book. Commit to a gentle process of taking charge of your life, of being proactive. Be creative. You could write out a plan for the day. If you decide that art will be a regular action for you, begin by organising your art room or corner. Look at what is missing in your life and take action in these directions, for example, more variety in your life, levity, fun, lightheartedness. Now, or further down the line if your level of selfhood is very low, consider a course that might further your education, or enhance or develop a new skill or interest.

One of the advantages of small actions is that we frequently experience completion. Completing tasks gives us a sense of satisfaction and relief and gradually enhances our self-confidence. Making actions a part of our routine, of how we live, enables us to experience completion regularly, thereby in time raising our self-confidence and changing how we feel for the better. Do not let your self-doubt stop you, for example, 'I don't know how to do anything', or 'there is no point trying any action as it will not work'. Do them anyway. Your self-doubt will only stop you if you let it. You may feel nervous about taking action, that's understandable. For the moment, you need to do it, and do it repeatedly (and gently), and gradually your anxiety decreases and your sense of satisfaction increases.

The importance of action is recognised by mental health support groups, including GROW. At its weekly meetings, GROW encourages participants to pick one action for the week and then try to ensure that participants complete that action, irrespective of how bad they are feeling that week. Many people allow how they feel to totally dictate what they do. If they don't feel good, they do very little. Their challenge is to become practised at taking action *irrespective of how they feel*. Otherwise, they risk losing out on the potential of action to change how we feel for the better.

Actions taken by two clients attending me have served as a useful living laboratory for the sort of changes they needed to make in their lives. Both men were quite unsure of themselves, took few risks, consequently experiencing life as dull and repetitive. One man loved playing chess, the other was in the process of renovating his home. With the chess-player, I used his love of chess as a testing ground for experimentation, including risk-taking. Through this experimentation, he experienced that he could indeed take more risks than he had realised.

He gradually extended this practice of more action- and risk-taking into other areas of his life. The man who was renovating his home was already in the process of experimentation regarding what he wanted in his home. He felt energised by this, particularly by the fact that he was making his own decisions, something he generally avoided, as he was afraid of making decisions. With my encouragement, he extended what he had learned about himself and his ability to take action through the renovation process to other aspects of his life.

The real test of how well a tree is rooted is not in fine weather, but when the wind is howling. The real test of a ship is not how it floats when safely docked in a harbour, but when it is out at sea, dealing with the various challenges nature throws at it. We humans need to be tested too, which is why our self-confidence tends to drop when we habitually withdraw from the challenges life presents to us.

Reflecting and revisiting

Regular reflection helps us to become more aware of how we are living. When combined with the information contained in this book, regular reflection will help you to increase your awareness and knowledge of yourself, your habits and patterns of dealing with yourself, others and life. Reflection is therefore a recommended action for every component of selfhood, as you will see. Reflection will also help you keep focused on your goals, including the actions you work with as outlined throughout section two of the book, and the overall aim of raising your sense of selfhood.

Cultivating the habit of regular reflection and revisiting helps you become increasingly in better contact with yourself, your feelings and your needs, important barometers and compasses as you journey through life. Regular reflection and revisiting will therefore ultimately benefit you considerably, leading in time to a non-critical, highly developed yet low-grade, non-intrusive ever-present awareness of yourself and how you are. You may resist the idea initially, particularly if the habit of escaping from contact with yourself is strong within you. In order to integrate the habit of reflection and revisiting within you, you need to deliberately bring the action of reflection and revisiting into your thinking several times a day.

Develop the habit of reflecting and revisiting situations at regular intervals during the day. The key point is to ensure that you do so several times each day. This approach roots the new habit within you, in time turning what used to be unfamiliar into what is familiar, second nature. This is a very good habit to cultivate, and will ensure over time that you become far more aware and mindful of how you live, and of the process of recovery of selfhood upon which you are now embarking. One approach would be to reflect in the morning soon after waking, midday-meal-time, in the evening around six pm, and at night, shortly before sleep. Or, experiment regarding reflection times that might suit you, and come up with a reflection routine that works for you. Each reflection is brief, a minute or so is enough. The topics upon which to reflect are discussed under each selfhood component. When reflecting at night, use the time to gently put the day that is just over to bed, and reassure yourself that you will be there to support yourself tomorrow.

Regular reflection enables you to develop a quality which is recommended in many spiritual and religious belief systems: becoming an observer of yourself, in all the situations you encounter, a low-key, non-intrusive state of being an observer of yourself as you go though your day, your life. During these moments of reflection, reflect on the interactions, thoughts and feelings you have experienced, the actions you took or did not take. Think about whatever tasks you are working on, and gently reflect upon whether or not you honoured these components of your selfhood during the previous few hours. This type of gentle questioning, done kindly, helps train you to become increasingly mindful of yourself, the components of selfhood, and the degree to which the components of selfhood are developed within you.

Reflecting on how you felt and how you responded to various situations and encounters during your day is a necessary part of the process of recovery of selfhood. Doing so helps you to increase your understanding of how you contributed to your experiences, consider the choice of actions you have at your disposal, and organise your sense of how you might take better care of yourself as you go through each day. If you do not revisit and reflect upon the day's events, you miss out on the opportunity to use your day and your life as a living laboratory, filled with opportunities to learn through experimentation.

Revisiting and reflecting overlaps with other topics in this book. For example, by becoming mindful of how you talk to and treat yourself, you will begin to notice just how self-critical and self-undermining you may have become. And by taking appropriate action, you begin to redress this situation.

Revisiting a situation that occurred with another person, when the dust has settled, can be an effective way of resolving conflict and misunderstanding, when done with honesty, each party sticking to 'I' rather than 'you' in the communication with the other. For example, if you reacted in anger to a loved one, come back later to this with the person, and explain what was really going on for you. Perhaps you felt hurt, translated the hurt into anger, and communicated just the anger. Now, consider risking to communicate the deeper truth of how you were really feeling, and you will find that this will help to heal you, the other person, and your relationship with them.

Writing

The benefits of daily writing have been known for centuries, hence the age-old practice of keeping a daily diary. Writing is a form of action, an important form of communication with ourselves. I regularly ask people who attend me to get into the habit of daily writing. Ten to fifteen minutes a day is plenty. Writing a little every day is far better than writing for two hours one day and nothing for the rest of the week. In order to integrate the habit of writing within you, it is necessary to write most days, if not every day. Many people report that, as they become accustomed to this practice, they look forward to their moments of writing. They increasingly find the experience of journalling as akin to communicating with a trusted friend.

Daily writing can be an unexpectedly enlightening practice. After just a week or two, many people report to me that they have been surprised at the insights about themselves that have surfaced in their writing. Write with the intention of communicating openly, honestly and directly to yourself, about yourself.

When I recommend daily writing to clients, many immediately become uneasy. They tell me that they are not good writers, that they are scared of being judged, that they generally do not write, and would prefer not to do so now. They doubt their abilities across many aspects of life, including their writing. I reassure them that this is not a test of anything, the quality of their English, their handwriting, or any other skill.

I suggest that you get an A4 notebook that you devote solely to this writing. Some people prefer to write on sheets they can later tear up, out of fear that others may read it. This is understandable, but if at all possible use a notebook that you can keep. If you use loose sheets and quickly dispose of them, your opportunities for later reflection on your writing are considerably reduced. Writing by hand communicates far more to us about ourselves than writing on computer or typewriter. It is a far more personal activity, in which aspects of your soul, your life experience, the essence of who you are, get expression.

Recently I discussed this with a client. He wanted to write on computer rather than by hand. He explained that whenever he wrote by hand, his writing was very tentative and controlled. He told me that he wrote by hand very slowly, as he gave great consideration to every word and sentence he wrote. I gently pointed out to him that his habits regarding handwriting reflected important aspects of how he lived – tentative, unsure of himself, vulnerable, afraid. He would come far more in contact with these important aspects of himself through writing by hand than by writing on computer, so I advised him to do the former. He would have much preferred to write on computer, thus avoiding contact with the painful emotions he seeks to avoid, like many of us. But he needed to come in contact with these emotions, feel them and work through them, so he can move on with his life.

The range of topics you can choose to write on is wide. The important thing is not the quality of your writing, or that you 'get it right'. The key point is that you *do the writing*. Within a short time, like water finding its own level, you will find your own style and topics upon which to write. So long as you keep your writing real, honest and as spontaneous as possible, there is considerable leverage regarding what and how you write.

Here are some ideas. I suggest you experiment with some or all of these ideas, and perhaps come up with some of your own. Some of the actions at the end of each selfhood topic later in section two involve writing also. Many of the suggestions below are explored in more detail under their own heading in the book:

> A diary of your day, describing what you did, how you felt, what happened in your day, and your reactions to the events of the day as experienced by you; your life story; the range of emotions you experience; your experience of painful emotions such as shame, sadness, loss, grief, fear, hurt, loneliness, worry, vulnerability, anger and rage; what you think and feel as you go through your day;

what you do with your emotions; write letters to important people in your life, both living and dead, saying what you need to say to them, which you do not post; reflections, insights that strike you; your strengths; your survival strategies; the parts of yourself you regularly banish or deny, the parts you have decided don't belong within you, that you have ostracised, shut down, rejected, or judged to be bad, such as your hurts, fears, insecurities, sadness or emotional pain; your sense of self, and the various components of selfhood described in this book, as you become familiar with them; your needs, the degree to which they are met, and possible ways to meet your needs; brainstorming regarding activities and actions you might partake in during your day; your doubts about yourself; your vulnerable side; the parts of your story that never get told; your patterns and habits of living; what strategies you have used to hide yourself; your experience of being hurt in life; what parts of you that you don't want others to see.

In your writing, work on using the language of feeling, of the heart. This is explored in detail in the section on dealing with emotions. You might find this hard to do, if you are not used to being in contact with the emotional aspect of yourself, but with practice you will manage it. Give your inner, private, personal self a chance to express itself in your writing.

Read over what you have written toward the end of each day. Reflect on your writing, and ask yourself if there is anything else that you have missed or avoided. Notice your reaction to what you have written. You may become aware of insights you hadn't previously noticed, such as subtle habits and patterns you live by that you have previously either not noticed or ignored, or beliefs about yourself or the world, or rules for living that you operate by but which have not been tested for truth or accuracy. An example of this surfaced yesterday with a client. At the beginning of our session, she said that any stress at all makes her 'crack up'. I wasn't at all convinced that this was the case. I asked her to think of situations in her life where this statement was clearly not true. Although there were several concrete examples in her life where this belief about herself was certainly not true, she could not think of any. I mentioned that she had just completed a year in college, and had done very well in her exams. She had not 'cracked up' under the stress of being in college and doing the exams. We discussed several other situations and challenges with which she had dealt effectively. During our discussion, she came to realise that what she was telling herself about cracking up under any stress was not based on fact, and that she needed to let go of this belief, as it was interfering with her progress in life. We need to be mindful regarding what we tell ourselves about ourselves.

Use your writing and what you have written to learn about yourself. For example, you may discover that you blame others, or procrastinate and find excuses to avoid, far more than you thought. You may find that you put others before you too much, or vice versa. Look out for areas in your writing where you have used 'you' or 'they'. Rethink the situation, bring your focus back to yourself. Rather than focusing primarily on what the other person might have said or done, reflect on how you handled the situation and how you felt. Consider what other possible actions and responses existed in that situation, and think about how you might handle future similar situations in ways that might work better for you, and write accordingly. At the end of each week, read over and reflect briefly on what you have written during the week. From time to time, read material you wrote several weeks or months previously. You are likely to notice changes in your writing that reflect increased awareness and an increased sense of selfhood.

Regarding when to write, I suggest you experiment, based on what might work for you. How you feel may vary at different times of the day, and your writing will reflect this. For example, many people whose sense of selfhood is low experience a great deal of anxiety in the morning, at the prospect of facing the day. At night, their level of anxiety is at its least, since the day is almost over and relief in the form of sleep is just around the corner. Write at different times of the day and see how it feels. If you decide to write in the evening, make sure that you include your morning experiences too. You may find that writing both in the morning and evening provides insights regarding how you feel and the actions you take at different times of the day.

Affirmations

An affirmation is a clear statement we make to ourselves, including ones that have not yet come to pass but which through repetition we gradually integrate into our worldview and our perception of ourselves. We make these statements in the present tense. For each component of selfhood, I have created a corresponding affirmation, all of which are listed in Appendix One. You are of course free to create your own affirmations. Affirmations are best written as positive statements and in the present tense. The language used should be powerful and definite.

Initially, the content of the affirmation may not correspond to your perception of yourself. Let's look at the affirmation 'I am safe. I protect me. I am the provider of my own protection and security' as an example. This affirmation corresponds to the self-generated security component of selfhood. If your level of selfhood is very low, you may feel that the opposite is the case, that you feel unsafe and unprotected far more frequently than you feel safe and protected.

Your mind can only focus on one thing at any given instant. By repeating an affirmation, you make your mind focus on the affirmation, and you bring an unfamiliar new possibility into your mind. You gradually become more aware of the concept of safety and being safe, since you are now consciously introducing this concept into your mind many times every day. You will become more aware of being safe as you go about your business each day, gradually incorporating it into your data bank through repetition. You will increasingly notice how you regularly take action to make yourself safe and to protect yourself, whereas previously you may have thought you were powerless to do so. Safety will increasingly become part of your vocabulary, your awareness, and you will therefore gradually feel safer within yourself.

You do not have to force yourself to believe the contents of your affirmations. Simply commit to repeating them, over and over. They will take effect in time, provided you keep up the work, including the work involved in raising your level of selfhood as discussed throughout this book. Consider writing out some or all of these affirmations as listed in Appendix One, so that you can access them easily during your day. Make a few copies and keep them in your wallet, pocket or handbag. Read the affirmations as part of your reflection times. Where possible, read them aloud, as hearing you say them in your own voice increases their impact. If you or someone you know has the ability to do so, consider making an audio recording of affirmations in your own voice, that you can listen to several times each day.

We now move on to a detailed consideration of each component of selfhood.

1. Spatial aspects of selfhood

The spatial aspects of selfhood involve or relate to space. The five components of selfhood in this category are boundaries and personal space, self-centredness, self-belonging, self-containment, and your comfort zone.

Boundaries and personal space

We begin by turning our attention to the bedrock of selfhood. Our boundary and personal space is pivotal to our sense of selfhood. The poet Gerard Manley Hopkins once said that 'your personal boundaries protect the inner core of your identity and your right to choices'. According to American writer Joseph Campbell, 'Your sacred space is where you can find yourself again and again'.

We each have our own personal boundary, which is roughly at an arm's length. I refer to the space within your boundary as your own personal space. It could be argued that your personal boundary is by far the most important boundary you possess, and that your personal space is sacred, your true home. Most people spend a considerable amount of time most days away from their physical home. From birth to death, we live our entire existence inside our boundary, within our personal space, which accompanies us everywhere, into every interaction and activity in which we partake. It therefore makes sense to be aware of and look after both our boundary and our personal space. We need to ensure that both are functioning to their highest quality, providing us with the most life-giving and nurturing personal environment possible.

We acknowledge our boundary and personal space in our thoughts, conversations and actions. When someone we hardly know stands too close to us, they have crossed our boundary and entered our personal space. We may feel a strong desire to remove them from our personal space immediately. We may sometimes feel we need to 'get some space'. Many of us know people who do not 'respect boundaries', or who have a habit of being 'in your face'. When faced by such people, we may feel the desire to 'hold our ground', to 'stand firm'. We may 'put up a wall' when we find ourselves in a situation we experience as threatening or challenging. We sometimes speak of people (including ourselves) as being 'out there', 'all over the place', often meaning that they do not appear to be well grounded in themselves and within their own space. As we get to know and trust another, we may decide to 'let them in' to our private world. We sometimes speak of 'drawing lines in the sand', meaning that there are certain lines which we have decided that people should not cross. Our boundary is an important example of a line in the sand. Managing our personal space and boundary effectively is essential if we are to live a contented, fulfilled and peaceful life.

We regularly encounter situations that illustrate the importance of boundaries. We are expected to respect the boundaries of people who are designated as carrying out important duties. Passengers are not allowed to enter the pilot's cockpit or the bus-driver's space, for example. Boundaries mark the end-point of our home and the beginning of other people's property. These boundaries are obviously physical, but they are also highly symbolic, demarcating what is ours and what is not ours, what is home and what is not home. Our feelings for all that lies within the boundary of our home tend to be very different to our feelings for what lies outside these boundaries. We understand that when we approach another's front door, it is not appropriate to open the door and walk into their house. We are expected to knock and to request entry rather than demand the right to enter or to take this right for granted. When a house is being constructed, setting out the boundaries that define the property is one of the first priorities on the plans. Boundaries also apply to our possessions. There is a general understanding in society that other people's belongings are 'off limits', 'out of bounds'. The entitlement of sovereign states to police their boundaries and protect their land and space within these boundaries is recognised worldwide.

Yet, our personal boundaries and personal space, which are so fundamentally important to us, receive little priority in comparison. I believe that every human being has the right to ensure that they manage their personal space effectively, under their sole governance. Our boundary and personal space deserve at least the same level of recognition and respect as physical boundaries, particularly from ourselves. Our boundary and personal space are illustrated in Diagram 5.

Having a solid, healthy sense of selfhood empowers us to manage our boundary more effectively, subtly opening and closing our boundary as we deem necessary, rarely feeling under significant threat or pressure. The following is also true, and forms the basis for the actions in this section: *learning to manage your boundary and personal space more effectively enhances your sense of selfhood.* A person with a solid sense of selfhood will instinctively manage their boundary and personal space effectively, making good contact with themselves and others, while generally maintaining inner peace within their personal space.

Successfully managing our boundaries, and living within our personal space is essential if we are to live a fulfilled and happy life. Boundary and personal space problems have knock-on effects on many other aspects of selfhood. This is why some of the components of selfhood in this book also include a task involving boundaries. Our personal space is like the pilot's cockpit: the controls we need to live effectively lie within arm's reach. It is up to us to ensure that we stay in charge and use the controls effectively.

When our level of selfhood is low, we may operate our boundary in an erratic fashion, swinging from one extreme to the other, fluctuating

BOUNDARY & PERSONAL SPACE

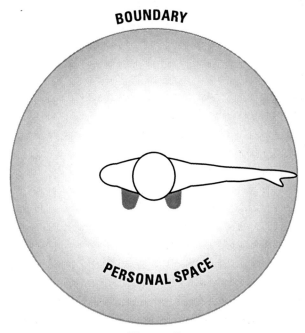

Diagram 5

between excessively open and closed boundaries, a reflection of our ever-present experience of fear and inner chaos. Or, we may shut down the boundary altogether, letting no one in and keeping us inside, in a relatively safe but dull and lonely prison.

Many people whose boundary is consistently and excessively closed experience a great deal of anxiety and agitation, a kind of hyper-energetic state. As human beings, we regularly experience a flow of energy within us, which we expend on a regular basis. As illustrated in Diagram 6, if our boundary is always closed, this energy has nowhere to go, other than to continue spiralling around within us, gathering speed like a tornado or vortex, resulting in us experiencing considerable ongoing agitation, excitation and distress. Making good contact with others and ourselves provides channels whereby this energy can be released.

In addition to providing us with a method of effectively controlling what enters our space from the outside world, when working effectively, our personal boundary minimises the excessive drainage from our

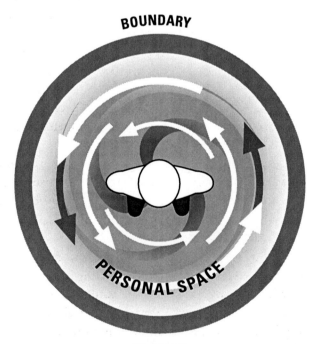

ENERGY

BOUNDARY

PERSONAL SPACE

Diagram 6

personal space of very important commodities such as our energy, attention and inner peace. When our level of selfhood is low, our energy may continuously drain from our personal space into the outside world through the gaping holes in our boundary.

Throughout the past century, we have become increasingly aware of the effects of pollution on our health and environment. Most developed counties now recognise the value of clean air, water, and unpolluted environments. This contrasts with the lack of appreciation of the importance placed on the quality of the environment within which each of us continually lives, our own personal space. I am regularly struck by people who are well informed about the world and current affairs, yet are oblivious to the key importance of their boundary and the quality of their personal space. The mother of one young male client of mine is an example. I know this woman, and my young client's description of how he experienced his mother is consistent with my sense of her. He described his mother as being virtually always irritated, bored, unhappy and giving out, blaming and judging others, leaning on her children, having a poor quality relationship with her husband, and few if any friends. It would appear that this woman is unaware that, irrespective of the cleanliness of the air she breathes and the water she drinks, she is living in an extremely polluted environment. Her own personal space is continually polluted by her own anger, frustration, irritability, low sense of selfhood, and lack of her needs being met. Crucially, she continues to choose to *do little or nothing to change*, despite her life being miserable and no end of advice and encouragement from her son and others. Such advice from another rarely works, unless the person themselves is prepared to work at getting their life back on track.

One male client of mine in his fifties described how he was affected by phone conversations with a friend who lived some distance away. His friend had been badly hit by the severe 2009–10 economic recession in Ireland. Typically, the conversation revolved around his friend telling my client in great detail how difficult things were. When the conversation was over, his friend generally felt much better, but my client felt deeply affected by the conversation. His friend had unwittingly offloaded his stress onto my client, whose boundary was excessively open, resulting in his friend's situation causing deep upset within my client's personal space.

Both men were unaware of these subtle processes, and his friend certainly was not deliberately attempting to use or to burden my client.

Nevertheless, what transpired every time they talked was a crossing of my client's boundary, an invasion of his personal space, and the subsequent changing (or 'polluting') of his personal space for several hours. My client fared much better in these conversations when, at my suggestion, he took charge of his personal boundary and his personal space right through the conversation without saying a word about this to his friend. He learned a very important lesson: it is possible to listen empathically without having the avalanche of the other person's distress plunge into his personal space like a tsunami. He consciously kept the other person's distress at the boundary of his personal space and dealt with it there, rather than open his boundary wide and let it all pile in on him as he had always unwittingly done previously. If someone came to your house, opened a window and proceeded to fill your house with smoke using a hosepipe, you would react immediately and take whatever steps were required to stop your home being polluted. Commit to maintaining a similar level of vigilance regarding the pollution of your personal space. Maintain this vigilance quietly, without conflict with others, or long-winded explanations or justification to others about what you are doing. The only person you need to convince about the importance of managing your boundary and personal space is you.

As depicted in Diagram 5 on page 69, people with a high sense of selfhood, whether they know it or not, tend to live very much from within their own space. In contrast, as illustrated in Diagram 7, people with a low sense of selfhood spend a great deal of their time and focus on looking beyond their boundary, outside of their personal space. For example, during a train journey, Belinda became quite agitated by conversations of other passengers. Twenty-four years of age, Belinda's boundaries were habitually wide open. She had no buffer to the sounds around her, which then flooded into her personal space. She therefore experienced these sounds as being much louder than they were in reality. A house where the front windows and front wall have been removed is a suitable analogy: people in the front sitting room of that house will experience external sounds as being much louder than their neighbours, whose windows and front walls are intact.

Trying to read other people's minds is a boundary and personal space issue. The lower a person's level of selfhood, the more likely they are to regularly attempt to read other people's minds. We need to remind ourselves that we have no authority or jurisdiction over another person's boundary and personal space. There is little point in becoming preoccupied with reading another person's mind. As depicted in Diagram 7, in attempting to do so, we try to leave our space, enter theirs, and figure out what is going on within their personal, private world, something that is both impossible and beyond our rights. It is far better to work on enhancing our sense of selfhood, and engage with others from a place of increasing power and strength, from *inside* our boundary, from *within* our own personal space. We have to live within our own space, even when we do everything in our power not to. Attempting to live continually outside our personal space is as impossible as seeking to defy gravity. Inevitably, when we try to do so, we end up tying ourselves and our lives up in knots.

If your pattern of behaviour has been to be excessively focused on others, then a core aspect of your work will involve shifting the focus of your attention away from other people and back to yourself. If you continually look outside of yourself to provide you with the components of selfhood, you will need to practise bringing your attention back into

INVASION & EXODUS

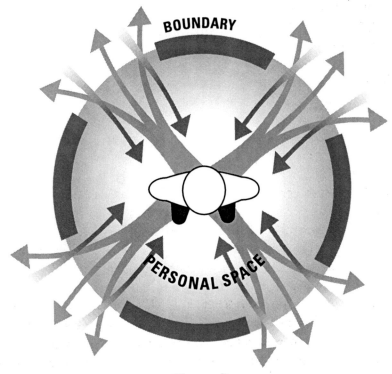

Diagram 7

your own space. You will need to make a serious and continuous commitment to this practice. Initially, this will feel quite unfamiliar to you, and that is to be expected. Carry on regardless.

As illustrated in Diagram 8, attempting to protect ourselves in a world in which we do not feel safe, we may create a reinforced, thickened boundary continuously as a frantic compensatory mechanism. Large, gaping holes frequently remain in our boundary, through which we continue to experience hurt and invasion, and repeatedly expend our attention and precious energy.

It is therefore understandable that people with a low sense of selfhood experience a feeling of emptiness, or as one client put it, 'I'm an empty vessel'. When our personal space is emptied of our attention, and of the components of selfhood, we feel that emptiness, that craving, often without realising that it is often our sense of self for which we are craving. Our personal space needs to be filled with the components of selfhood, and when it is, we experience inner peace and contentment.

REINFORCED BOUNDARY WITH GAPING HOLES

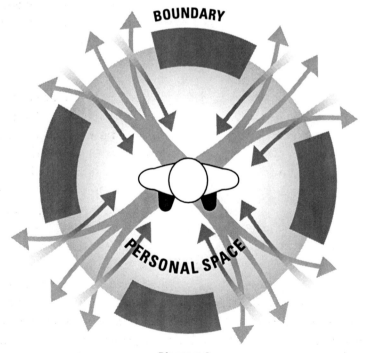

Diagram 8

We may alternate between leaving our own personal space to enter other people's space and excessively allowing and inviting others to cross our boundary into our personal space, which subsequently becomes crowded and tension-filled. Our personal space becomes invaded by the views, opinions, needs, demands and expectations of others, real or presumed.

An analogy may help to demonstrate how impossible living outside one's own space and boundary really is. We know how important it is to have a sense of 'home' in our lives. We experience our home as being an extension of ourselves, our place. We are familiar with the boundary around our home. Imagine that, at the end of your day, you head home as usual. On this occasion, you do not go home, but to your neighbour's house. You enter the house without knocking, kick off your shoes and throw yourself on the sofa. You are going to make yourself at home here. You are going to eat in your neighbour's kitchen, use their toilet, have a lovely relaxing bath, sleep in their bed, and generally treat their house as if it were your home. However, your neighbour's house is unfamiliar to you, and it is not your home anyway, so you cannot do a whole lot there. You do not have the authority to make many decisions in or about your neighbour's house. You do not belong there and you never can belong there because, by definition, you are in someone else's space, though this does not stop you from trying.

You are restless all night, but you cannot figure out why. You do not sleep properly because you are not in your own bed. Your neighbour and their partner are also in the bed, and they are not one bit happy about your presence in their home and particularly in their bed. The next day you leave your neighbour's house, head off to work, and in the evening come back to your neighbour's house again and the saga continues.

This scenario sounds implausible, even ridiculous. No one would consider it appropriate to live in someone else's house as if it were their own home, eat at their dinner table, watch their TV, and sleep in their bed. Yet when our level of selfhood is low, we repeatedly try to enter other people's space, seeking from outside ourselves that which can only be provided from within. Explicit in terms such as self-confidence, self-belief, self-trust, self-reliance, self-esteem and the majority of the qualities referred to in this book is the reality that they refer to the presence of these qualities *within ourselves*. For example, your level of self-confidence is the degree to which *you* have confidence in *you*. It is not a measure of how confident other people are in you. Yet many of us spend a major portion of our lives searching outside of ourselves for what we can only truly find within.

Imagine the chaos that would occur if there were no boundaries between people's houses, or if these boundaries were ignored by everyone. This is precisely the situation you experience when your boundary is fractured and fragmented.

Gordon's story illustrates the central importance of personal boundaries in our life. Gordon attended me in his mid-fifties. He had been diagnosed as suffering from depression fifteen years previously. Gordon's experiences of personal boundaries in his home of origin helped to define how he dealt with boundaries throughout his life. Gordon had three siblings. From his early childhood, one brother effectively ruled the household. This brother was unpredictable, causing considerable disturbance at home throughout Gordon's childhood and teenage years. Gordon's brother regularly invaded Gordon's boundary. Eventually, Gordon's bedroom became his only sanctuary. His bedroom became a metaphor for his personal space, the walls and door of his bedroom had become a prized boundary. He did not like people entering his bedroom: it was *his* space. However, even here, Gordon's boundary was regularly crossed and his space invaded by his brother, who thought nothing of barging into his room whenever he chose and paid no heed to Gordon's requests for privacy. Eventually, Gordon took to locking his bedroom door, an attempt to reinforce his boundary. He came to regard his bedroom as being like a round tower, providing three hundred and sixty degree visibility. This enabled him to maintain vigilance over any potential 'enemies' who might seek to invade his space, his bedroom. In his bedroom, Gordon felt safe. Out there in the world, he felt unsafe, under threat.

Throughout his life, Gordon continued to live in accordance with this experience of boundaries and safety. He was generally hyper-vigilant regarding any possible invasion of his space, as he equated this with being inevitably hurt. He had no sense of being able to effectively employ his boundary and protect his personal space out there in the world. Consequently, he lived a narrow, safe life, taking few risks, missing out on a great deal of potentially fulfilling opportunities. Gordon attended me on five occasions, principally to help him cope with an upcoming major change in his life, moving house. Our work revolved around boundary and personal space work. Gordon found this to be helpful and practical, and he was quite excited by the small but successful steps he took, and looked forward to a gentle and gradual expansion of his life in accordance with the ideas within this book.

While the importance and role of the self receives little attention currently within psychiatry, one occasionally finds references to issues described in this book as being aspects of selfhood. For example, according to the psychiatry textbook, *Companion to Psychiatric Studies 2004,* in a reference to schizophrenia:

> Many of these hallucinations and delusions can be interpreted as a result of a failure to distinguish between ideas and impulses arising in the patient's own mind and perceptions arising in the external world, a so-called 'loss of ego boundaries'.

People who become diagnosed with schizophrenia have an extremely low level of selfhood, not least in regard to their boundary and personal space. If your level of selfhood is extremely low, you may not feel at all sure of who you are, and therefore who you are not. It makes sense that you may not be sure where your thoughts are originating from, since you have such a fragile sense of yourself to begin with. Nor should it be so surprising that a person with an extremely low sense of self and consequently without healthy boundaries, without any sense of inner power or confidence in their ability to protect themselves in this world, might constantly worry that others can invade their space, read their thoughts or have power over them in various ways.

As one man in his mid-twenties diagnosed with schizophrenia currently attending me says, he 'disintegrates' on a regular basis, particularly when he is around people. His sense of selfhood is so fragile that he experiences himself collapsing under perceived threats, such as being in the company of others. When a person has no experience of having boundaries, and no confidence in their ability to protect themselves or to generate their own inner security, such a reaction makes perfect sense.

The experience of people diagnosed as having schizophrenia demonstrates the relevance of our personal boundary and personal space to our mental health. Feeling unsafe is one of their most frequent feelings. As illustrated in Diagram 8 on page 74, their boundary tends to contain a mix of great thickness and gaping holes, often simultaneously. Parts of their boundary are extremely open, allowing the world to pile in on top of them as they regularly experience overwhelm, repeatedly leave their space, becoming preoccupied with what other people are saying and doing. Other parts of their boundary are very thick, as they desperately seek to protect themselves by withdrawing and shutting down. There will be more on this in my future book on schizophrenia.

ACTIONS

1.   Familiarise yourself with your boundary
Stand up, and stretch out your hands in front of you, like a policeman stopping traffic. Your boundary is where your hands are. Turn slowly around, three hundred and sixty degrees, keeping your arms outstretched. You have just traced your boundary. Visualise this boundary being all around you, from the top of your head to your toes. Picture this boundary as being transparent, strong and solid, about three inches thick. This is *your* boundary. Visualise many doors in your boundary. Only you can open these doors and let stuff in, or yourself out, since it is your boundary, and you are the gatekeeper of your boundary. You have little or no control over anything outside your boundary. However, whatever comes toward you, once it reaches your boundary, you decide how you are going to deal with it. You always have decided how to deal with what comes toward you, even if you are not aware that you are doing so. From now on, you will do so with far greater awareness, with an inner knowing that you are now consciously taking charge of your boundary. Carry out this exercise at each reflection time.

*2.   Become aware of the current state of your boundary and personal space,
     and how you manage your boundary*
Become an observer of what happens at your boundary, how you are affected by interactions with others. What kind of boundary do you have? If you are very sensitive, if you are generally preoccupied with other people and how they feel about you, then your boundary is likely to be very open, leaving you vulnerable to repeated hurt many times every day. Your boundary may be quite closed, with prison-like walls, letting very little in. Perhaps your boundary alternates between these two poles, which may also co-exist simultaneously. The aim here is to become aware of the type of boundary you have created.

Commit to noticing when you cross your boundary, either seeking the qualities of the components of selfhood from outside yourself, or in an attempt to read other people's minds because you do not feel safe. Work on noticing when you have allowed others to cross your boundary and invade your space, whether they intended to or not.

What does your personal space feel like? How does it feel to live within your personal space? Is this space predominantly calm and peaceful, or is it generally filled with pressure and tension? Who or what apart from you is in this space? Is this a crowded space where you can hardly breathe? Does it feel hectic, frantic, empty, lonely, dead, stagnant? Does how it feels change much during the day or on different days of the week? If your personal space is predominantly peaceful, then your level of selfhood is quite high. If it is generally filled with anxiety, tension, fear, unhappiness or other difficult emotions and experiences, then your level of selfhood is low.

3.   Creating a healthy boundary and peaceful personal space
Resolve to take charge of your boundary. From now on, determine that you will live inside your own boundary, in your own personal space. Make a commitment to gently and repeatedly bring your attention back into your personal space, within your personal boundary, and to provide yourself with what you need from within your own space. Become aware of your boundary and your personal space, roughly an arm's length all around you, as described above in action 1. See this as your lifetime home. Commit to being the pilot, in charge of the cockpit that is your personal space, within your boundary, having all of the controls within arm's reach. You decide what does and does not penetrate this boundary. You also decide what leaves you and your personal space through this boundary, for example, the degree to which you choose to enter the space of others as you communicate and connect with others. You are in charge, both of your personal space and of your boundary.

4.   Everything inside this boundary is yours, and yours alone
You are the ruler of your personal space. You decide what comes into it. Your boundary is there to keep you safe and secure, to keep hurt and threat out. Visualise perceived threats coming at you, hitting off your boundary and falling harmlessly to the ground, your personal space remaining untouched by the threat.

Keep your boundary in mind throughout your day. Bear in mind the difference between a perceived threat and a real threat. When our level of selfhood is low, we may frequently perceive threats where objectively there are none. A perceived threat certainly *feels* real, and you may be inclined to react accordingly. This is not at all to diminish the experience of feeling threatened. It is reassuring to know that often, when we feel unsafe, we actually *are* safe.

5.   Think of your boundary and personal space as a game of tennis
Tennis is a useful analogy in relation to boundaries and personal space. On the tennis court, each player has their territory, their space. The net and the lines on the court depict the boundary between what area is in play and what is out of bounds. See yourself as a tennis player. The net and the lines on your side of the tennis court is your boundary. Your side of the court equates with your own personal space. When the ball crosses over the net into your side, the ball is in your court. You are the decision-maker regarding how you play your next shot.

6.   Be the boss. You are anyway, whether you realise it or not
You live your life from inside your own personal space. In that space, you alone are the boss, the decision-maker. Risk taking small steps toward taking charge of the situations you encounter. Doing so will in time enable you to risk trusting in your ability to decide what is good for you, and to take charge of the situations you encounter.

7.   Gently push what is not yours, what is not current or real, out of your space
There will be times when events and exchanges are so significant to us that they penetrate our boundary and alter the state of our personal space. Nevertheless, we can take action to minimise the invasion of our boundary. Whenever you are affected by situations or encounters, you have allowed them into your space. Gently remind yourself that you are not buying into this way of living anymore, and gently direct that thought, feeling or reaction to the outside of your boundary. Similarly, when you become preoccupied with the future or the past, gently push these thoughts to the outside of your boundary and let them go. With practice, you will become good at this.

8. *Conscious control of boundary exercise*

At each reflection time, practise taking conscious control of your boundary. Sit for a few moments, and get a sense of your boundary, at arm's length. Visualise yourself closing your boundary tight, all around you. Notice how that feels. Then, picture your boundary relaxing, opening, allowing the outside world to enter your space. Notice how this feels. Do this exercise three or four times on each occasion.

Several times each day, notice how your boundary feels, and experiment with opening and closing it. With practice, you will become more aware of your boundary. You will considerably increase your conscious control of your boundary, rather than your boundary responding and reacting to events without your conscious control. Take charge of your boundary, and you will soon learn that you have the ability to open and close it *as you see fit*.

9. *Personal space exercise*

At each of your daily reflections, and any other time you like, carry out the following brief exercise. Sitting comfortably, close your eyes, and become aware of your boundary all around you. Turn your attention to your personal space. Notice how this space feels. Does it feel tight, under pressure, claustrophobic? Does it feel like there are worries or people in this space? Identify who and what is in your space. Pick one. Get a sense of where they are within your personal space. Place the palms of your hands in front of them, and gently push them forward by extending your arms until they are at the point of your boundary. Notice them at your boundary. Bring your hands down. Notice how your personal space feels now, a little freer perhaps. One by one, gently escort every person, every worry and stress that feels inside your space to your boundary in the same fashion. Move the people and things you are happy to have in your space to the outside of your boundary also. Notice how it feels after you have removed each person from your personal space. With practice, you will notice that your personal space becomes more peaceful, less crowded. You will continue to keep those you want close to you, while becoming more aware of your own private, personal space. Use this exercise at each of your reflection times, and any other time you choose. Use it to clear your space after contact with people where your peace has been disturbed.

10. Evaluate what people say and do from outside your boundary
Decide that as a general rule you will only evaluate what others say and do once you have ensured that you are keeping their words and actions outside your boundary. That way, you preserve the environment of your personal space. You decide who and what to let in, and you increasingly deal with people's words and actions from a place of inner power and calm. Before, during and after contact, be mindful of your boundary and your personal space, and what happens to your boundary and personal space during and after contact.

11. Practise staying at home
Do not cross your boundary and leave your space, either in an attempt to figure out what others are thinking of you, or to people-please. This is a total waste of time, energy and attention, and you will get it wrong most of the time anyway. When you notice yourself doing this, bring your attention back home, into your personal space, where it belongs. You have no business in other people's space. Everyone lives in their own world. Ensure that you stay within yours.

12. Practise not taking things personally
The vast majority of incidents where we take offence are not intended to hurt us. Of the few that are intended to hurt, the fact that there was an intention to hurt does not mean that you have to go along with this and feel hurt. It takes two to tango. How you react to a particular situation is largely up to you, since you make your choices and decisions. You can decide that you will not allow the actions or words of others, whether intended or not, to penetrate your boundary and pollute the environment of your personal space and dictate how you feel.

13. Boundary and personal space declaration
Read this declaration to yourself at every reflection time, out loud if possible.

> 'Wherever I am, I have a boundary. My boundary is always with me. My boundary is solid, strong and firm. I live within my personal space, inside my boundary. My personal space is my home. My personal space is safe, peaceful. It is mine and mine alone. I decide who or what gets through this boundary into me.

I am in charge of my boundary. I alone am the boss. Other people's boundaries, space and worlds are not my concern, so I will not attempt to go into their space. I will stay within mine. Whatever comes at me, I am in charge of my reaction. I will not let the words of others enter into my space unless I choose to. I am always aware of my need to live within my own space, my own boundaries. I am vigilant about this. I notice when I leave my space, and I quickly take restorative action, and come back into my own space and boundary. I notice when I allow others to cross my boundary and invade my personal space. Again, I quickly take restorative action. I gently and firmly push what has entered my space back where it belongs, outside my boundary. Through these actions, I restore calm, peace and space within my boundary, in my own personal space.'

14. Don't leave home without your boundary
Your boundary is at least as important as your coat, keys, umbrella and anything else you make sure to bring with you on leaving home during the day. Remind yourself many times every day of your boundary, and of your power within your boundary, both during your daily reflections and staying mindful of your boundary and personal space throughout your day.

15. Reflection
At each reflection time, consider how you have handled your boundary and personal space since your last reflection. Your reflection times are an ideal time to do the exercises described within these actions. Commit to be mindful of your boundary and personal space until your next reflection time.

16. Affirmation
'My boundary is intact, and I am in charge of it. I live within my boundary, in my own personal space as I go through the day. My personal space is peaceful and calm.'

Self-centredness
Many people immediately react negatively to the idea of self-centredness, equating it with undesirable characteristics such as selfishness. I use the

term simply in the context of space, and how we organise ourselves in terms of our own space in our dealings with the world.

The centre of something is its mid-point, the fulcrum around which it revolves. The centre-point is often a key aspect of the object, the heart of the unit, without which it may not be able to function. For example, the hub is an essential part of a wheel. The importance of words that depict the centre, such as hub, pivot or fulcrum, is illustrated by the fact that their use has extended beyond the world of physics, engineering and mechanics, being widely used in everyday language. One definition of a fulcrum describes it as a thing that plays a central or essential role in an activity, event or situation. For example, it is widely recognised that research is the fulcrum of the academic world. The word 'hub' is widely used to describe the centre of operations of organisations.

Whether we realise it or not, each of us is at the centre of our life, the fulcrum around which our life revolves. Healthy self-centredness is therefore a quality worth developing. Healthy self-centredness means that your awareness is centred within yourself, providing a springboard for healthy and effective action, for contact with others and the world. In decisions and actions taken by you and others, you ensure that you bear in mind your own wellbeing, and the impact on you of those decisions and actions. Do not lose sight of yourself and your needs in the various interactions and encounters you experience. As depicted in Diagram 9, healthy, functional self-centredness is a balanced, calm state, where you interact effectively with the world from a place of being centred and grounded within yourself.

Pilots sit at the centre of the cockpit, equidistant from all of the plane's control systems, all of which are within arm's reach. If pilots sat to one side of the cockpit, then some controls would be out of reach while others might feel uncomfortably close for the pilot. The centre-point of the cockpit is the optimum position for the pilot. Similarly, being at the centre of our personal space is the optimum position for us to repeatedly return to.

The state of selflessness is sometimes recommended as a way of life, particularly in religious and spiritual contexts. This works for some, particularly people with a solid sense of selfhood who manage to combine an attitude of selflessness with being well centred within themselves. They have chosen to streamline their lives and their needs to a selfless way of life. For others however, particularly those with a low sense of selfhood, living in a selfless state is a recipe for deep unhappiness, brought about by years of unmet needs, having little hope of this ever changing.

Living with healthy self-centredness ensures that unhealthy, more extreme positions are avoided, including excessive people-pleasing. In such situations, the balance between self-centredness and placing one's attention on others is skewed greatly in favour of other people, at the expense of neglecting oneself. Selfishness is the other extreme, another state of major imbalance, where the person's attention is always focused on themselves, to the exclusion of the needs, rights and wellbeing of others. As is usually the case, balance is the key.

People experiencing emotional and mental health problems may spend a considerable amount of time on themselves, their thoughts and feelings, frequently interpreted by others as selfishness. Generally, this is more accurately described as self-obsessiveness or self-preoccupation rather than self-centredness. It is often a consequence of experiencing a great deal of fear, insecurity, self-doubt, and considerable lack of

HEALTHY SELF-CENTREDNESS

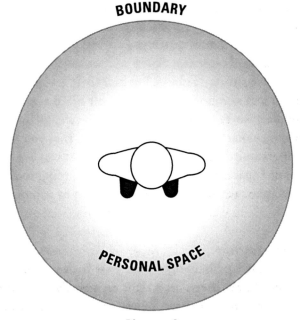

Diagram 9

confidence in one's ability to relate effectively to other people. This is quite different from and not to be confused with healthy self-listening, self-observation, or healthy self-centredness.

ACTIONS

1. How self-centred are you?
As you go about your day, gently pay attention to where your attention goes. You are seeking to become aware of your habits and patterns regarding self-centredness. Notice whether you are well centred within yourself. You may find that you are not centred within yourself, but instead your attention regularly scatters to the four winds so that you are literally all over the place.

2. Becoming centred within yourself
See yourself as being the centre of your world, a king or queen sitting on a throne at the centre of your personal space, the ruler of your territory, your world, your personal space that lies inside your boundary. This may require quite a shift in your thinking, especially if you have tended to be outwardly-focused, so be patient with yourself. Turn your attention in a different direction, toward yourself. Remind yourself gently and often, several times each day, that wherever you are and whatever you are doing, you are at the centre of every experience, contact and interaction you have. Do this not in an egotistical fashion, but because it is a fact. Factor 'I' into every equation and situation you find yourself in, in a balanced way, of course. Your life revolves around you. Accept this fact and live accordingly. When you notice that you are not well centred, that you have become somewhat ungrounded, gently remind yourself that you live at the centre of your personal space, and visualise yourself returning to the centre of your personal space again. Do this as many times as you need to during the day.

3. Self-centering exercise
Sit comfortably, preferably upright with your back straight and relaxed. Eyes open or closed, whatever feels right for you. Extend your hands in front of you, and picture your boundary all around you, at your fingertips. See yourself as being right at the mid-point of your personal

space, centred and grounded. Keep this image in your mind for a few minutes. When you are finished, keep this awareness of being centred within your personal space with you.

4. Reflection
At your reflection times, remind yourself of the *fact* that you are always at the centre of your world. During your reflections, gently consider how centred within yourself you were over the past few hours since your last reflection. Commit to being consciously centred within your own personal space until your next reflection time. Remind yourself that your experience of people and the world revolves around you, not around other people.

5. Affirmation
'I am centred within myself in all of my interactions and activities.'

Self-belonging
Definitions of the word 'belong' include being a part of something, being in an appropriate place, situation or environment, being a member of something, to be included, to fit in naturally, to have a home, a rightful place, to be owned by or in the possession of something. Self-belonging therefore refers to the felt sense of being a part of yourself, experiencing the appropriateness of living within your personal space as your rightful place, to feel at home within yourself, at one with yourself, happy and content in your own skin.

If your sense of selfhood is low, you may regularly experience the feeling of not belonging, not being a part of anything, whether you are alone, with family, friends or in a crowd. Even if you have good relationships and are a member of groups of various types, you often feel the absence of that sense of belonging that you believe you should have and that you desperately want to experience.

Generally, the core problem is an absence of a sense of self-belonging, an inner knowing that you belong to and within yourself. This is often at the root of the repeated experience of not belonging within relationships and groups. Unwittingly, you may be projecting your lack of self-belonging into the world, which reflects and mirrors exactly that experience right back to you, a boomerang effect.

Many of us attempt to compensate for lack of self-belonging by excessive involvement in and identification with our communities, our material possessions and our various roles. This may seem to work to some degree for a while, but if these are taken away, we feel this loss of belonging acutely, as we have little or no felt sense of self-belonging.

A major contributor to the lack of self-belonging, which is such a part of low selfhood, is the fact that attempting to live outside your own personal space and boundary is also an ever-present feature of low selfhood. It is pretty impossible to experience a sense of self-belonging when your focus and attention is rarely inside your own space. Instead, your attention is almost constantly outside your own space, on everyone and everything else but you. Any attention you do give yourself is generally filled with considerable self-criticism and judgement.

Think of it in terms of your home. The key reason that you regard it as home is because you live there. When you are at home pottering around, you do not constantly think about other people's homes. If you did, this preoccupation would seriously diminish your feeling of being at home. Rather, you are usually very much at home, experiencing that comforting sense of feeling and being at home. This comfort and familiarity comes from your accumulated experience of being in this place, this building and all it currently contains and has contained in the past, including the people and pets that have lived or currently live with you.

Any home that has not been cared for or lived in for many years will show all the signs of the years of inattention and neglect. The longer you are away from home, staying somewhere else, the weaker that inner-felt sense of home becomes. Imagine that you return to your home, having been away for ten years. During this time, the house was vacant. No one kept a check on it or looked after it. You enter the house. Everything is exactly as you left it, but it does not feel like home. It feels quite lifeless, with almost an eerie silence and emptiness. The signs of neglect and the passage of time are obvious throughout – broken windows, thick cobwebs, paint faded and peeling, and the musty smell of dampness.

You decide that you want to turn this house into your home again. Your first challenge is to tend to the considerable amount of cleaning up and repair work that has built up during the ten years you were away. This will take some time. You then need to redecorate the house. You sleep there for the first week, but the house still does not have that cosy, comforting being-in-my-own-familiar-home feeling. It takes quite a considerable amount of time to clear out the place, carry out repairs and decorate it to your liking again. Only then does it even begin to feel like home.

Beginning the journey of recovery of self-belonging after years of not really being at home in yourself and your own personal space involves a similar process. Initially, when you bring your attention back into your own space on a regular basis, you experience feelings of emptiness, strangeness, almost an eerie feeling. You may feel tempted to get out of there as quickly as you can and shut the door behind you. As you persist with coming back into your own space, you might not like some of the initial emotions and reactions that surface within you. Feelings of sadness, abandonment, emptiness, hurt, anxiety may rise within you as you re-experience the space that you left and have neglected for many years. Stick with it, and in time you will come to belong within and to yourself again.

ACTIONS

1.   To what degree do you feel you belong within yourself?
Reflecting on this question will give you a sense of where you currently stand on the issue of self-belonging.

2.   Spend more time 'at home', where you belong
If you want to experience greater self-belonging, then you need to live 'at home' more, within your personal space, inside your personal boundary. You need to get to know yourself and this space, in the same way that you know your physical home well. As you go through your day, gently remind yourself that you belong in your personal space and within your boundary.

Letting your emotions surface is an important step toward becoming more comfortable in and ultimately belonging within your own personal space. Keep coming back into your own personal space. Be prepared to stay with and work through all that surfaces within you as you do so. If you persist, gradually your personal space will take on the feelings and qualities of home. You will increasingly be at peace within yourself and your space. You will know, a knowing that becomes increasingly strong and well rooted, that you really do belong to and within yourself. Then you will be in a much better position to experience belonging with others.

3. *Reflection*

At each reflection time, consider the degree to which you were mindful of the issue of self-belonging since your last reflection. Simply considering the issue very briefly at each reflection will keep this issue in your mind as you go through your day.

4. *Affirmation*

'I belong to and within myself, within my boundary, in my personal space – my home.'

Self-containment

To contain means to keep within limits, to hold or be capable of holding within a fixed limit or area, to keep or have inside (for example, this box contains a pair of shoes). To me, self-containment means holding and keeping ourselves generally inside the limits of our boundary, within our personal space.

People with a strong sense of selfhood are generally self-contained, whereas people with a low sense of selfhood tend not to be. People with a high level of selfhood deal with self-containment in a balanced way. As they go through their day, they sense, evaluate and work through situations from within their own space. They contain the process of figuring out things within themselves predominantly. A person with a high sense of selfhood will generally know instinctively when it is appropriate for them to share their thoughts, feelings, needs, ideas, fears and concerns with others. They won't get the balance right on every occasion and they are okay with that, since they recognise that they are human and not a machine.

In contrast, people with a low level of selfhood tend to operate either at one of the two extremes, or flitting between both extremes. These extremes are:

1. Total self-containment, where they contain absolutely everything within themselves, rarely if ever reaching to others for help or support. A gradual build-up of pressure arises within, as a consequence of the excessive containment. For many, this build-up of pressure results in an inner-felt experience of great

stress, which spills out forcefully when the strain gets too much. This may occur in the form of a major reaction that seems out of context to the situation, as perceived by others.

2. No self-containment, where they feel the need to constantly spill out their feelings, needs, thoughts, fears and concerns to others. Often, the person selects a small number of people they trust deeply, and repeatedly relies on these people to come up with solutions and advice. Some people with low selfhood regularly pour out very personal and intimate information to others, including those they have just met.

ACTIONS

1. Identify your patterns of self-containment
Identify where you stand on the spectrum of self-containment depicted in Diagram 10. As with all components of selfhood, it is your patterns

SPECTRUM OF SELF-CONTAINMENT

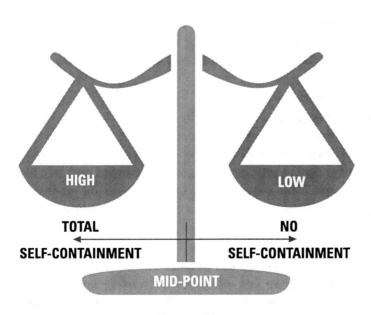

Diagram 10

and habits that matter, not one-offs. If your patterns are balanced, if you are truly happy with them and they are effectively meeting your needs, great. If you are toward either extreme, then this needs attention.

2. Risk adopting new patterns of self-containment

If your patterns of self-containment are causing you problems, risk adopting new patterns of self-containment. If your pattern has been one of little or no self-containment, then take baby steps toward greater self-containment. This will not be easy. You will frequently feel a strong impulse to pour out your fears and anxieties on to others. Pouring them out in your daily writing is a good compromise initially, allowing you to defuse the pressure build-up inside you without increasing your dependency on others. If you are at the other end of the spectrum, rarely sharing anything with others, consider taking small steps toward sharing ideas, concerns and worries with other people, if there are such trustworthy people in your life. This will feel frightening initially, and may bring up emotions such as sadness that were previously kept at bay. Do it anyway and go with the emotions as they emerge. You will soon come to the realisation that you can handle both greater self-containment and whatever emotions you have been avoiding. You will feel happier, more connected both to yourself and to others, and more liberated. Writing in your journal about your fears, worries and other issues you self-contain excessively can be a helpful way to offload them.

3. Be gentle with yourself

On many occasions, you will not be able to contain your anxieties and fears within yourself. That is to be expected, and it is perfectly okay. It takes some time to develop confidence in your ability to self-contain effectively, and in any case the goal is balanced and not total self-containment. This process of adjustment must be gradual, since it involves a fundamental shift in how you deal with yourself and others.

4. Reflection

At your reflection times, ask yourself to what degree you were self-contained since your last reflection. Depending on what side of the mid-point you are on, reflect on how you managed your particular challenge regarding self-containment during the previous few hours.

Renew your commitment to balanced self-containment between now and your next reflection time.

5. Affirmation
'I practise balanced self-containment in my actions and interactions.'

Your comfort zone

A person's comfort zone refers to the range of situations and experiences in which a person operates in which they feel secure, safe, in control, at ease, without experiencing undue stress, fear or anxiety.

The creation of comfort zones is a common practice for us human beings. Through the sensing process described earlier, the child arrives at certain conclusions about themselves, people and the world, about which aspects of life they experience as comfortable and uncomfortable. Aspects that the child is comfortable with constitute that child's 'safe world', their comfort zone. Elements of life with which the child is uncomfortable, that the child experiences as unsafe and threatening, lie outside the child's comfort zone. As we go through our childhood, adolescence and into adult life, we each maintain a comfort zone within which we feel safe and secure.

The lower our sense of selfhood, the smaller this comfort zone will be, and the fewer people and things will be in it. A person with a high sense of selfhood will have a comfort zone that is wide and expansive, encompassing the majority of the situations and challenges they encounter. They rarely feel as if they are frantically close to the edge of their comfort zone, in danger of falling off a cliff into an abyss. They generally feel pretty comfortable being close to the edge of their comfort zone on a regular basis. They do not feel threatened or become frantic at the edge, since they know they have themselves to rely on, unless the situation itself is one of considerable danger. They generally feel little or no desire to reduce their comfort zone, because for them there is no need. They feel safe anyway.

People with a low level of selfhood are regularly frightened by life and its challenges. They tend to withdraw from challenge rather than tackle it. For them, life is like living continually in a hurricane, so they habitually batten down the hatches. People with a low sense of selfhood frequently withdraw deeply into the cocoon of their limited comfort zone. They rarely emerge from the safety of their cocooned comfort zone, seldom coming close to the edge of their safety circle. They are terrified of this, fearing they will fall off the edge of the world and into an abyss from which they may never return. This process may continue throughout life unless they address it, often becoming more entrenched the older they become. The longer they live within a small safety circle, the more challenging it is to break out of it. The contraction and expansion of our comfort zones is illustrated in Diagram 11.

There are parallels here with the training of elephants. Baby elephants whose owners want to train them for captivity are methodically trained into submission. The training process involves chaining the young elephants to fixed objects. Initially, strong chains need to be used, as the animals resist being restricted in this fashion. In time, the elephants come to realise and accept that the chains are stronger than they are. They give up the fight, and no longer struggle against being chained. They in effect become institutionalised, equating the experience of being chained with submission. Gradually, the elephant trainers can use less powerful restraints, eventually reaching the point where fully-grown elephants

COMFORT ZONES

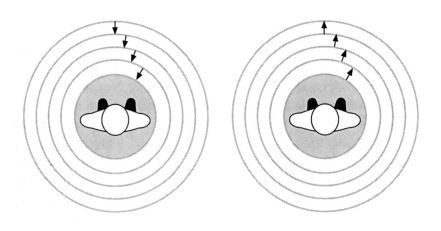

CONTRACTING COMFORT ZONE

EXPANDING COMFORT ZONE

Diagram 11

acquiesce when a flimsy string is attached to their leg. We humans have the ability to figure things out a great deal more than elephants. If we commit to it, we can gradually break free of and go beyond the chains that bind us.

Apparently, when a horse refuses a fence, they lose confidence, and the fence seems bigger next time. This is similar to what happens to humans. When we refuse to jump a hurdle, by declining to go beyond our comfort zone, our sense of selfhood slips a little. Problems arise for us when refusing new fences becomes a habit. Our comfort zone and our sense of selfhood shrinks, and our anxiety, fear and defensive living increases.

We need to be tested in the world. When we are tested, we find resources within ourselves to deal with the challenges that face us. If we continue to avoid being tested in the world, our comfort zone and sense of selfhood diminishes accordingly. We feel increasingly unable to face even the ordinary everyday chores and activities, which now feel anything but ordinary and safe. People who have fallen off a horse, or have been involved in a car accident are advised to get back in the saddle or driver's seat as soon as possible. The longer the person avoids returning to what now may seem outside their comfort zone, the more difficult it becomes. By withdrawing deep into one's comfort zone as a reaction to such an accident, the person gets some semblance of relief, but paradoxically their level of fear, anxiety and lack of feeling safe escalates.

It is as if we are being carried on the conveyor belt of life, slowly but surely, from birth, through the various stages of our life, to death. This conveyor belt frequently brings us to a tunnel, the tunnel of the unknown. If we avoid entering the tunnel, the conveyor belt of life will tend to bring us back repeatedly to the entrance to the same or similar tunnels of the unknown. We will therefore either choose to enter the tunnel eventually, or we will have to find ways of either repeatedly jumping off the conveyor belt or walking against it, which consumes great amounts of our energy. We will likely have to continue this process of avoidance for life, or most of it, so that we do not inadvertently find ourselves being conveyed into the tunnel. We incur great losses as a result, lost opportunities and possibilities, which generates immense sadness within us. These feelings may tempt us to further embellish our forms of escapism, sometimes reaching the point where we avoid any contact with ourselves or the world that might remind us of what we are doing, and what we are missing out on.

Being at the edge is where growth happens for us, where there is challenge, excitement and anxiety at encountering the unfamiliar. Retreating temporarily into our comfort zone enables us to catch our breath, ground ourselves and re-group. We generally do best when we have a healthy balance between being within our safety circle and stepping outside it, a healthy flow between the two.

When our level of selfhood is low, we may be sorely tempted to live deep within our safety circle, in the depths of our cocoon. This cocoon is safe and does not itself provoke anxiety within us, although we may still experience considerable undercurrents of anxiety caused by our patterns of avoidance of our own feelings and our pervasive sense of fear, terror and lack of feeling safe. The cocoon is stagnant and boring, with little growth and fulfilment. Our comfort zone becomes progressively smaller. We become increasingly dependent on the few people, things and activities that exist within our safety circle, often in quite tension-filled relationships. When someone or something precious leaves our life as will inevitably happen, it affects us profoundly. There is now a large void in our already sparse comfort zone. Our challenge is to risk going to the edge and beyond, and staying there, albeit briefly in the early stages, and to feel whatever emotions surface, the common ones being anxiety, fear, sadness and anger.

When our level of selfhood is very low, we find it difficult to expand our comfort zone. We may have stopped trying to expand it years ago, like the elephant becoming convinced that it is a pointless exercise. Or, as Jimmy's history exemplifies, we may resort to self-delusion and self-dishonesty, two alluring and seductive bedfellows. Now in his early fifties, Jimmy has never had a sexual relationship. His level of selfhood has been low throughout his life. In his twenties he did briefly date one girl, but this quickly fizzled out. He found the uncertainty and risk of the unknown too much to handle. Jimmy consequently became very anxious in her company, and the girl soon ended the relationship. When Jimmy began attending me, his level of selfhood was very low. Nothing in his life seemed to be working. He was in a state of almost constant distress, paralysed by his experience of life. Since then, he has made considerable progress in many areas of his life. He got his business up and running, very tentatively initially. Previously a doormat in all situations, he has developed considerable confidence in his ability to work effectively and deal with the wide range of people with whom he does business. He is a man of considerable integrity. He gets a good reaction from the people with whom he does business. He still lives within a narrow comfort zone, with few people in this circle, principally his father, his siblings and their children. His mother and sister died four and eight years ago respectively. His inner life still revolves around his mother and sister. Jimmy has not moved on and does not want to. He has not filled the enormous voids, both those that were always there for decades, and the deaths of the two women he most loved in the world. He finds it easier to think about them than to seriously go about making new female contacts.

Relationships with women is an aspect of life he has not yet addressed. Greatly lacking confidence in his attractiveness to women, he has not asked a woman out on a date for over twenty-five years. As far as Jimmy is concerned, it is a risk too far. Jimmy deludes himself into thinking there is little point in dating a woman because if he did, he might see another woman the following week that he might prefer. This is self-delusion. The seductive power of self-delusion is reinforced by the fact that Jimmy is fundamentally an honest and sincere person. Jimmy is not a fickle man. He would be loyal and respectful to any woman he dated. Deep down inside, Jimmy knows the truth: it is terror of risk and rejection associated with putting his heart on the line that holds him back.

Alternating between the edge and the cocoon is perfectly okay, especially in the early stages of this work. At the beginning, we do not know if we can survive outside our comfort zone. We make progress when we stay outside for as long as we possibly can, and then withdraw into our safety circle to catch our breath and regroup. If we persist with this approach, we slowly build up a series of little successes that gradually generate self-belief. We expand our comfort zone and consequently the richness of our experience of life. Our level of selfhood increases. When we consistently do the opposite, it has the opposite effect. Our safety circle continues to contract further, leading to stagnancy, the absence of growth in our lives, and a wide range of distressing feelings and experiences.

As our level of selfhood rises, we become more comfortable around the edge of our comfort zone. Through repetition and practice, we become more confident at engaging in activities that lie outside our comfort zone. Our comfort zone increases as we become more practised at and secure about crossing the edge of our comfort zone.

ACTIONS

1. Identify your comfort zone
You may struggle with this, as we often block what we are uncomfortable
with out of our awareness, or at least we try to, often not fully succeeding.
Draw a circle, and over the next few days add who and what is in your
comfort zone to your circle, and what lies outside of your comfort zone.
This will give you more clarity regarding what lies inside and outside your
comfort zone, and make this more real for you. For example, you may
feel comfortable being with and talking to one person, whereas you might
feel quite uncomfortable being in and speaking in a group of three or
more people. You might feel relatively comfortable chatting to people,
but asking someone out on a date might be outside your comfort zone
and therefore be very anxiety-provoking. Bear the idea of your comfort
zone in mind as you go through your day and you will come up with
several examples that are within your comfort zone and others that lie
outside it.

*2.   What are your patterns regarding your comfort zone, living at its edge
       and crossing over into the unfamiliar?*
Do you routinely avoid what is outside your comfort zone? Perhaps you
stay so deeply within your comfort zone that you generally do not come
close enough to its edge to notice it or to feel that anxiety. The healthiest
pattern is where you are living within your comfort zone most of the
time, but you regularly step outside this comfort zone into the unknown,
into zones of life with which you are unfamiliar and perhaps fearful, but
which offer potential for growth and fulfilment. The lower your sense of
selfhood, the more fearful the unfamiliar will be.

3.   Commit to expanding your comfort zone
Learning by experience, and risking to expand your comfort zone is a
prerequisite for the development of a solid sense of selfhood. You
accomplish this by testing yourself, by developing the habit of stepping
outside your comfort zone, small steps that may feel big. Be prepared to
feel the uncomfortable but inevitable anxiety that comes with putting
yourself where you do not feel safe. Make this a medium-term project
that you pursue every day, with self-honesty and avoiding self-delusion.
If your level of selfhood is low, you are likely to feel unsafe every time

you step out of your comfort zone, experience a surge of anxiety, and a strong urge to retreat into your comfort zone. Do your best to stay in this new place, outside your comfort zone, for as long as you can. Withdraw into your comfort zone when you feel you really have to.

Spend some time over the next few days getting a sense of what you tend to be drawn to, and what you tend to avoid. Try to expand your experience by beginning things you have not previously done or tend to avoid. You will be able to come up with ideas if you think about it sufficiently. The actions discussed on page 58 may help in this regard.

4. Many attempts will be needed

Retreating into your comfort zone after making an effort to do something that is outside your comfort zone is perfectly natural. Doing so is not evidence of failure. It is to be expected as part of the process, a sort of insurance policy or safety net. A child learning to ride a bicycle will fall off many times. They will in time master the art of riding a bicycle, provided they persist with their efforts. Withdrawing into your comfort zone having stepped briefly out of it is never a problem. Return without undue delay to the process of stepping out of your comfort zone. You soon realise that you are indeed able to step out of your comfort zone, survive there, and in the process, expand your comfort zone.

The edge of your comfort zone may feel like the edge of the world. Crossing that edge may feel terrifying, as if you are risking falling off the edge of the world into oblivion. There is solid ground on the other side, you just don't know that yet as you haven't sufficiently tested the edge of your comfort zone. Become practised at testing this edge, gently, one step at a time, and you will come to realise that the edge is actually more like a paper bag than the edge of a cliff. With practice, you learn to punch your way through, and increasingly experience that there is indeed solid ground on the other side, and that you are safe there too.

In the Chinese language, precisely the same symbols are used for the word 'crisis' as for 'opportunity'. How wise this is. A crisis, when handled properly and seen for what it truly is, often presents immense opportunities for change and growth. Similarly, what is often called a 'breakdown' can become a 'breakthrough', when it is properly understood and managed well. I have seen this many times with clients with whom I have worked.

5. Do one thing that scares you every day
I saw this sentence on a t-shirt when on holidays recently. It is good advice. Getting into the habit of doing things that scare us helps us to expand our comfort zone. Doing one rather than, say, ten such actions a day emphasises the importance and wisdom of taking small steps, one at a time. These can be quite simple actions, such as making a phone call you have been avoiding, or reaching out for help and support when you feel low.

6. Reflection
At your reflection times, consider whether the issue of your comfort zone has arisen since your last reflection time. If it did, did you notice it, and how did you manage it? Commit to being mindful of your comfort zone and of the occasions when it comes up as an issue in your life. You do not have to become preoccupied with this issue. A gentle, focused awareness of it will do just fine.

7. Affirmation
'I balance living largely within my comfort zone with a willingness to go beyond my comfort zone when doing so is genuinely for my own good, my own growth.'

Case histories
Here are two stories of people I have worked with, for whom the spatial aspects of selfhood were central to our work together.

Alan's story is a good illustration of the key importance of our boundary and personal space. He was in his mid-forties when he began attending me as a client. His life was falling apart. His wife wanted a separation, he had developed an alcohol problem, he had recently become unemployed and money was quickly running out. Having become overwhelmed, Alan was admitted to a psychiatric hospital, and he began attending me soon after being discharged from hospital.

Alan had experienced a great deal of anxiety and depression for much of his life. He frequently turned to alcohol for comfort. He continued into his adult life with patterns of living that he had developed as a child. For example, he tended to lean excessively on other people. The buck never stopped with him. He always passed it on to someone else, wanting others to make the hard calls, the decisions, to make everything all right. Alan did not generally persist with anything, either as a child or an adult. For example, when away from home on boy-scout trips in his childhood, he regularly came home early, homesick, rather than stay and experience the understandable anxiety and uncertainty of being away from home. He quickly ran back to safety of home. All this continued to further undermine his sense of self, as he repeatedly searched outside himself for the components of selfhood, which as I have discussed, does not work.

As we worked together, he gradually took ownership and responsibility for himself and for his own wellbeing. He surprised himself, increasingly realising, through experimentation and practice, that he could provide his own self-esteem and self-confidence, that he was the primary creator of his own sense of selfhood. One day, when we were discussing personal space and boundaries, he summed up his situation in a few sentences. Alan said that all his life he was 'out there', holding his hands wide apart in front of him, signifying being out there, outside of himself. He said that he always put himself outside of his own space and repeatedly let others into his space. He was literally all over the place. His attention was on others, what they thought of him, how he might get their approval, and to whom he could turn to make everything okay and help him feel safe.

Now, he continued, he realised that his primary focus needed to be within his own boundaries, inside his own space. His outstretched hands met, fingertips touching, signifying a boundary between him and the outside world. He went from initially feeling he would collapse without his marriage to knowing that in fact it was appropriate for his marriage to end. He felt that it had not been a great marriage, and that he deserved better. Alan reported feeling far less anxiety, greater empowerment and inner peace, and more control over his life. He reported having some really good days, despite the fact that there were such major challenges in his life. For the first time in a very long time, he was feeling joy and energy.

Stella's story demonstrates the importance of self-belonging. In her mid-forties when she first attended me, Stella had been diagnosed over the past five years with both depression and obsessive-compulsive disorder, both of which were clearly related to her loss of selfhood. She had been attending psychiatrists regularly for the previous three years and was being prescribed copious amounts of medication, including high doses of an antidepressant and several tranquillisers daily. She felt that the medication definitely helped her, but it did not seem to be getting to the root of the problem. Her doctors were not recommending any other course of action, so she attended me to discuss other possible options.

Within five minutes, it was obvious to me that Stella's level of selfhood was extremely low, though no previous doctor had ever mentioned that her sense of self was a relevant factor in her situation. Although in her mid-forties, she came to see me accompanied by her mother. Every time I asked Stella a question, she looked to her for reassurance and approval of the way she had answered that particular question. She frequently asked her mother to answer my questions for her.

Stella's fundamental problem was her very low level of selfhood. This accounted for her recurring anxiety, her enormous fear of almost everything. Her obsessive-compulsive tendencies and her tendency to become depressed were the direct result of her low sense of selfhood. Stella could not recall what it felt like to belong anywhere. Although reared in a loving family, she had never really felt that she belonged at home. There was nothing to suggest a major trauma in her childhood that caused her loss of selfhood, though the gradual accumulation of immense self-doubt certainly had occurred within her. Stella had no memory of ever belonging to or within herself, a natural consequence of never feeling 'at home' within her own personal space.

Stella tried to live her entire life outside her boundary and personal space. Her attention perpetually went out to other people, how everyone else felt. Were they okay, happy? Was she tending to them sufficiently? What did others think of her? What would other people think of her if she did this, or that? As long as other people were okay with what she was saying and doing, she could relax, a little. But she never really relaxed because she felt so fundamentally unsafe and insecure.

As is always the case in people whose level of selfhood is very low, any risk seemed overwhelming for Stella. She therefore avoided even minimal risks, steering well clear of bigger risks, which was why she had never been involved in a relationship in her entire life. The very idea of being in a relationship was terrifying for her although she desperately wanted to be confident enough to risk entering a relationship. Stella was the epitome of the enormous unnoticed and often excruciating losses and great conflicts experienced by people who have a low level of selfhood.

Toward the end of our first session she was sobbing with relief at being understood. 'He gets it, he gets it!', she exclaimed excitedly to her mother. In our first few meetings, we focused on some important principles of the work necessary for a person with low selfhood. I listened carefully and respectfully to Stella's story. I helped her to come into better awareness and contact with her emotions, and to grieve for her many losses. I regularly demonstrated my empathy for her, my understanding of her life story and how difficult life has been for her.

In our work together, we used the components of selfhood as a framework. I encouraged Stella to be aware of the components of selfhood as she went through her daily life. She reported that her understanding of herself was growing, that she could see how her low level of selfhood contributed to the stress and difficulties she experienced. She has experimented with aspects of selfhood, such as regularly bringing her attention back into her own personal space, minding her boundary, self-referral and self-empathy. She is excited by the fact that she is entering a whole new world of understanding herself, raising her level of selfhood, and dealing with the world far more effectively. In the process, she is attending to her needs to a far greater extent. My approach makes sense to Stella, consequently she is willing to work hard on raising her level of selfhood.

Stella's life had become stagnant over time. Preoccupied with fear, for years Stella had engaged with few new activities or ventures. I had been suggesting to Stella that she needed more enjoyment and fulfilment. She tentatively tried one or two things, without much success in terms of enjoyment for her. Then, she discovered horse-riding. Initially tentative and fearful, she went for a horse-riding lesson. As always, fear was her dominant emotion, but on my advice she persisted. After five lessons, she began to relax into it. Within three months, Stella was buying books on horse-riding and seeking out TV programmes relevant to her new interest. Such behaviour was unprecedented: Stella had not felt interested in anything for decades. Her sense of selfhood began to rise. She felt good during and after her horse-riding lessons. New channels of social contact opened up through the horse-riding centre.

While horse-riding one day, Stella saw a bull in an adjacent field. She was in no danger from the bull, but over the ensuing days she wondered whether she should give up horse-riding, in case she did ever encounter a bull. Stella acknowledged that she focused on the bull issue because it gave her an acceptable way out, a means of giving up the horse-riding for an apparently legitimate reason. This is an example of how the old habits and patterns of sabotaging potential progress that frightens us can and will surface, often so subtly that we do not see them for what they are. She decided to continue.

Stella's sense of self-belonging has steadily increased since we commenced working together. She is consequently less fearful, takes far less medication, and experiences considerably more inner peace than at any other time of her life.

2. Self-awareness

In this section, we consider aspects of selfhood that are particularly related to self-awareness. Self-talk, the rainbow of emotions, dealing with emotions, self-attunement, self-knowledge, self-contact and sexuality are explored. Given its importance, the issue of self-awareness also arises to a lesser extent in several other aspects of selfhood.

Self-talk

Each of us experiences our own personal internal dialogue, the ongoing conversation we have with ourselves. This internal dialogue is what you are thinking, feeling and saying to yourself about yourself and your life. If your level of selfhood is high, then your self-talk will reflect that, being largely self-supportive, calm and self-affirming. If your level of selfhood is low, your self-talk will mirror that too, typically being self-critical, self-judgemental, and filled with tension and irritation. To experience peace and contentment, your self-talk needs to become self-supporting and self-affirming.

Self-critical self-talk is a habit we develop over time. It often seems easier to berate ourselves continually than to risk talking softly and gently to ourselves, showing ourselves compassion and thus feel the depth of our emotional distress, grief and sadness. With time, attention and gentleness, we can change how we talk to ourselves. I have worked with many people for whom self-criticism and self-deprecation have been subtle protective mechanisms, protecting them from taking risks that scared them. Self-criticism serves to distance ourselves from ourselves. In our internal dialogue, this distancing is sometimes reflected in the change of language from the first person ('I') to the second person ('you'), for example 'you stupid fool, what were you thinking?'. Functional self-talk helps us to keep things real and in perspective, to live in accordance with things as they are rather than as we wish them to be.

A moment in Hugh's life illustrates the importance of the quality of our self-talk. Hugh began attending me in his sixties. He had been diagnosed in his late twenties with bipolar disorder. All the components of Hugh's selfhood were low, not least his self-talk, his inner dialogue. An experience prior to driving to an appointment with me was a typical example. Five minutes before his scheduled departure, he could not find his spectacles, which he needed for the seventy-mile drive to my office.

In such situations, Hugh would immediately begin to berate himself severely with comments, such as 'you fool, you stupid idiot', and this was his initial reaction to being unable to locate his glasses. He then noticed what he was doing, that he was talking to himself in extremely derisive terms for something as innocuous as mislaying his spectacles. He became aware that his words were typical of the type of criticism he had been regularly subjected to by his father. Hugh had heard such criticism so frequently that criticising himself had become second-nature to him. He had internalised and continued the style of his father's commentary on him. Realising what he was doing, Hugh resolved to cease regurgitating his father's words and create his own way of communicating with himself, using self-supporting and self-validating self-talk.

He immediately began to talk to himself in this fashion, and as a result became more relaxed. He had done nothing wrong. So what if he was late for his appointment with me? It would not be the end of the world. He was also able to separate what he had done from who he was, a feat he would never have been able to do in the past. Hugh managed to say to himself and believe that, yes, he had mislaid his glasses, which was indeed unfortunate, but this was something he had *done*, it did not represent who he *was*. There was no need for him to undermine his own person because of this innocent action. Hugh's action interrupted the usual cascading, escalating chain reaction of major self-criticism that catapulted him into immense inner despair and distress for several hours at least, and often for days. He worked his way through it in minutes, stopping the chain reaction in its tracks, quickly getting himself back to a place of inner peace and control. He was thrilled with this 'breakthrough'– his description. Taking his time, Hugh had another look around the house for his glasses and quickly found them. He set off to his appointment with me, delighted with himself. Taking charge of the situation in this manner had a positive effect on his sense of selfhood.

As they are aspects of how we communicate with ourselves, self-approval and self-affirmation are explored in this section. In people who are primarily driven by the need for approval outside of themselves, it is their lack of selfhood that is driving this need for external approval. Working on self-approval and self-affirmation gradually tips the balance away from seeking approval and affirmation from others, toward being the provider of these important qualities for ourselves. By cultivating the habit of self-affirmation, you become more effective at dealing with the world. Self-affirmation means actively making statements to yourself about yourself, such as the affirmations included throughout this book, listed in Appendix One. Such affirmations repeated over time help to change your perception of yourself.

People with a strong sense of selfhood tend to be spontaneously and effortlessly self-affirming. They encourage themselves as they go through life, often without realising that they are doing so. People with a low sense of selfhood tend to do the opposite, repeatedly undermining themselves. There is a spectrum, ranging from one extreme to the other. At one extreme, there are people who rarely affirm themselves, who pander to the needs, wants, words and actions of others, either expressed or presumed. They live in an ever-present state of inner turmoil, repeatedly berating themselves for things they have but should not have done, or have not but should have done.

At the other extreme are people who constantly self-affirm, often to the exclusion of their real needs and the needs and rights of others, of their responsibilities toward others. Having lost touch with self-honesty and perspective, they convince themselves of the rightness of their every word and action. They refuse to acknowledge that we all make mistakes, that our words and actions can sometimes hurt and cause pain for others. These people do not apologise very often. Some people who choose to live like this seem to be happy. However, they are rarely truly content. They tend to alienate others, and therefore their potential for personal growth, connecting with people and maintaining healthy relationships is often significantly diminished. They are reducing their availability to access and therefore to benefit from opportunities for satisfaction, growth, fulfilment and satisfying relationships that may cross their path as they journey through life.

ACTIONS

1.   Become familiar with the tone and content of your self-talk

Notice how you talk to yourself. What is the general tone and content of your self-talk? If your level of selfhood is low, the tone will generally be harsh and self-critical, and the content is a virtually continuous flow of self-criticism and self-judgement. By paying attention to this inner conversation, you learn to notice put-downs and replace them with self-supportive and self-affirming words and language, as Hugh did in the case history above. Do the tone or content of your self-talk change in particular situations, or at certain times of the day or year? If so, gently explore why that might be. Might you be unintentionally using critical self-talk as a way of avoiding difficult realities or emotions? Notice the words you use toward yourself, the self-critical comments you make, and gently replace them with more tolerant ones. Stick at it and you will change how you talk to yourself.

2.   Are there subtle benefits from your current self-critical self-talk?

There is often a pay-off for our internal dialogue. Our critical self-talk may be protecting us from taking risks due to fear of failure, success, or of becoming overwhelmed with fear, sadness, grief or other distressing emotions. We deserve our own compassion for ourselves as we work toward changing our self-talk and seeking to understand why we have adopted this pattern of talking to ourselves. Sometimes, we unwittingly use self-critical self-talk to keep ourselves in a powerless or 'victim' mode, so we do not have to take ownership and responsibility for ourselves.

3.   Reassess specific examples of critical self-talk

When you get frustrated with yourself, you may beat yourself up regarding why you did or did not do a particular thing. There is another way of handling such situations. Explore *why* you reacted as you did, what purpose might your reaction have served. You will increasingly realise that your critical self-talk served a purpose, perhaps an attempt to avoid hurt or exposure in similar future situations. For example, fear and great self-doubt are driving forces behind obsessive-compulsive disorder. The person's self-talk reflects this, often being filled with fear, dread, and rigidity, in a frantic attempt to minimise risk.

You need to gradually let go of the self-critical self-talk as it is causing you significant problems. You cannot see beyond the present and into the future, and know the outcome and the consequence of your actions and decisions, so stop creating such unattainable standards from yourself. Ask yourself what you can learn from what happened that might help you in future situations you may encounter. In this way, you become more practised at talking to yourself in a more productive fashion.

4.   *Substitute gentleness, understanding, acceptance, compassion, in place of self-criticism, self-judgement, self-depreciation*

It is time to cease self-talk that is self-critical, self-judging, self-depreciating or self-loathing in any way. Gently replace these with self-acceptance, self-understanding and self-tolerance. Adopt the qualities of gentleness, compassion and understanding toward yourself. You may initially find this difficult, since it may feel unfamiliar. You may resist this, since being gentler with yourself may highlight the absence of gentleness and compassion in your life up to now, and this awareness may bring you in touch with your emotions. This is necessary for the healing of emotional distress and therefore for increased mental wellness.

5.   *Barrister for the defence*

If your level of selfhood is low, then you probably need a counter-voice to speak on your behalf. You already live with an aggressive barrister for the prosecution in your head, one who is adept at using every possible opportunity to criticise and undermine you. This barrister has won so many cases, hundreds every day, that you have probably thrown in the towel and no longer even attempt to defend yourself. It is time to balance things out a little: you need a barrister for the defence.

Repeatedly bring a counter-voice into your thinking. When you notice yourself yet again viciously beating yourself up for not getting something right, deliberately speak up for yourself, as though you were a barrister acting on your own behalf. Make a case for yourself to yourself. Outline the scenario as it unfolded, from start to finish. You will generally find that (a) you did the best you felt you could in the circumstances, (b) you could not have known the outcome since you cannot see into the future, and (c) what you did was not all that bad, being quite reasonable and understandable in the circumstances.

Initially, you will have to force this, as it will not come naturally to you. When the prosecuting barrister gets into full flow, you need to defend yourself and your actions. That barrister keeps going over your past, trawling for anything it can interpret as a mistake or a bad decision, in an effort to gather evidence to convince you that you really are a terrible person. Identify some reasons that validate and vindicate yourself. For example, you did what you thought was right, given the amount of information you had at your disposal at the time. It is easy to criticise yourself with hindsight, when the situation is over or has advanced further. When you made your choice or decision, this later information was not available to you. Even when you have all the information available to you, the choice you make may not work out. You are human and all you can do is your best. Then, let it go. The trial is over and the case is closed.

6. *Commit to being your own primary source of validation, affirmation and approval*

Make a commitment to notice whenever you invalidate or undermine yourself. When you catch yourself behaving like this, gently say to yourself: 'Aha, there I go again'. Then, summon up a counter-voice, as discussed in the previous action, to validate and affirm both yourself and whatever thought, feeling or action prompted you to undermine yourself. Be mindful of the language you use toward yourself. Refrain from language that contributes to you invalidating, disapproving and trivialising yourself. By summoning up this counter-voice on a regular basis, you sow the seeds of change toward self-validation, self-affirmation and self-approval. You do not have to believe the counter-voice initially. Belief will come over time and as a result of persistence and perseverance.

7. *Risk holding on to your perspective*

Your perspective on things *is* valid, though if your self-talk is filled with self-criticism, you may find this hard to believe. Check with yourself regarding what your perspective and opinion is, how you feel about things. When you meet others who hold a different perspective, listen to what they say, and risk holding on to your perspective. You do not need to justify, explain or even state your perspective, or have others accept your opinions. Let your view, your perspective, become in time a solid foundation for you in your dealings with people.

8. *Reflection*

At your daily reflection times, reflect on how you talked to yourself since your last reflection time. Note the times when you took your eye off the ball, when your self-talk became self-critical, self-judging and self-rejecting. With repetition of this practice of reflection on how you talk to yourself, the previously unfamiliar becomes the familiar. You integrate this new way of talking to yourself into your reality and into your relationship with yourself. During your daily reflections, consider how you have handled the issue of self-approval and self-validation since your last reflection. Renew your commitment to validate and affirm yourself on an ongoing basis.

9. *Affirmation*

'I talk to myself with gentleness, respect and understanding, which I deserve. Every aspect of me is valid. I continually affirm myself. I approve of me.'

The rainbow of emotions

A rainbow is a breathtaking example of an important principle in life: the majestic beauty and balanced harmony of the whole, each individual aspect making an important contribution to the harmony and aliveness of the whole. A rainbow embodies the entire spectrum of colour, each individual colour contributing to its awesome splendour. This principle applies across the spectrum of human experiences and endeavours. The orchestra functions best when all members operate effectively, interacting with each other in harmony. Similarly, individuals function best when the entire spectrum of who they are is alive and vibrant, including the range of emotions they experience. Colours are not good or bad, positive or negative. There are just colours, each with different qualities. Similarly, there is no such thing as a good or bad, or a positive or negative emotion. There are just emotions, each of which has its own value.

The healthy management of emotions is a prerequisite for mental health. Each emotion has its purpose and its place. The ability to access the full range of emotions, as appropriate, is a characteristic of a high level of selfhood. If feelings are not managed well, they can wield enormous power and be quite destructive. If you become practised at hiding your feelings from others (unexpressed feelings), you may eventually become able to hide your feelings from yourself (unacknowledged feelings). Sometimes, you may confuse a desire to think positively with the wish to deny your feelings. You give your feelings power over you when you deny their existence.

How an individual handles emotions frequently undergoes a major transformation during adolescence. Young men tend to be in a particularly difficult position. During adolescence and even earlier, many boys learn that it is not acceptable to cry or to appear anxious or unsure of themselves in front of others. They also learn that it not socially okay to show affection to other young men through touch, as girls do with other girls, hugging, linking arms as they walk down the street, arms around each other in friendship. Many young men often seem not to care about anything, themselves included. This is frequently a defence. Many care a great deal, but do not feel they have permission to express this. Many reach a point of giving up caring because it is too risky and exposes them to repeatedly experiencing hurt.

Being able to access the wide spectrum of feelings helps us to live life more fully. Having access to feelings is not the same thing as acting out those feelings. For example, while it is normal and healthy to feel anger, this does not give us the right to translate our anger into verbal or physical aggression. Anger is an emotion felt within. It is a valuable ally. Some of us quickly convert our anger into aggression, bypassing assertiveness. We cross other people's boundaries, invading others with an onslaught. Or we stay silent, fuming inside for hours. Many people anger easily. Some use anger to control others. They know their expression of anger frightens and bullies others into submission. Others never feel anger, and are deprived of the benefits associated with this emotion.

The following experience from my own life illustrates the value of anger. It also demonstrates the importance of connecting with what lies beneath the surface within us, as explored under the human iceberg heading later in this section. One Sunday seven years ago, I delivered a day-long seminar on mental health in Dublin, Ireland. Afterwards I was tired, as I had been speaking for virtually the whole day. The organiser asked me if I would drive a person back to Limerick where I lived, a three-hour drive from Dublin. Without thinking, I happily agreed. As I continued chatting to other people, I became aware of a powerful wave of anger surging within me. The suddenness and force of this emotion really took me by surprise. I took a few moments to tune into myself, trying to understand what was going on within me.

I soon became aware of the source of my anger. Having been with people without a break for over seven hours and speaking continuously throughout, I had been looking forward to driving home alone, in order to prepare myself for the beginning of a busy working week the following morning. I needed this alone-time to recharge my batteries after a long, intense, enjoyable day. By agreeing to give that lift, I had neglected my own needs. I would probably be talking for a further three hours in the car. My anger was my ally, reminding me that I was not attending to my own needs. Initially, I directed my anger at the person who made the request. How dare they make such a request, I thought. Realising that my anger was about me and not the other person, I brought my attention back to myself, to what my anger was trying to communicate to me, my need in the situation. Since my anger involved me communicating with me, I did not need to communicate my anger to the two people involved. I needed to own my own anger, listen to it, identify what it sought to communicate, and take appropriate action to meet my need.

My choices were to either suppress my own need and give the lift rather than risk their disapproval, or to honour my need and tell them both that I needed to travel alone. I chose to honour my need. The person to whom I was to give the lift had already come and thanked me. I communicated to them both that I needed time and space alone after the intensity of the seminar. Within seconds my anger dissolved instantly and totally, as rapidly as it had arisen. Peace returned within me. I had taken steps to meet my needs. I did not need anger any more. Like warning lights on the dashboard, anger has a purpose. Attend to the issue, and the warning light switches off. Neither of the two people concerned knew that I was angry. They did not need to know. They had every right to ask for the lift. It was up to me to decide what to do with their request.

Saying 'no' meant risking their disappointment and disapproval. As it happened, I received neither. The woman had a return train ticket anyway, though I did not know that when I retracted the offer of the lift. Had they been disapproving of my action, I would still have honoured my need. I was not responsible for how that woman got home, but I was responsible for taking care of myself and ensuring that I was properly prepared for the upcoming working week. Had I suppressed my need, I'm sure we would have had a pleasant trip. The conversation would have been flowing, but that was not what I needed. I would have arrived home late at night, exhausted and all talked out, facing unprepared into a demanding week early the following morning. Instead, the silence and aloneness of the trip enabled me to gently leave the seminar behind me and focus on my own wellbeing for a while, and on preparing for the week ahead.

Some people regularly express anger and aggression as a response to experiencing hurt. They feel the hurt for an instant, quickly translate it into anger, and often go beyond anger into aggressive words and behaviour. This protects them from feeling the full impact of their hurt and from risking exposing their vulnerability to others. They may be frantically hoping that the other person will recognise and honour their well-disguised hurt. The other person, feeling threatened and entrenched in self-protection mode to survive the force of the aggression, may be in no position to see through the camouflage. The angry one, having distanced themselves from others in this fashion, feels deeply upset and alone, their hurt, loneliness, and sadness multiplied. Their core issue, that they are hurting, remains unexpressed and unresolved. Clear communication has vacated the premises. Their fundamental needs in the situation go unmet, hidden and heavily disguised within the familiar safe cloak of anger. Ultimately, there are no real winners.

In my opinion there is no such thing as a negative feeling. Negativity lies in the denial of feeling.

ACTIONS

1. Familiarise yourself with the rainbow of emotions
Become more familiar with the range of emotions that we human beings can experience. In alphabetical order, commonly experienced emotions include alienation, anger, anxiety, apathy, bliss, boredom, confusion, connectedness, contempt, contentment, dejection, depression, despair, desire, devastation, disappointment, disconnectness, disgust, distraction, distress, dread, elation, envy, excitement, exhaustion, fear, fury, gratitude, grief, guilt, happiness, hate, hope, hopelessness, hurt, interest, jealousy, joy, loneliness, love, loss, lost, numb, overwhelm, panic, pain, pleasure,

pride, rage, regret, resignation, sadness, sorrow, shame, surprise, tenderness, terror and wonder. There are other emotions that derive from the above list. For example, feeling cheated is usually a result of feeling hurt or loss.

2. How many colours are in your rainbow of emotions?
Identify the emotions that you do feel. Reflect on the degree to which you allow yourself to feel the full range of emotions, from deep sadness, hurt, grief, rejection and loss, to great joy, laughter, bliss and peace at the other end of the spectrum. Through honest self-reflection on the spectrum of emotions just outlined in action 1, you will become more familiar with the range of human emotions. You will then be able to identify which if any of the rainbow of emotions you may be experiencing either to a great degree, or not at all.

3. Name and articulate your feelings
All of your feelings make sense. Your feelings are a barometer, an accurate pointer to how you are. If you are generally unfamiliar with the feeling side of yourself, develop the habit of naming your feelings. The accuracy of the words you use is important. Think more about your feelings and what it is you are feeling. Instead of imprecise words such as tired, down, lousy, stupid, terrible, miserable, unstable, not in good form, put accurate feeling words on to how you are. You may struggle with this initially, since it may be very new for you. Persist, and in time you will experience greater clarity regarding precisely what it is that you are feeling. Use the emotions outlined in action 1 for reference. For example, 'I'm feeling frightened, nervous, unsure, hurt, lonely, sad, jealous, lost, rejected, abandoned, angry, furious, happy'.

4. Reflection
During your daily reflection times, consider the rainbow of emotions, the emotions you felt and the emotions you tended to avoid feeling, since your last reflection time. Resolve to notice and to name your feelings to yourself.

5. Affirmation
'I have free-flowing access to the entire rainbow of my emotions.'

Dealing with emotions

Broadly speaking, I regard emotions as being one of two types: primary and secondary. Primary emotions are the core, pure, spontaneous emotions that arise within us as we engage with life, such as joy, sadness, tears, anger, jealousy and fear. These generally reach completion soon after that moment or situation is complete. Secondary emotions occur when we avoid or change the primary original feeling into a different emotion. Secondary emotions often arise when we perceive experiencing a primary emotion as too overwhelming or terrifying. We may withdraw from the challenge of feeling primary emotions to what we believe to be the relative safety of secondary ones. Secondary emotions are likely to be ongoing, pervasive, without an obvious trigger and with little resolution, one step removed from primary emotions. If you experience powerful and distressing primary emotions such as grief, hurt and sadness, you may unwittingly block them by superimposing a secondary emotion. You may then regularly avoid full and real contact with yourself, your emotions and other people. The emotion or experience that you are most aware of is a secondary emotion such as anxiety, apathy, depression or numbness, for which you might decide to seek professional help. Beneath this secondary emotion there often lies a well of unexpressed primary emotion.

Prolonged or recurring anxiety, irritability, restlessness, boredom, confusion, depression, feeling flat, disconnectedness, distractedness, numbness, deadness and tiredness are examples of secondary emotions. Many emotions can be both primary or secondary. For example, anger is a primary emotion when it is the core, original reaction, as was the case in my experience of anger described above. Anger is a secondary emotion if it is employed to deflect away from the core, original emotion felt. For example, if we have felt hurt and immediately transmute the hurt into anger, in this situation anger is a secondary emotion. Similarly, while sadness is often a primary emotion, some people regularly change other primary feelings such as anger into sadness. These people, being more comfortable with sadness and inaction than with anger and its associated energy to take action to resolve the situation, are using sadness as a secondary emotion, albeit without realising they are doing so. There are times when it is entirely appropriate that anger would accompany and at times temporarily supersede the hurt we feel. Such anger helps us to take appropriate action in the circumstances. Once we have taken this action and the need for anger has passed, it is important that we feel and work though the original feeling of hurt.

A person who feels a great deal of secondary emotions may rarely if ever feel primary emotions. This is why many people who feel a great deal of numbness, depression or anxiety do not generally feel or express their deep sadness fully, nor do they experience much joy.

Connecting with primary emotions and releasing them is an effective way of alleviating experiences of prolonged anxiety, depression and numbness. You may be able to do much of this work on your own, gently exploring behind the secondary emotion you are experiencing, asking yourself what primary emotion might lie hidden behind it. Usually, the primary emotion is grief, loss, sadness, anger or hurt. You may need to do this work with a person you trust, such as a good counsellor.

When a person feels tired, there may of course be no underlying emotional issue. However, if tiredness is a recurring and unresolved issue, it might be worth considering whether unfinished emotional business might be a contributing factor, as was the case with Peter. In his mid-fifties, Peter and his wife were attending me for counselling regarding their relationship. At one meeting, Peter mentioned that he felt tired and drained. I sensed there was more to his tiredness, so I asked him to tune into himself, and try to notice what else might be there. Nothing came to him. I asked if sadness or loneliness might be in there along with tiredness. Peter immediately said no. He then said 'fear', so we explored that. His wife held his hand all the while. Peter's demeanour changed quickly. I asked him what he was feeling. Now, he had no doubt about what he was feeling: great sadness and fear. I sensed that communicating directly to his wife might help Peter to fully express this emotion, and bring this piece of grieving to completion. I asked Peter to look directly into his wife's eyes and speak to her from his heart. He struggled with this initially, and then he said to his wife that he felt he was unlovable, that he did not deserve her love, that he was terrified that he would never again feel loved.

Without speaking, his wife immediately stood up, moved toward him, and held him very tightly. Over the next twenty minutes, Peter experienced deep grief and sadness, sobbing intensely, then becoming gradually more peaceful in the arms of his wife. Afterwards, Peter reported feeling a surge of energy and heat in his chest area. I felt that this may represent a flow of heat and energy to an area previously somewhat blocked: his heart. Unwittingly, Peter had been using tiredness as a secondary emotion, as a way of avoiding contact with both his own feelings, and with his wife. Real emotional contact with his wife would have brought him into more direct contact with himself and his sadness in particular, which he preferred to avoid.

Anxiety may be a primary emotion if we find ourselves faced with an immediate threat. When anxiety is a primary emotion, it generally recedes quickly, unless the threat is ongoing or has caused considerable upheaval. Anger is often secondary to other emotions, usually hurt, sadness or fear. When a person is expressing great anger or rage, as this wave of emotion passes, it is often followed by great sadness and tears, reflecting the hurt and sadness that lay beneath their anger.

Risking feeling our emotions fully is a pathway to living in the realm of primary emotions and experiencing the rainbow of emotions. Experiencing primary rather than secondary emotions involves resisting the temptation to avoid painful emotions, such as sadness, loss, grief, overwhelm and loneliness. It means staying with raw distressing emotions. When we allow ourselves to feel the full impact of our feelings, they often lose their intensity surprisingly quickly. Experiencing the full extent of the emotion serves to release and diminish it. This may prove to be tough going for a while, but with it comes a sense of feeling alive that is in sharp contrast to the sense of deadness that often accompanies secondary emotions.

We may believe we cannot cope with the intensity of our primary emotions. We may express this belief as 'I'm afraid to cry, because if I start, I may not be able to stop, or I might lose control'. A man who attends me recently used this logic as a reason not to cry, for resisting tears that were obviously just beneath the surface. I asked him if he had ever met anyone, or heard of anyone who, when they allowed themselves to cry, continued to cry without ever stopping. He acknowledged that he never had heard of such a situation. Such statements and beliefs are avoidance strategies. The real reason is generally that we are afraid of doing so. There is no need to fear that you will never be able to stop crying if you start. When we do express emotions, we tend to do so in pulses, only allowing a certain amount to surface at a time. This is wise, enabling us to deal with powerful emotions and very difficult situations in a phased manner rather than all at once. This helps us to adapt more gradually to changing circumstances. We have far more power and control over our emotions than we might think.

In keeping with our general societal failure to fully understand emotions, there are many misguided expectations regarding how people should feel in certain situations. If their feelings are in contrast to the expected ones, the person may experience disapproval, often feeling considerable guilt for having that feeling, or that there is something seriously wrong with them. Yet, people's feelings always make sense. Here are some examples.

At the birth of his first child, Simon felt overwhelmed by a range of emotions. Along with joy, a feeling he would have expected to feel at this time, he felt great sorrow. He felt upset that his little baby might have to experience distress and sadness in life. Simon was attending a psychiatrist, having been diagnosed as suffering from depression. The psychiatrist told Simon that these feelings were not normal, that they were further evidence of his depression. On hearing the story, which occurred eighteen months prior to my meeting Simon, it made perfect sense to me. Simon had known considerable sorrow in his own life. It is not surprising that he would feel upset that his child might also experience such sorrow.

Amanda's husband died when she was in her early sixties. Her husband had a stroke three years prior to his death. The stroke seemed to take away much of his personality and spirit. Their relationship inevitably changed following the stroke, Amanda becoming more of a carer for her husband than experiencing him as a partner. When her husband died, Amanda experienced great sadness. She understood why she felt this emotion, but she was very upset that she also felt a sense of relief, as Amanda thought it was totally inappropriate to feel relief in the circumstances. When I explained to her that relief was an understandable reaction, as well as sadness, she relaxed about it, and proceeded to deal with her grief. Amanda's transient reaction of relief made sense at several levels. Her grieving for her husband actually began when he had the stroke. Seeing him in his compromised, post-stroke state filled her with sadness. Every day since the stroke had been a difficult existence for both of them. Part of her relief was because her husband was no longer suffering.

Beatrice had her first baby four months ago. Reflecting on her experience of pregnancy, labour and being a mother, she looked at it as 'a big secret'. Beatrice felt that there are expectations placed on a pregnant woman, and that her experiences were expected by others to match these expectations. She recalled people saying to her during her pregnancy 'you must be so excited!'. She felt that the expected answer was implied in the question: 'yes, I am so excited, it is all just so wonderful'. She would have liked to reply in accordance with her experience, her truth: 'well actually, I feel tired, unsure of myself, and I'm terrified about what lies ahead, the labour, whether I will be a good mother, and how all this will affect my life and my relationship with my husband'. Rather than risk the other person's reaction to this, Beatrice replied that yes, it was indeed wonderful, as she saw little point in any other response.

Lara was in her mid-forties when she began attending me. Separated, with three young children, Lara attended me because her self-confidence was very low and she felt stuck in her life. Our work together revolved around the principles outlined throughout this book. Within weeks she was feeling somewhat better. Lara arranged to travel to France for a weekend with two friends, the first time she had done anything like that for twenty years. On the day of departure, Lara was surprised that she felt a sense of sadness, shock and horror at how little she had looked after herself and her own needs during the preceding twenty years. She did not expect to feel like this on the day of departure for a fun weekend with her best friends. I explained the rightness of her reaction to Lara, that the presence of this weekend in her life was highlighting how such acts of self-care, how moments of fun and joy had been missing for all those years.

These are just a few examples to demonstrate that it is incorrect to presume that in a given situation, all people should feel the same emotion, or feel just one emotion. Another example is the fact that, on suddenly hearing shocking news, some people immediately burst into laughter, as a part of their shock reaction.

Unless they have experienced considerable fear, hurt and threat, most young children tend to have full access to the range of primary emotions. They may cry uncontrollably one minute, and two minutes later they are laughing heartily. This is a healthy expression of the flow of emotions, and they are consequently free to fully experience life. Having experienced high levels of fear, hurt, trauma, or loss of selfhood, many children learn to hide their primary emotions under a cloud of secondary emotions such as anxiety, depression and numbness. They may create other forms of escapism from reality, such as fantasy worlds where they are the star. In these worlds, their needs are met and life is good for them, the opposite of the real world as they experience it. Such reactions are understandable, but the child is at risk of becoming ever more distant from reality, thus making a return to the real world increasingly challenging and terrifying.

Many young men in western society are disconnected from their feelings. Aspects of western culture encourage such disconnection. For example, in many westernised societies, anger is one of the few emotions that it is publicly acceptable for a man to express. Two problems may arise as a consequence. They may translate other emotions and experiences, such as hurt, sadness, loneliness, jealousy and other distressing emotions into anger. Doing so deprives them of the experience of the original feeling, and the healing and learning that comes from working through a feeling to completion and integrating the messages that are inherent in that feeling. These messages often concern our needs, particularly our unmet needs.

Secondly, they may translate the anger into aggression, toward others or themselves. While anger often serves an important purpose, aggression crosses a line that none of us has the right to cross. Anger is a valid emotion. Aggression is not an emotion, it is a behaviour: it is an attack. Some young men suppress their anger, experiencing what they perceive as a more acceptable primary emotion such as sadness and crying, or more commonly convert it into a secondary emotion such as anxiety, depression or numbness.

Certain situations may act as triggers for the release of pent up or suppressed emotions. Premenstrual tension and alcohol are two such triggers. A woman's premenstrual experience often reflects aspects of her emotions that are generally kept beneath the surface. Women who become aggressive in the premenstrual phase of their cycle tend to have an undercurrent of suppressed aggression. When they do not deal directly and effectively with their needs, their hurt, pain and sadness as they arise, anger and aggression fester. A pressure cooker situation develops, and the premenstrual time becomes a regular release valve. The underlying cause of the build up of pressure isn't dealt with, so the cycle continues. Similarly with alcohol, once described as 'truth serum' by a client. Whatever we have suppressed may come to the surface as a result of the ingestion of alcohol, albeit in a somewhat distorted fashion.

If you do not feel your feelings and process them fully, then you may find other ways of dealing with your emotions. You may express your feelings through your body, for example, through nervous repetitive movements, patterns of eye contact, tension held within the body, posture and general body language. As illustrated in Diagram 2 on page 12, you may channel your emotions through other routes, such as your psychological aspect. You may have an extremely busy mind, always thinking, finding it difficult to shut off or slow down your thinking. By allowing yourself to feel your feelings more and therefore open the emotional aspect of who you are, you may well find that your mind becomes calmer and more peaceful. You may also find that you are holding less tension in your body.

Many people who suppress or avoid emotions experience physical symptoms and stress-related illnesses. In many such instances, the person's body does the talking for them, since they are not dealing effectively with their emotions, or effectively meeting their needs. There is considerable truth in the saying 'the body never lies'. When emotions are not worked through to completion, this can manifest in the body as physical symptoms, sometimes progressing in time to physical illness.

Sometimes we train ourselves to block our feelings for the sake of others. Many of us believe that we should be 'strong', which really means 'show no emotion'. We may feel we cannot show any emotion to anyone, including ourselves. The very use of the word 'strong' implies that it is 'weak' to feel and express emotion. Many people will do anything to avoid being seen by others as weak, sometimes even ending their life rather than risk showing emotion or anything that might be interpreted as weakness or vulnerability. Often, while we are convinced that we are blocking our feelings for the sake of others, we are actually doing so because *we* are afraid of making full contact with our painful emotions. We need not be so afraid of this. It is true that allowing ourselves to feel the peak of our emotions will not be easy. However, in doing so, we help to release the emotion, and by its very nature, the peak of the emotions does not last long. It passes, often followed initially by exhaustion, usually then followed by a feeling of relief and some peace.

ACTIONS

1. Identify your beliefs regarding emotions and their expression
Do you have strong views regarding people expressing emotion? Are there some emotions you would classify as good or bad, as positive or negative? If there are, then you probably do everything in your power not to feel 'bad' or 'negative' emotions. When you feel them, you may repeatedly berate yourself for feeling such emotions, perhaps concluding that you must be a bad person to be experiencing them. Revise your approach to emotions. Do not place value judgements on them. Every emotion has a

purpose. Look at your patterns of dealing with people, life, loss, fear, change, and hurt. This will help you to identify the emotions with which you are most, and least, comfortable.

2.   *Identify your strategies for handling emotions*
If you are anxious, depressed, numb, detached, or if you regularly create fantasy worlds, ask yourself honestly and without judgement, what feelings, risks and challenges you may be seeking to avoid. Gradually, provided you persist with this, you will become increasingly aware of feelings that you have previously sought to avoid. Allow yourself to experience these feelings. Common strategies used to avoid feeling our feelings include repeatedly distracting ourselves, withdrawing into a secondary emotion, medicating ourselves with prescription and non-prescription substances including alcohol, changing the feeling to ones we find more palatable, and projection of the feeling onto someone else, for example becoming angry with someone else when you are really angry with yourself.

What are your patterns of handling your emotions? Do you feel them or block them? Do you transmute them into other emotions with which you are more comfortable? Do you channel your emotions through other aspects of your being, such as your body or your thoughts? Do you express your emotions when you really want to or need to, or do you suppress them? Do your emotions come full circle, to completion and relief, or do you interrupt the normal healthy cycle of the emergence, experiencing and resolution of your emotions? You may need some time to think about this, as you may have developed your patterns of handling emotions many years ago. You probably have not given this matter much attention for years.

Take note of your patterns in relation to how you handle emotions. Become familiar with these patterns. Resolve to work on them over time. If you can, take immediate corrective action on your patterns of behaviour regarding how you express your emotions. If it is not possible to do so immediately, do so as soon as you can. If you stick with this practice, slowly but surely, you will become more efficient at feeling the full spectrum of emotions, and you will be able to deal more effectively with your emotions.

3.   *Observe your feelings*
Work on developing a clear sense of your flow of feelings as you go about your day. As with any language, you become familiar with the language

of emotion by working on it, by thinking, feeling, learning and talking in that language. Pay more attention to the part of you that feels.

4. Keep a diary of your emotions
Every day, spend a few minutes writing about your day, from an emotional perspective. Use the list of emotions in action 1 on page 113, in the rainbow of emotions section as a reference. Use the language of emotion. For example, 'I felt frightened when…I felt hurt when…' Write in your daily journal about the feelings you experienced that day.

5. Identify the degree to which you experience secondary emotions
As mentioned earlier, prolonged or recurring anxiety, irritability, restlessness, boredom, confusion, depression, feeling flat, disconnectedness, distractedness, numbness, deadness and tiredness are examples of secondary emotions. Also, any emotion you regularly go to in order to avoid contact with the primary emotion you are experiencing is by definition a secondary emotion. For example, as mentioned earlier, anger is a secondary emotion where hurt, sadness or grief is the primary emotion. Notice which if any of these feelings you experience, and the degree to which you experience them. If these are frequently recurring feelings, you need to work on them, which is the subject of the next task.

6. What primary emotions lie beneath your secondary emotions? Commit to experiencing the underlying primary emotions
Using the list of emotions in action 1 on page 113, explore which unexpressed primary emotions lie beneath the secondary emotions you experience. Likely possibilities include hurt, loss, grief, sadness, anger and rage. Go through the list several times and see which emotions fit for you. Commit to feeling the primary emotions you identify, as opposed to whatever emotion you might otherwise transmute it into.

7. Allow yourself to feel the full range of your feelings
Having identified the emotions you block, give yourself permission to feel these emotions. As you go through your day, be gently aware of these emotions, and notice situations that might ordinarily provoke these emotions in others. Note what emotions you feel, if any. Perhaps you did actually feel a glimmer of that emotion before quickly blocking it or changing it into another, more comfortable feeling. Be similarly vigilant

regarding emotions that you experience a great deal of, perhaps because you feel more comfortable with them, such as anger or sadness. This varies from person to person. Become aware of your own patterns regarding these emotions, and write about this regularly in your journal.

8. *Bring the feeling back home, and ask yourself what need of yours is being expressed through that emotion and through your behaviour*

We tend to project some emotions onto others. For example, when we feel anger, jealousy or fear, we may feel angry or jealous toward others, or see people as major threats to our safety. Bring your attention back home, to yourself. Ask yourself what this emotion might be trying to communicate to you. Anger is often about an unmet need we have, or feelings such as hurt that we have not acknowledged and worked through. Jealousy is often about an unmet need or desire, that becomes heightened when we notice it elsewhere. Jealousy can be secondary to an underlying fear of losing someone or something very important to us. Our challenge is to be honest with ourselves, identify the issue, our underlying feelings, our unmet need, and to take whatever action is appropriate to the situation. Consider how your behaviour might be reflecting how you handle your emotions.

9. *Reflection*

During your reflection times, consider how you have handled the issue of your emotions since your last reflection time. Commit to become increasingly aware of the range of emotions within you, and to deal with them effectively.

10. *Affirmation*

'All of my feelings make sense. I accept whatever feelings I experience, and I work through them.'

Self-attunement

To attune means to make aware or responsive. Attunement is the quality of being in tune with something. Self-attunement therefore means being aware of, in tune with and responsive to one's self. We need to be tuned in to ourselves, in touch with and aware of how we are feeling, thinking and acting. We need to be aware and mindful of our individual needs.

Being self-attuned offers the optimum platform for life and for living purposefully and effectively. Being attuned to ourselves can be distressing at times. Often without realising it, we may block our self-attunement in various ways, including numbing or avoiding our feelings, submerging ourselves in activities and distractions.

The importance of the practice of mindfulness, which encourages self-attunement and self-awareness, is demonstrated by its acceptance across a wide spectrum of life, ranging from psychiatry, psychology and counselling to spiritual and religious groups. Becoming attuned to yourself and how you live enables you to be more aware of your patterns and habits of living. These are the little (and sometimes not so little) habits you have developed over the years, including those that keep creating problems for you. Having identified them, you can take corrective action as appropriate.

See mindfulness and self-attunement in a positive light, not as a pressure to always get things right, or pressure to be watching everything you do like a hawk. Balanced mindfulness is a gentle, low-key self-observing activity, with the minimum of judgement. This is something you can gradually train yourself into, a gentle ongoing self-awareness. As with self-centredness, self-awareness is not to be confused with selfishness and self-preoccupation.

Self-attunement involves becoming aware of yourself and how you go about your life. It is a gentle pattern of observation, noticing and listening to yourself, not a critical form of self-analysis. It means becoming more aware of your habits and patterns of feeling, thinking, doing, your ways of relating and communicating, dealing with stress, pressure and everyday life. It entails gently bringing your attention back to the present moment. Mindfulness involves gentle self-reflection on how you think, feel, act and live. Honesty is necessary in order for mindfulness to be effective. One of the first things many people who adopt mindfulness in their lives become aware of is their tendency to subtly hoodwink and deceive themselves, often as a surprisingly frequent occurrence.

I recall a middle-aged woman who attended me some years ago, whose lack of self-attunement and mindfulness was causing significant problems for her. When I first met her, I was immediately struck by the speed at which she walked, faster than some people run. When I pointed this out to her, she was quite surprised: she had never noticed it before. As we discussed this, she mentioned how she did on occasion notice herself flying past other pedestrians, but never attached any significance to it. Some time later, she told me of a revealing interchange she had with a friend. Taken aback by her speediness on the golf course, as she yet again raced from a green to the next tee, her friend said, 'you know Mildred, we are meant to take our time and to enjoy this'.

Mildred's speediness was indeed highly significant. Her attention was always on to the next shot, the next hole, whatever was next, rather than whatever was current. Not surprisingly, exhaustion was one of her main problems. Her style of walking was one of many examples of her recurring tendency to unnecessarily burn up enormous amounts of energy. It took her some time to successfully slow down the pace of her walking, perhaps because always being on the run was one way of avoiding contact with herself. Slowing things down meant coming more in contact with her emotions, including her fears, anxiety, sadness, grief and losses. Her walking speed was a dysfunctional maladaptive coping mechanism.

ACTIONS

1. Become self-attuned

Become an observer of yourself. Practice noticing the subtle stuff that goes on continually in and around you. Become mindful of how you talk to and treat yourself and others. Pay more attention to the various aspects of yourself, your physical, emotional, psychological, social, relational, sexual and spiritual aspects. How are they? How are you treating them? Commit to being more aware of what goes on inside you as you go though your day, in the present moment, in the 'now'. Increased awareness of your patterns of feeling, thinking, acting, your expectations of and beliefs about yourself, and your habits and patterns of living, is an important step toward a more productive and enriching life. You notice aspects of yourself that you might choose to change, aspects that may no longer serve any meaningful purpose in your life. You become more aware of responses and actions that are more likely to lead to satisfactory resolutions to the challenges you face.

2. Awareness exercise

Once every day (more often if you wish), take about five minutes to sit alone. You don't need to time it, stop when you think five minutes is up.

Sit upright, eyes closed. Take gentle deep breaths in and out, and tune in to yourself. Notice any sensations, feelings or thoughts that come immediately to your attention. Scan your body gently from top to toe, noticing how each part of your body feels. Become aware of the points of contact between your body, the chair and the floor. Tune in to how you are feeling for a moment or two. Then, turn your attention to your thoughts. Do not analyse, engage or otherwise interfere with your thoughts. Simply notice your thoughts, let them cross the horizon of your mind like clouds crossing the sky. They come, and they go. Let them go. Now, turn your attention to your feelings. What feelings if any are you aware of within you? Just notice your feelings, you do not have to do anything with them. Then, look around you, briefly noticing your surroundings. Notice what is around you: the furniture, the colours, scents, sounds. Don't analyse, just observe. Next, bring your attention back into yourself, your own personal space, for a moment. Then, go about your business, resolving to be more mindful of all aspects of yourself during your day, a gentle observer of yourself.

3.   Develop an alarm system, and take action
Develop an inner alarm system similar to the lights on the car dashboard that alert you to an impending or current problem, advising you to take corrective action before the problem escalates to a major situation. The woman who habitually moved rapidly needed to become more aware of her tendency to speediness and take corrective action. You too need to become aware of your own patterns and habits, by adopting an attitude of gentle observation and mindfulness. Commit to noticing them when they surface. Take charge of the moment yourself, and take whatever corrective action is appropriate, one step at a time. Resolve to take such actions gently, over time. Your patterns and habits are set down within you over many years, and take time to change. Accept this as part of the reality of the situation.

4.   Reflection
Use your daily periods of reflection to remind yourself to be mindful of and attuned to yourself, to reflect on your level of mindfulness over the previous few hours, and to again commit to being mindful and aware in the present moment.

5. Affirmation for mindfulness and self-attunement
'I am attuned to and mindful of myself, my thoughts, my feelings and my needs.'

Self-knowledge

If Sir Frances Bacon's assertion that knowledge is power is correct, learning about ourselves offers considerable possibilities for self-empowerment, the development of inner power. According to Chinese philosopher Lau-Tzu, 'knowing others is wisdom: knowing yourself is enlightenment'. Committing to the process of coming to know oneself is one of the greatest endeavours that any human being can undertake. Knowing more about yourself, who you are and therefore who you are not, greatly helps you to shape your sense of selfhood and enhances your ability to deal effectively with the world.

Through increasing your self-knowledge, you become more intimate with yourself, more aware of aspects of yourself that you may need to address. For example, there may be several reasons why you might believe that you are not good at a particular activity. You may have little aptitude for that particular endeavour or you may simply have no interest in it. Alternatively, there may be something about the activity that you find intimidating or threatening, and you may be tempted to avoid it. For example, you may seek to convince yourself and others that you do not speak in public because you are no good at it. In truth however, the real reason is probably that you are terrified of standing up and speaking in front of others. If you decide not to address this fear, it may have quite an impact on your life, and will limit your options for growth and fulfilment.

If you decide to address this fear, you will initially experience considerable anxiety, but you will have conquered and overcome the fear. You will also have recovered an important part of yourself, the self-confidence to express yourself in front of others. You will also experience a sense of being more powerful, and therefore more able to live a full life. I am not suggesting that if you have a fear of public speaking that you should address it now. This would be several steps too far for most people with a low sense of selfhood. Lesser fears should be tackled first. Increasing your self-knowledge decreases your likelihood of making choices that are excessively defined by outside influences. Being honest with yourself, you will minimise your attempts to pull the wool over your own eyes regarding your patterns of avoidance and self-deception.

Perhaps over the years you have allowed your values, pursuits or interests to be dictated or restricted by those around you. Reclaiming your sense of self involves asking yourself whether the life you are living truly reflects your own values and interests. Perhaps you have a long-buried interest in dancing, singing, writing or travelling, any activity or pursuit that meant a lot to you, old and perhaps forgotten hopes and dreams. Increasing your self-knowledge involves exploring these important questions, and taking appropriate action.

Getting to know yourself affords you the opportunity to understand yourself better, and the opportunity to take action and make changes toward raising your level of selfhood. Cultivating a desire for greater self-knowledge enables you to understand and resolve your subtle habits and patterns. For example, you may find that emotions and unfinished emotional business are expressed in your body. This is especially likely if you have shut down those feelings with which you feel least comfortable. Learning about what your body might be communicating to you is an important step toward re-opening channels of communication within you that may have been blocked for years.

Sometimes we can get clues about our inner resources, qualities and abilities from things that other people say about us, particularly comments that are made by more than one person. People with a low sense of selfhood tend to dismiss compliments and positive feedback. They rarely let this inside their boundary, however they dwell on any negative commentary. They will not risk seeing themselves as the capable or talented people that others may see. This does not fit with their view of themselves and so it is rejected. The pursuit of self-knowledge involves risking being open to the possible truth in other people's experience of us, including the positive aspects of how they experience us.

ACTIONS

1. Commit to getting to know yourself better
You may think that you already know yourself very well, and you may indeed be right. However, it is more likely that there is much about yourself that you do not know. Make a commitment to get to know yourself better.

2.   Get to know your habits and patterns of living
You will learn a considerable amount about yourself by paying attention
to your habits and patterns of living. This may take some time, as your
habits and patterns are by now second nature to you. Make a heading in
your journal for habits and patterns of living, and enter them when they
strike you. Be open to spotting clues that will reveal more about your
habits and patterns, such as triggers for anxiety, your patterns of
conversing and relating. How do you generally handle risk-taking? Are
you proactive in your decision-making or do you like to surrender this
power to others? Does your body tend to be tired, sore, tense? Do you
habitually put things off or avoid challenge? Do you have a strong need
to be in control, to be able to control your surroundings and contact with
others? If so, is it because doing so helps you feel safer? Your habits and
patterns regarding how you handle emotions are dealt with in the section
on dealing with emotions.

3.   Peel back the onion, one layer at a time
When you notice habits, clues or triggers, and you will, peel back the
onion. In other words, go a little deeper. For example, say you become
aware that you frequently start things but rarely see them through to
completion. Ask yourself why this might be, how this habit may serve
you, since you would not adopt and keep a habit unless it served you in
some way. Initially, no answer may surface. Consider possible reasons.
Might ceasing activities before completion serve to protect you in some
way? An activity or project that is not completed cannot be judged or
criticised, by yourself or others. Might you be protecting yourself from
judgement or failure? Sit with the question, and in time the answer will
bubble up from inside you. Gently continue the process of peeling back
the onion. If you now feel that you avoid completion due to fear of
failure, explore your ideas and opinions around failure, especially as you
apply them to yourself. Then go deeper again, and ask yourself where you
might have formed these opinions. Might you have regularly experienced
failure as a child and felt judged, criticised or rejected for having failed?
Might this suggest that by ensuring you do not bring things to
completion, you may be avoiding contact with the painful feelings of fear,
anxiety and sadness that originated in the past but which might re-surface
now if you changed this habit and began completing tasks? This is just
an example of how tracking a clue, trigger or habit by peeling back the

onion leads to increased self-knowledge. Don't worry if in the initial stages this feels confusing. You are just beginning this process. Do not come to major new conclusions about yourself prematurely. Do the work, and gradually you will become more confident about who you are and what you are learning about yourself.

4. Keep a daily journal

Daily writing in your journal and reading back over it a few times a week is an excellent way to come to know yourself better. I have outlined many possible areas that are worth writing about on page 63. Writing about your habits and patterns, the recurring triggers and clues mentioned above, helps deeper truths to come to the surface.

5. What does your life and how you live reveal to you about yourself?

While of course external events beyond your control may have had a considerable impact on you, nevertheless where you are in your life and how your life is now is largely the product of your choices and decisions, including how you responded to the external events of your life. What does your life tell you about yourself, the choices you have made, your fears, your strategies of protecting yourself? Simply keep the question in your mind. Answers will surface within you in their own time, often popping into your mind when you are least expecting them to.

6. Do things differently

Having identified your habits and patterns, gradually try doing things a little differently. For example, if you are in the habit of beginning tasks and not persisting through to completion, make it happen that you see some things through to completion. A man who is currently attending me has for decades consistently abandoned all projects, apart from those he absolutely had to complete for work. Every class, course, hobby or activity he initiated never went beyond the second session. He has now completed a series of eight guitar classes. I have been encouraging him to complete the classes, which would be a first for him. The very fact of completing the lessons is changing how he feels about himself, and he is learning a lot about himself in the process.

7. Reflection

In your daily reflection times, ask yourself if you have learned anything new about yourself since your last reflection time. Often during these reflections, nothing in particular will strike you, but there will be many occasions where you will have learned important things about yourself. As you come to know more about yourself, you can decide what if anything you need to do about what you have learned about yourself.

8. Affirmation
'Every day, I come to know myself a little better.'

Self-contact

Self-contact refers to the connection we have and level of contact we make with ourselves. The greater our level of self-contact, the more aware of all aspects of ourselves we become, increasing our potential to live a full life. Many people live their lives making little contact with important aspects of themselves, such as their feelings and unfinished emotional business from the past that still affects how they currently live.

I am often struck by the similarities between freezers and how many of us handle painful emotions. When you put food into a freezer, it hardens over a period of several hours, becoming rigid and inflexible. Previously, it was fresh, soft, malleable, ready to be eaten. Now it is rock hard, frozen solid, unusable in its new state. When you put food in the freezer and close the door, you forget about the food and the process of freezing. Your frozen food remains there until you decide to take it out. Whether the food is in the freezer for two days, two years, or twenty years, it remains largely unchanged over time, rigid, silent, unnoticed, and immobile. It has become significantly heavier than it was in its original fresh, malleable state, weighed down by water that has turned into ice.

Imagine what would happen if you kept putting food into your freezer every day but never took any out. It would soon reach bursting point. In the lead up to that point, there were warning signs that the freezer was struggling to cope with its ever-expanding burden. If we do not pay attention to these warning signs, the freezer eventually hits crisis point. It becomes overloaded, stops functioning, reaching a point where the doors can't even be closed, such is the level of overload and congestion within.

If you decide to defrost the freezer, a major thawing-out process begins. For the first several hours, not a lot appears to be happening.

Then, water flows from the freezer at an increasing rate. Eventually, the water previously contained within the food as ice has all been released. The defrosting process does not go on forever, there is an end to it. The food returns to its original malleable state, ready to be eaten.

When we experience shock, hurt or other painful and distressing experiences and emotions, one of two processes generally occurs. We can fully work through the distress at that time. Alternatively, we may choose not to deal with our emotions and distress. The situation may seem so overwhelming that we feel we have little choice but to become numb, to freeze the experience. We block it and hold it within us. Our emotions and hurts then go through a process similar to the freezing that occurs in our freezer. Within us, the emotions become silent, hardened, heavier over time. They weigh us down. We have closed the door on the emotions within us, just as we close the door of the freezer and immediately forget about what is going on inside.

If we do not deal with our hurts as they occur, or if we allow a considerable build-up of unresolved hurt, pain and emotion to accumulate within us, all this heaviness eventually makes its presence felt, despite our efforts to deny its existence. Some will experience this in their body. I recall one man who, during his immensely difficult childhood, repeatedly experienced great irritation on his skin. He was taken to several doctors. No cause was found and no problem was identified. On one occasion, returning home from yet another doctor's office, this boy said to himself that he was giving up. He concluded that there was no point in trying to communicate to anyone that there was something major wrong in his life: immense pain regarding his relationships with both his parents and the family situation generally.

Much of our accumulated unresolved hurt and emotional distress arises during childhood and adolescence. Children may experience difficult emotions as too overwhelming to deal with fully, particularly because we live in a society that does not generally support the intense feeling and processing of painful emotions. Painful events and moments are felt initially for a brief few seconds. Overwhelmed by the emotion, the child may choose to disengage from it and forget the experience, but the hurt and pain will have registered. It stays within the child, not fully dealt with, without reaching the point of closure and completion. The pattern of blocking pain, hurt and other distressing emotions is now established. This pattern continues into and throughout adulthood.

With the ever-increasing weight of emotional pain within us, like the overloaded freezer we may reach a point of overload and breakdown. It is not we who break down: it is our dysfunctional methods of handling life, including our distress, that reach breaking point. The result is a major flood of emotion, or emotion-infused behaviour, that may take you and others by surprise and be misunderstood and misinterpreted. You may have hidden your emotions away so well within you that others, and perhaps you too, were taken by surprise by the intensity of your emotions or your behaviour. This 'breakdown', when properly understood and dealt with, contains within it the seeds of a breakthrough, the creation of new, more effective ways of being, of living, of relating, especially to one's self.

A mother who once attended me became upset when in the course of our work she became aware of the reason why she always avoided playing with her young children. She cried deeply as she remembered how in her own childhood, her parents generally did not engage with or play with her. Playing with her own children risked bringing this painful memory out of the freezer within her and into her awareness. It seemed easier not to go there. By grieving for the loss of good contact with her own parents, she was able to enjoy playing with her children and the good mutual contact that resulted from this interaction.

As with food removed from the freezer, when you deal with your unresolved hurts, water may flow from you too, tears that you did not realise you had within you. Allow these tears to flow. Releasing these tears will gradually lead to you feeling much freer, lighter, more flexible and ready to engage far more fully with life. This was the case for Luke, a man in his thirties who endured immense emotional distress without ever releasing this distress in tears. Within weeks of commencing to work with me, he noticed that he was regularly becoming tearful while watching sensitive emotional scenes on television. His emotional freezer was beginning to thaw out. This coincided with a change within him that was no coincidence: he felt that he was coming alive, having felt 'dead' inside for years.

In ways, there are similarities between icebergs and us human beings. Only just over ten per cent of an iceberg is visible to the naked eye, the rest lies beneath the surface of the ocean. It is the unseen underwater aspect of the iceberg that is most powerful, that sinks ships. Without this knowledge, we would not understand how ships are sunk by icebergs, generally without coming into direct contact with the part of the iceberg that lies above the water surface.

We human beings are aware of the aspects of ourselves that are 'above the surface', including our thoughts, feelings, our bodily sensations and the contact we make with others and the world through our five senses. We are affected by what lies beneath the surface, of which we are far less aware. As illustrated in Diagram 12, such factors include: our unmet needs; our overall level of selfhood; our level of the individual components of selfhood; our emotional fragility; our avoidance strategies; our databank of previous experiences; our insecurities and our level of self-doubt; our habits of living and patterns of behaviour; the level of fear we experience, or avoid experiencing as much as we can; blocked and unprocessed experiences and emotions such as shock, grief, loss, hurt and anger; our creative drives and how we channel our creativity.

Becoming more aware of 'what lies beneath' can feel challenging and frightening. Yet, becoming aware helps us to understand ourselves better, enabling us to take corrective action, and address the real issues rather

THE HUMAN ICEBERG

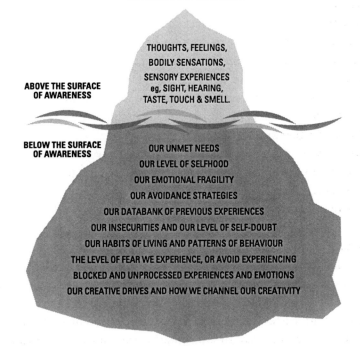

Diagram 12

than the surface ones. As a result, we tie up loose ends, which would remain dangling and incomplete if we continued to just deal with what is on the surface.

The human iceberg concept helps us to understand the experience of people who become diagnosed as suffering from mental illnesses such as depression, obsessive-compulsive disorder, bipolar disorder and schizophrenia. As an example, let us consider schizophrenia. On the surface, hearing voices, becoming paranoid, experiencing delusions and major withdrawal may not seem to make sense. This conclusion fails to take into account the reality that we experience life not as it is but as we are. For example, if I feel constantly unsafe and vulnerable, I will either be on constant red alert for potential threats everywhere, or I will do my best to avoid all contact with situations that might risk increasing my sense of not feeling safe.

The person who becomes paranoid and consequently chooses to withdraw greatly from life does so because they are feeling extremely unsafe. They are convinced that they are unable to make themselves feel safe or protect themselves. Beneath the surface lies enormous loss of selfhood, resulting in a range of consequences such as great dread, terror and insecurity. The person projects these on to the screen of life, just as the cinema projector projects the film images on to the screen. These people are often more aware of the surface experiences, such as hearing voices and delusions than with the aspects of the experience that lie deeper. Without the cinema projector, there would be no images on the screen. Without the loss of selfhood and consequent terror, there would be no paranoia or withdrawal.

Many of us spend much of our lives trying to avoid peak anxiety, and attempting to avoid showing major expressions of fear and anxiety to others. This is largely because as a society, we have deemed public expressions of anxiety to be unacceptable, and those who do so risk public rejection and all that goes with that. Indeed, our society supports the avoidance of real contact to quite a degree. For example, silence is now a rarity in public places. Coffee shops, bars, and hotel lobbies routinely have music systems, televisions or radios on, often quite loudly. Within homes, silence and stillness, necessary conditions to make true contact with ourselves, are becoming increasingly rare commodities, with an ever-increasing array of audio and visual machines with which to occupy and distract ourselves. Many people wittingly or unwittingly use various chemical substances to avoid contact with themselves and their feelings, including alcohol, cigarettes, over the counter, prescribed and illegal drugs.

The resistance to feel deeply-held feelings pervades our lives more than we might realise. For example, now in his mid-fifties, one of Joseph's main traits is that he is a fixer, a problem solver. This pattern began in his childhood. Both parents had major alcohol problems, and his childhood was frequently chaotic. No one seemed to fix things at home, to ensure that all was well and that the children felt safe. Joseph adopted that role as a child, and continued it throughout his life. The role helped him to feel safer, since things were at least being fixed and sorted out to some degree, albeit by himself. In reality, Joseph had for decades held great sadness in his heart around his childhood, in particular about not having his emotional needs met.

Becoming a problem-solver became a way of relating, a role in which he felt safe, confident and powerful since he had so much practice and experience as a fixer. When he becomes upset, he generally chooses not to communicate this to his partner. He wanders off on his own as he has always done, as if licking his wounds, often taking 2-3 days to become aware of his feelings, and several more days to communicate what he experienced to his partner. My suggestion that he risk expressing to his partner what he is going through *as he is experiencing it* filled him with terror. Doing so would likely result in him coming into contact with his own deep long-held and unexpressed feelings of great sadness, so it is much easier for him to not go there. Indeed, he often says 'I don't want to go there'. Working through his sadness will likely liberate him, if he is prepared to do so.

The process of disconnection from one's self occurs in three stages. Initially, the child has feelings and needs, and articulates them. If the child's needs are generally met, and their feelings listened to and respected, without judgement or disapproval, the child will generally continue to stay in good contact with themselves. If the need is frequently not met or their feelings are not listened to, respected and validated, the child feels hurt and saddened, and may withdraw somewhat. This leads into the next stage, where the child is aware of their feelings and needs but does not articulate them, leading to further pain and withdrawal. This often progresses to a third stage, in which the child does not feel either the need or the pain. They are in effect numbed and anaesthetised, disconnected from and out of contact with themselves and their feelings. Many people remain at the second stage, and do not experience the third stage.

Secondary feelings such as irritability, numbness, anxiety and depression generally lie above the surface, as do the primary emotions we allow ourselves to feel, while the primary emotions we choose to block, often with secondary emotions, lie beneath the surface. Overcoming our distress often involves re-connecting with these primary feelings, with which we have sought to avoid contact by pushing them under the surface.

Avoiding contact with our most difficult feelings can be very tempting. Driving them underground means that we avoid direct and raw contact with the peak experience of painful emotion, particularly when deep down we are terrified that we may not survive this experience. As one woman who attends me put it, whose heart had been broken in a relationship, 'what happens when you reconnect with love?'. In asking the question, she revealed her intense fear about fully opening her wounded heart, reconnecting with her partner, and in the process connecting with her deeply held sadness and grief regarding the loss of trust that had occurred within the relationship.

For similar reasons, she struggled with saying 'I love you' to her partner. In fully reconnecting with love, she would also connect fully with intense hurt, grief, anger and rage, feelings that she had avoided for several years, well hidden from her own awareness, within the dungeons of her human iceberg beneath the surface. For her to truly reconnect with love for her partner again, she needed to experience these feelings, work through them and let them go. Doing so would enable her to either really come into this relationship again, or to leave it. Either option seemed terrifying, another reason why she hesitated to come into full contact with herself and her emotions. It sometimes seems easier to sit on the fence than to take any action that might lead to major and terrifying change in our lives.

She has made considerable progress on this in recent weeks. For example, following a week in which she took a lot of action and made very good contact with herself and others, she felt the need to withdraw. For two days, she made little contact with others, remaining in good contact with herself, experiencing much grief and sadness. She felt much lighter following this release of grief and sadness, and reconnected with people again. This period of withdrawal was now over, and she had handled it well.

It is often stated that we continue to avoid feeling, expressing and taking risks as adults because we fear further rejection. While there is some truth in this, there is more to it. We often know deep down that things have changed, that we are now in situations where we are not likely to be rejected. What we are often really afraid of is making direct contact with the pain involved in experiencing feelings of great pain that remain within our freezer, associated with previous experiences of rejection, abandonment, loss, trauma and other distressing experiences. By avoiding possible triggers, we minimise the risk of feeling these intense and difficult feelings. Sometimes, we really need this avoidance of contact, in order to survive. However in time it can become counter-productive to avoid dealing with aspects of ourselves that lie deep within us and continue to cause problems.

Kathy, Malcolm, Mel and Betty are further examples of the significance of what lies beneath the surface and its impact on our daily lives and experiences. Twenty-year-old Kathy had gone through a very hard time during her teenage years, enduring several years of bullying. This had hurt her deeply, and for years Kathy kept this grief from others and indeed from herself. Kathy found it extremely difficult to hug her parents and siblings, even though she loved them very much. It upset her parents greatly that Kathy would not hug them, and they blamed themselves. They concluded that they must have made some big mistakes in their parenting for Kathy to seem to want to avoid any expression of affection with them.

In fact, Kathy craved physical affection from her family, but she avoided hugging because it would open her heart and bring Kathy into close emotional contact with *herself* though loving physical contact with members of her family. Kathy would then come into direct contact with her own painful emotions, possibly bursting into tears. She wanted to avoid such intense contact with her feelings, so she chose to avoid hugging those who loved her. Her desire to avoid contact with herself was so strong that she was willing to lose out on something so important as the giving and receiving of the expression of love and affection. Kathy also tended to avoid conversations with her parents that might lead to increased contact with herself and her emotions. She especially avoided such conversations with her mother because her mother would ask 'pertinent questions' that brought Kathy into contact with her feelings. By avoiding contact with her feelings in this way, she also unwittingly ensured that her painful feelings remained within her and continued to affect her everyday life. With my encouragement, Kathy risked expressing and receiving physical affection within her family. As I expected, this loving physical contact with her family initially triggered major expressions of sadness and grief within Kathy. She continued with this new way of connecting with her family, and as a result she has come into much better contact with herself, releasing a great deal of emotion in the process. These emotions have now been fully released, and Kathy is now able to enjoy the benefits of a palpably closer relationship with herself and her family.

Malcolm attended me on one occasion. Aged forty-five, the appointment was arranged by his sister, who persuaded him to attend me. However, Malcolm himself did not seem to want help. Although according to his siblings Malcolm had been at crisis point, in a very dark place for many weeks, he utterly refused to engage with me in a meaningful way. Malcolm spent the consultation time avoiding contact with me, but also with himself. He kept looking out the window, and hardly answered a single question with any degree of real communication.

Every question I asked him, he either evaded or reflected the question right back to me. When I asked him about how much fear he experienced, he asked me 'how much do you experience?'. I replied that yes, I sometimes do experience fear in my life. He replied that he felt no fear, that his confidence was high. I knew that neither of these assertions was true, and when I attempted to explore them with Malcolm, I was met with a stubborn silence. He was adamant that things in his life were fine, despite the fact that he was now so housebound that special arrangements had to be made with the state social services because he felt unable to leave home to cash his weekly disability cheque, such was his desire to avoid all contact with people.

Malcolm also employed another deflection technique, talking around a subject rather than respond as it applied to his own life. For example, when I asked him if he was happy, as he continued to look out the window he said 'what is happiness?' and spoke briefly on the subject in a detached, theoretical way. When I attempted to bring the issue back to himself within his own life, he again stopped talking and would not engage with me.

Talking about sport was another deflection technique he employed. Malcolm must have brought sport into the conversation on about twenty occasions, as something he was interested in. And yet, when I sought to explore this with him, he again ended the conversation very quickly.

While sport is an important and healthy aspect of life for many people, Malcolm used sport as a way of avoiding contact with me in that meeting. He certainly was practised at avoiding contact.

As we only met once, I was not sure which of the two of us Malcolm was being the most dishonest with, probably me. I suspected that Malcolm had over the years become quite dishonest with himself too, refusing to acknowledge the level of his distress and seek help for it. I offered him a further appointment. Malcolm said he would think about it. That was nine months ago, and I haven't heard from him since then. I believe Malcolm deliberately set out to avoid contact with me. Over the years he had also become practised at avoiding contact with himself, with his emotional pain, his challenges, including the challenge of shaping a fulfilling life for himself.

The common tendency to avoid deeper contact with both ourselves and others is often not helped by the collective attitudes of the society in which we live. For example, a male client of mine once told me that he had to leave work one day because he felt that he was on the verge of tears. Part of his reaction was fear of feeling his own feelings, but he was also understandably concerned regarding how his work colleagues might react.

Mel, now in his late forties, habitually avoided contact with himself and others. Every Saturday he visited his mother's home, as did his four sisters. While his sisters would remain in the downstairs sitting room, chatting away with each other and their mother, Mel always went to an upstairs bedroom and read, having said a brief 'hello' to the gang in the sitting room. As we discussed this, it emerged that he repeatedly chose to avoid contact with his family because he would feel uncomfortable in their company. His brief 'hello' followed by his disappearing act served to minimise his unease while also avoiding contact with his family and with his own feelings.

His challenge is to stay in the room with his family, feel whatever uncomfortable feelings arise within him, and risk engaging in conversation. Why would anyone resist this, it sounds so simple, ordinary and pleasant. Actually, Mel had several reasons. He would have to consider letting his guard down and reveal more of himself in the conversations. He would have to consider that these are indeed good people, that perhaps he was wrong in his judgements about them. Mel might also then come in contact with his own emotions, including sadness, loss, regret and guilt regarding how he has lived, the sadness he has experienced, and some of the decisions he has made. So every

Saturday, he chose to keep up his guard, to maintain his belief that he has been hard done by the world, and that he had not contributed to his isolation. It was everyone else's fault.

In her mid-thirties, Betty attended me with the intention of making progress toward recovery of her mental health. Betty had been diagnosed as suffering from schizophrenia seven years previously. On the surface, Betty was genuinely keen to make progress. Indeed, at times she became quite impatient with the pace of her progress. However, beneath the surface within Betty lay a great deal of fear and self-doubt. Many of her habits and patterns of living were designed to minimise her exposure to risk. For example, currently doing a post-graduate academic course, Betty mentioned that she usually studies in her own room and always has done, because she feels very insecure and self-conscious when there are others in the room with her. This was a significant revelation, because it revealed an important contradiction within Betty. On the one hand, she was keen, impatient even, to make progress, but on the other hand, she was continuing to choose to live in ways that were counter-productive in the context of recovery. Becoming aware of this apparent contradiction was the first step for Betty. She now needed to address her fears if she is to make real progress, through self-reassurance and taking different actions, such as studying more in the room with others, reassuring herself over and over, before, during and after studying in that room. Self-reassurance is explored in more detail in the Self-support section on page 173.

ACTIONS

1. To what degree do you make or avoid contact with yourself?
Commit to be mindful of this question as you go about your day. You do this by being the observer, as discussed in the section on self-awareness. Pledge that you will be more observing of yourself, your habits, patterns, tendencies, what you are attracted to, and what you seek to avoid. This will help you become more aware of and familiar with the degree to which you make or avoid contact with yourself.

2. Consider the process of disconnection from yourself as it might apply to you
As discussed on page 137 in this section on self-contact, broadly speaking

there are three levels of connection with or disconnection from one's self, and a range in between. The first stage involves the process of withdrawal, having felt hurt when articulated needs and feelings went either unnoticed, unresolved or disrespected. The next stage is being aware of our feelings and needs but not seeing either through to completion. The third stage is where we become unaware of our feelings and our needs. Where are you on this scale?

3. The iceberg: What may lie beneath the surface within you?
Reflect on what if anything may lie beneath the surface within you. Fear, sadness, unresolved emotions, low sense of selfhood and the great self-doubt that accompanies this, are examples of what may lie deeper within you. See the iceberg diagram on page 135 for more ideas on what may lie beneath.

4. Consider your habits and patterns of living
Be prepared to notice your habits and patterns of living as you go about your day. What are your patterns of handling challenge, risk, hurt, rejection, failure, success, or other experiences? Do you tend to process your emotions and work difficult situations through to completion when they happen, put them on hold for a while and then deal with them, or put them in the freezer and leave them there? Do you like or dislike and avoid stillness or silence, which is likely to bring you into contact with yourself? What strategies do you use as patterns of avoidance? What you habitually avoid? What are your habits in regard to removing yourself from immediate contact with yourself and others, such as distraction, avoidance, withdrawing, putting things off, daydreaming, racing off into either future or the past? As with the woman who habitually avoided playing with her children, the man who became a fixer, the girl who avoided hugging, you may have developed some habits and patterns that are designed to keep you from making contact with yourself, particularly with your painful emotions. By becoming aware of your habits and patterns around contact, you become more aware of the subtleties of what you do habitually and why, and you consequently become more informed about yourself.

5. Look for apparent contradictions
Like Betty in the example described on page 142, you may genuinely want to progress, yet be behaving in ways that suggest otherwise.

Becoming more aware and mindful of your habits and patterns of living will help to reveal such apparent contradictions within your life.

6. Do you have a freezer inside you?
If you have been in the habit of blocking many of your emotions and having many unmet needs, the chances are that you have created your own freezer within you. Consider what you might have put into the freezer over the years. What emotions, experiences and unmet needs might remain frozen within you to this day? Are you experiencing or have you experienced signs of freezer overload, such as panic, anxiety, surges of emotions that seem inappropriate to the situation, or recurring stress symptoms? Do you feel weighed down, burdened, frozen, tired, exhausted, numb, cold? If so, weighed down with what?

On reflection, have there been times in your life when your emotions or your behaviour reflected the process of freezing, overload and thawing out? Reflect on your life. Were there times when your freezer became so full that stuff spilled out, or that you took drastic or major action to try to keep the freezer door closed, such as taking substances to numb yourself, or other forms of escape and avoidance?

7. What secondary emotions or other consequences do you experience as a result of avoiding contact with yourself, or trying to keep the freezer door closed?
Consider the degree to which you experience secondary feelings, as discussed in the section on dealing with emotions. The degree to which you experience secondary feelings reflects how full your inner freezer is, and the level of intensity of your need to store unexpressed feelings and experiences in your freezer. Other consequences of avoiding contact with yourself include withdrawing from life, risk and challenge, not committing or persisting, and drifting through life, lacking passion and energy.

8. What are your triggers, and how do you deal with them?
If you are in the habit of avoiding contact with yourself, you will nevertheless encounter situations that may potentially bring you into closer contact with yourself. Such situations include those likely to bring up emotions such as fear, sadness, grief, and anxiety. Become more observant of your reactions to situations. You may be quite practised at

dealing with such triggers, and have a well rehearsed routine, designed to ensure that you quickly put a stop to any possibility that the trigger may lead you to make better contact with yourself. Notice the triggers, and notice your reactions to them.

9. Be mindful of your level of honesty with yourself

Self-delusion can be a way of maintaining the avoidance of contact with ourselves, keeping contact with our difficult emotions at bay, but they remain, lurking, like a dark cloud on the horizon. Reflect on your reasons for avoiding things. For example, 'I don't like hugging' may actually mean 'I avoid hugging because it brings up difficult emotions in me, but I would love to give and receive more hugs'.

10. Write in your journal

In your daily writing, write about the issue of contact with yourself, bearing the actions in this section in mind. Doing so will help you become aware of your habits and patterns around self-contact, including your often subtle methods of side-stepping contact with yourself.

11. Take different actions

Having identified your habits and patterns regarding self-contact, you may need to take different actions in future. For example, Kathy, who as described earlier avoided any degree of hugging within her family, had options regarding different actions she could take. She could risk expressing to her family the truth about her avoidance of hugging. She could write in detail about it. Both of these would be progress, bringing her into greater contact with herself. But the greatest progress would be made by going ahead and doing it, by hugging and being hugged, and letting whatever emotions surface within her to be expressed. This would initially feel challenging, and may therefore provoke anxiety. She needed to carry on regardless. This is precisely what she did. And after an initial intense experience and expression of sadness and grief triggered by making real contact with herself through the hugging, Kathy experienced great relief. She also experienced a sense of joy, not least because she and her family felt much closer to each other, now that hugging was again an acceptable form of loving contact between them.

12. Reflect on your childhood, your past and write about it
Do you recall times when you felt great distress and then numbed it out because it was too big, too painful to handle? In your childhood, did you develop patterns of blocking pain and hurt that was just too much to endure at the time?

13. Self-contact exercise
I suggest you do this exercise once a day. You can do this exercise at any time, especially when you are experiencing feelings or emotion within you. Sit upright in a comfortable chair, in silence. Place one hand over your heart, and your other hand on your tummy. Notice what is going on in your mind, your thoughts, your feelings, your body. Make good contact with yourself, with whatever way you are feeling. Name whatever it is you are feeling. Stay with the feeling. Breathe gently into it. Don't try to change it, let it be. Ask yourself what might lie beneath the feeling, if anything. Do this for a few minutes. Then, end the exercise, and carry on with your day, remaining more mindful of being in good contact with yourself.

14. Reflection
At your reflection times, reflect on the level of contact you made with yourself since your last reflection time. Gently re-affirm your commitment to make good contact with all aspects of yourself in your life.

15. Affirmation
'I make good contact with myself, including the aspects of myself I might prefer to avoid.'

Sexuality
The term 'sexuality' is a broad concept that includes aspects of our physical, emotional, psychological, social, spiritual and sexual make-up, including sexual orientation, the capacity to feel sexual feelings, the state or quality of being sexual.

You don't have to be sexually active to be in touch with your sexuality. Some people with a high sense of selfhood and a strong and comfortable awareness of their own sexuality choose not to engage in sexual relationships. Of course, this is perfectly okay and healthy, as long as this choice is made honestly, without trying to deceive oneself when the real reason is something else, usually fear.

Becoming comfortable with one's sexuality is an important aspect of selfhood. How young people experience the emergence of their sexuality in their late childhood and especially in their teenage years is closely linked to their level of selfhood. Coping with this major change in their experience of themselves and of life is challenging enough for young people with a solid sense of self.

Young people with a low level of selfhood question virtually everything about themselves, such is their level of self-doubt. Some tend not to experiment sexually, because of their high level of self-doubt, their great fear of risk, and their frantic need to stay within their significantly reduced comfort zone. They are left contemplating their sexuality in a theoretical bubble. Others, whose level of selfhood is low though usually slightly higher than those who seek to totally avoid contact with sex and their sexuality, become promiscuous, having little regard for themselves, their body or their sexuality. As a person's level of selfhood rises, they become more confident about who they are, who they are not, and what they really want. This applies across all aspects of selfhood, including sexuality.

Adults with a solid sense of selfhood, being generally comfortable regarding most aspects of themselves, tend to be at ease with their sexuality too. Irrespective of the presence or absence of sexual relationships in their life, they are aware that sexuality is an aspect of who they are, and they are comfortable with this reality. In keeping with the pervasive sense of self-doubt they live with, most people with a low sense of selfhood experience considerable self-doubt and inner conflict regarding their sexuality. They have difficulty accepting their sexuality, and have little confidence in their ability to satisfactorily experience and express their sexuality.

Some young people are quite unsure of themselves around their sexuality, going though extended periods of being confused around sex and sexuality. 'Am I straight or am I gay?' is a natural question many young people ask themselves. The intensity with which a person poses this question can sometimes be a reflection of both their level of selfhood and the intensity of their struggle with the emergence of their sexuality. Gaining clarity regarding their sexuality tends to parallel the raising of their selfhood.

Responsible, satisfying and respectful sexual behaviour is a good indicator of a strong sense of selfhood. People with a high sense of selfhood express their sexuality in keeping with their beliefs, values and their high sense of self. Rarely will they dishonour themselves in their sexual expression. If they do, they realise it, and resolve not to do so again. People with a low sense of selfhood may be disconnected from their sexuality, rarely experiencing themselves as sexual beings. Many fear sex and intimacy greatly, either avoiding them, engaging in sexual practices without emotional input, or creating an extremely strong, fear-based emotional connection to their sexuality. Many people, who have been promiscuous at times in their lives, later acknowledge that they were not happy during that time, that their promiscuity did not make them happy, and that their sense of self was very low at that time. For some, sex becomes a way of making some level of contact with others, while protecting one's heart by attempting to ensure that an emotional relationship does not develop that might later end, and also ensuring that they avoid making real emotional contact with themselves, their own feelings and distress. This type of sexual behaviour may work for some, but it can result in considerable dishonouring of one's self, and damage to the person's sense of self that can take quite some time to heal.

When a person's level of selfhood is very low, they may feel that the whole area of sex and sexuality is way beyond them, and attempt to suppress or ignore this aspect of themselves. This approach may seem to work for a while, but on occasion they will become aware of their own sexuality, as one cannot totally shut reality out forever. They may experience their sexual urges as bad, even evil, as very distressing, throwing them considerably, as they have been trying so hard to banish this aspect of themselves. Their sexual urges may feel like extreme surges within them. Lacking spontaneous and ever-flowing expression, these surges are often imbalanced, out of proportion, extreme at times, rarely reaching satisfactory completion. They feel helpless and hopeless regarding their sexuality, because they may not have the confidence to see to it that their sexual needs and their need for love are met. They may judge themselves very harshly for experiencing such feelings. They may feel overwhelmed, angry, guilty, anxious, not knowing what to do with these feelings or how to handle them. The distress of this experience may tempt them to disconnect even more from their sexual aspect and withdraw further from this aspect of themselves and of life. The real issue here is that the person has been suddenly reminded of an aspect of themselves which they have been trying to deny. This raw contact with reality upsets them greatly, reminding them of who they really are, of what they are missing out on. Reclaiming this aspect of themselves seems extremely daunting.

As described earlier and depicted in Diagram 2 on page 12, loss of selfhood is generally accompanied by a shutting down or an imbalance in some of the aspects of our being. Some people shut down their sexual aspect, which increases the pressure on the other lanes. If a person shuts down their sexual and emotional aspect, there is a corresponding increase in the levels of activity and pressure within the remaining lanes. Others go to another extreme. For them, sex becomes increasingly important, one of the few lanes that remains open, receiving increased traffic, if for example they have closed down their emotional aspect. For some, sex becomes a way of temporarily expressing and defusing emotions such as anger and loneliness without actually addressing the core issues. They remain unhappy and disenchanted, as their sexual encounters remain fundamentally superficial and empty, which may be what they choose, but perhaps not what they need.

There is a considerable body of evidence to suggest that maintaining a healthy love and sexual life into old age contributes to health, happiness and longevity. Healthy, self-honouring sex and sexuality enhance one's sense of wellbeing, aliveness and connectedness, both to ourselves and to others.

In many relationships, sex and sexuality diminish considerably within many relationships as the years pass. While many people have no problem with this, for others it is a great loss. It is possible to work on your level of acceptance and aliveness of your sexuality.

ACTIONS

1. Take your time

Take your time on this one. Sexuality is a pretty intimidating subject when we have lost our sense of self, so be gentle with yourself. Actions in this area therefore need to be taken with considerable care. Working on generally raising your level of selfhood as outlined throughout this book will help you to gradually make considerable progress, increasing your awareness of all aspects of yourself including your sexuality.

2. To what degree are you aware of your sexuality?

Consider the degree to which you are aware of, experience and express your sexuality. Give this question some honest consideration. Refer to the first paragraphs of this section on sexuality if you are unclear about what sexuality means. Perhaps you are disconnected from your sexuality. Explore these issues in your writing and reflections, noting your reactions to moments where matters relating to sexuality arise.

3. Consider your habits, patterns, feelings and beliefs regarding your sexuality

Reflect on how comfortable you are regarding your sexuality, how you view your sexuality, your desirability or attractiveness. Do you view your desirability purely in physical terms, or do you see it in terms of the totality of your being, the person that you are? Is it frightening to think of being sexually intimate with someone? Do sexual encounters leave you feeling lonely or unhappy? Consider what feelings come up within you regarding your sexuality, any judgements you make about yourself regarding sexuality, sexual thoughts or activities, including masturbation. Such feelings might include fear, terror, dread, anxiety, guilt, shame, and an immediate desire to change topic. Explore these issues further, noting your reactions to moments where sexuality comes up as an issue around you. Masturbation is often fundamentally a comforting or tension-releasing act, or an attempt to compensate for lack of sexual contact, which is why many people feel sad and empty after masturbating, if this is the case for them.

Consider what messages you may have received regarding sex and sexuality, and to what degree you may have internalised the views, beliefs and biases of others. If you have internalised the beliefs of others toward sexuality, consider whether you might work on gradually creating your own attitudes, and let go of the opinions of others that over the years you may have internalised as your own.

4. Write about your experience of sexuality in your life

Write a diary of your sexuality, how you experienced its emergence, and the difficult emotions you may have experienced as you tried to deal with it. Explore what have you done with your sexuality over the years, and whether this has changed over time. This is *you* telling your story to *you*, how it really was for you. Honour, respect and have compassion for yourself and for this important part of your life story.

5.   Do you have ownership of your sexuality?

Do you take charge of your sexuality, or do you regularly surrender it according to the wishes and desires of others? To what degree do you shape your sexuality and sexual behaviour in accordance with what you really feel is best for you, or for other reasons such as acceptance by others, because others want you to behave this way, or because you think they want you to behave in this way?

6.   Resolve to be self-respecting and self-honouring regarding your sexuality

Prize your sexuality. Do not reduce its importance in your own eyes, and do not give permission to others to disrespect you by disrespecting your sexuality, if you know this is not what you want or need. Own and honour your sexuality.

7.   Reflection

At your reflection times, gently bear in mind whether any issues relating to your sexuality surfaced since your last reflection. Commit to noticing and honouring your sexuality to yourself as you go about your day.

8.   Affirmation

'I am connected to, aware of, and proud of my sexuality.'

Case histories

Here are two stories of people I have worked with, for whom the recovery of self-awareness aspects of selfhood was central to the recovery of their sense of selfhood, and consequently, their emotional and mental wellbeing.

Margaret's story is an example of how many of us censor our emotions, the price we pay for so doing, and the benefits we experience when we stop blocking emotions we experience as painful or difficult. Margaret began attending me in her mid-forties. She been suffering from depression for over ten years, and had been taking Cipramil, an antidepressant drug. She tried unsuccessfully to come off this medication on several occasions during this ten-year period. On each occasion, within weeks of stopping the drug, she experienced intense emotions including sadness, tearfulness, anxiety, fear and regrets about the passing of time, wishing desperately that she was back in her youth again. Her sense of selfhood had been low since her childhood. Fearful of change and of new experiences for decades, Margaret had structured her life around her great need for safety and security. She had some confidence in certain aspects of herself, such as her mothering qualities and her book-keeping abilities. She seldom strayed beyond these arenas, rarely initiating new activities in her life.

Margaret wanted to explore what might be causing her depression. She hoped she could live contentedly without medication. After a few sessions, I was satisfied that it was appropriate to begin reducing her medication, and I weaned her off Cipramil over a period of six months. Within weeks, she began to experience intense emotions. This continued for over two months. Margaret experienced despair, anxiety, fear, tearfulness and great self-doubt. She obsessed about the passing of time, a mirror image of her previous experiences of coming off medication. I used our sessions to facilitate this expression of emotion, supporting her as she went through this difficult and painful time. She knew that I was at the other end of the phone if she needed to talk. Margaret had not had such support on the previous occasions she attempted to come off medication. While Margaret was always diligent and conscientious about her career, over the years her work had become boring and repetitive. She wanted to resign, but was scared of the changes this would inevitably create to her lifestyle and her finances. Having little experience of successfully dealing with change, and having for years studiously avoided change, she greatly doubted her ability to survive such upheaval.

One day without warning, Margaret's employers informed her that because of the economic recession, she was being made redundant. Mindful of the advice I had been giving her, Margaret chose not to accept her employer's invitation to leave immediately, instead deciding to deal with the situation in ways that were unfamiliar to her. She felt that she needed to work through the customary ten days' notice. Margaret had been off all medication for three months. Being on no medication, she experienced the full impact of her emotions during this ten-day period. This was her choice. She knew that she could at any time re-commence the medication if she wished. She chose to feel the experience fully, to work through it, and through the wide range of accompanying emotions.

Initially, Margaret was deeply shocked at the news that her career had come to a sudden end and, predictably, she went through a rollercoaster of emotions including fear, anxiety, anger, sadness, and frequent crying.

She made a conscious decision to let herself be seen to be upset, something she had never done previously. Choosing to stay on for those ten days proved to be very beneficial for Margaret. She knew that this time she was not running away, either from her challenging new reality or from her emotions. Many of her work colleagues acknowledged their sadness and upset at losing her. She had ample opportunity to express her gratitude for the friendships and comradeship she had experienced in the company over her twenty-five years there. By the end of her ten final days, she had ensured that she had no unfinished business with either the company or her colleagues. She brought closure to the entire situation. When she walked out the door for the last time, having honoured herself so well, she felt a strong sense of completeness.

Margaret came to see me three weeks after her last day at work. She had not felt the need to contact me sooner during this trying period of her life, I only heard about it after it was all over. I was struck by how well she looked. There was a sense of peace, strength and power about her that I had not previously noticed. She confirmed this sense of wellbeing, and she was surprised that she had coped so well with such enormous change. She described how, during those intense final ten days at work, her feelings were running at an all-time high. She had grieved deeply, experiencing a wide range of emotions. Margaret was now determined to take care of herself and to create more fulfilment in her life. During the previous six months, at my suggestion Margaret had become involved in new activities that she was thoroughly enjoying, including creative writing and bible studies. Margaret had been curious about these activities for years but had not previously mustered up the courage to participate.

During those final ten days at work, Margaret felt catapulted into living in the present because of the seriousness of the situation. Consequently, she felt more alive during those days than she had for years. She also experienced joy and laughter like never before. Once she allowed herself to fully experience her emotions, she opened herself to the entire range of emotion, thus experiencing a level of aliveness that only full openness to emotions can create. This contrasted with her previous decades-long experience of feeling depressed, flat, numb, stuck and bored. Her self-perception has changed forever. She now has an inner knowing that she can cope with change, while honouring herself and her needs during the process of major life changes.

Clara's experience demonstrates how the lack of self-knowledge can cause us to feel lost when confronted with overwhelming emotions which, when equipped with greater self-knowledge, make perfect sense. Clara described her childhood and teens as happy and free. Within twelve months of completing her university degree, she got married and started a new job. She was twenty-six years of age when she first came to see me. By then, she had endured a horrific twelve months. All had seemed well in the months prior to her wedding. However, during the week just before the big day, she experienced a great deal of anxiety and sadness. She couldn't understand why, because she loved her fiancé very much.

In the three months following the wedding, she became extremely distressed. Her GP referred her to a psychiatrist, who diagnosed depression and put her on Prozac. After a few months, the dosage was increased, as Clara was making no progress. At our initial sessions, she would visibly shake with anxiety and terror, crying continually, without any understanding of the cause of her distress. As I got to know Clara, I came to understand her situation clearly. She had always been extremely close to both parents. She relied greatly on her mother, always seeking and taking her advice. She also loved her family home, feeling very safe and secure there. The distress she endured around the time of the wedding made sense. She was terrified of moving on with her life, but she had suppressed this terror, so it found another way to express itself, through her overwhelming anxiety. Getting married was a definite statement, to herself and to the world. Clara was now moving on, separating from her parents, leaving her home of origin forever. She knew that moving on also carried with it the onus and expectation of becoming a competent adult. She, on the other hand, felt much more like a child than an adult woman.

It was only when Clara had been confronted with the reality of moving out of her old home that the degree of attachment to her parents finally surfaced. While her sense of selfhood had previously appeared strong, areas where she was vulnerable had never been really tested up to that point in her life. When they were, her sense of selfhood crumbled drastically and dramatically, as it had been constructed on shaky foundations. Clara cried a great deal during her initial sessions with me. I was glad to see that. I felt she was grieving for the illusion of always remaining a child, safe and secure in her home, always having a mother and father to mind her and keep her safe in this world. As the months progressed, Clara gained a significant degree of self-knowledge. This gave her hope, as she could now understand the painful journey she was going through. Eighteen months later, Clara had successfully made the transition from child to adult, from a protected life with her parents to a full life with her husband. She has been off all medication for over two years.

3. Caring for yourself

The components of selfhood discussed in this section have self-care as a common theme. They include self-care itself, your relationship with yourself, self-love, self-empathy, needs and need-meeting, self-support, self-regulation and self-comforting.

Self-care
Self-care is a right, not a privilege. Self-care means taking care of yourself and your needs, including your need to foster a solid sense of selfhood. It includes nurturing and nourishing all aspects of yourself, including your physical, emotional, psychological, social, sexual, relational and spiritual aspects.

If your sense of selfhood is low, you probably don't take sufficient care of yourself. You may not know how to best take care of and nurture yourself. You may feel so hurt, so disheartened, that you no longer care enough to look after yourself. Perhaps you believe that you do not have the right to self-care, or that others may react angrily toward you if you were to care for and about yourself. When our level of selfhood is low, our efforts to care for ourselves may be somewhat dysfunctional. We compromise ourselves in order to survive, getting our needs met as best we believe we can. Avoidance, escapism, withdrawing, saying either no or yes almost constantly are examples of dysfunctional acts of self-care. These acts of self-care may be the best we feel we can do, as seen from our personal perspective but they do not meet our core needs and often create even more problems for us. How saying either no or yes can be dysfunctional acts of self-care is described on page 198.

Self-care can be as ordinary as organising yourself to be punctual in your life without rushing, ready and prepared for what lies ahead. A central aspect of self-care is knowing and acknowledging when you need the help of others, and then seeking it out. Healthy self-care is not at the expense of caring for others as appropriate, or denying others the right to take care of themselves. A person with a healthy sense of selfhood generally does not feel the need to control, manipulate, or put others down.

It can be erroneously considered selfish to take care of ourselves. Doing so is sometimes frowned upon by others. In order to help other people, you need to become experienced at nurturing and taking care of yourself. A stark example of this occurs every time you fly. Before take-off, the cabin crew inform passengers that in the event of oxygen masks being required, adults should put on their mask first before helping their children with theirs. If parents do not take care of themselves and instead put on their child's mask first, the parents will not have enough time to put on their own masks. The child will survive all right, but the parents may quickly lose consciousness and die, as their children may be too young to realise the importance of putting the mask on their now unconscious parent. If the adult puts their oxygen mask on first, they can then put on their children's mask for them. While we are on the subject of flying, would you feel safe in a plane if you knew that the pilot did not take good care of him or herself?

Scott's story illustrates the importance of balancing self-care with caring for others. A successful businessman in his mid-fifties, Scott attended me for counselling as he had reached the point of burnout and he was afraid for his mental health. A key aspect of Scott's problem was a major imbalance in his self-care and care for others equation. Heavily involved in many business and social projects, helping others was enormously important to Scott. Through our work, Scott began to take care of himself. We worked toward balancing the equation. Consequently, Scott again experienced happiness, contentment and fulfilment, qualities that had increasingly eluded him in recent years in proportion to his lack of self-care.

ACTIONS

1. *On the spectrum of self-care – other-care depicted in Diagram 13, where are you?*

Observe the degree to which you take care of yourself. Do you give yourself enough time every day to take care of yourself, including enough time to eat well and tend to the little things in your life? Is self-care generally a consideration as you plan ahead? Do you take good care of your body? How frequently, due to failing to take good care of yourself, do you put your physical, emotional, and mental wellbeing excessively at risk? Make self-care a constant in your life. Then you will be in a good position to care for others also.

2. Accept that you deserve to take care of yourself
Risk accepting that you are deserving of your own self-care and self-nurturing. Expect that you may initially feel some sadness as you persist with this, an example of the presence–absence phenomenon described on page 38. In this situation, as you begin to employ self-care as a principle in your life, sadness may arise within you. This may happen as you may become aware of how absent self-care has been in your life, and perhaps also of the absence of others in your life to care for you, either now, in the past or both. This may cause you to feel sadness in the early stages. Not accepting that you are deserving can be a form of self-protection, often from direct contact with your own painful emotions.

3. Take care of the little things, and of yourself, as you go through your day
In your interactions with others, bear in mind your own presence. Be mindful of your needs, of taking care of yourself within each interaction and situation.

4. Make time for you
Make time every day for yourself. What you choose to do with that time

SELF-CARE – OTHER-CARE SPECTRUM

SELF-CARE   **OTHER-CARE**

Diagram 13

is up to you, whatever you feel would be best for you. If you live a busy life, you can still make some time for yourself every day, if you are prepared to prioritise this. Ensure that at regular intervals you take a day or at least several hours in a day for yourself, for something you would or might enjoy. Consider doing this weekly or certainly once every two weeks, since anything less may not be sufficient to keep up the momentum of a felt sense of ongoing self-care. If you are so out of touch with yourself that you do not know what you might enjoy, experiment. Have a go at a number of things. Give each a chance, do not dismiss them after one or two attempts. If you try five things, the chances are that you will find at least one that has some promise for you.

Patrice had given birth to her first child ten weeks previously. She felt overwhelmed by the constellation of changes involved in becoming a mother. Following a general discussion about her likes and dislikes and what might work for her, among other things I suggested to Patrice that every Saturday she take two–three hours to herself. Her husband took the baby out of the house for these few hours. I suggested that she use this time to reconnect with herself. During this three-hour time slot for herself, Patrice decided to cook herself a lovely breakfast, creating nice smells in the kitchen, while listening to her favourite music. She removed all watches and clocks from her vision, giving her a sense of timelessness. Patrice felt relieved and more in touch with herself afterwards, and consequently with her child and husband also. She was happy to make this a weekly event as was her husband, who could see the benefits of this practice.

5. *Striking a balance*

Is there a healthy balance between the degree to which you take care of yourself and of others? Many people whose sense of selfhood is low revolve their lives around caring for others, paying little heed to caring for themselves. If this is you, then it is time to risk taking better care of yourself. If you are at the opposite pole, always focusing on yourself, this generally does not work well either. You end up isolated, lonely, without good connection to others.

6. *Reflection*

During your daily moments of reflection, ask yourself 'how well have I taken care of myself so far today, both when I was on my own and when

I was with others?' Make a gentle commitment every morning to balance self-care with the care of others. In the evening, reflect on the day, and the degree to which you took care of yourself that day. The purpose of this reflection is to learn, not to criticise.

7. *Affirmation*
'I take good care of myself in every situation and interaction.'

Self-relationship
From birth to death, the only ever-present relationship in your life is the relationship you have with yourself. The quality of this relationship is a key element of mental wellness. It is both a determinant of your level of selfhood and a reflection of it.

Communicating and relating are core characteristics of relationships. We relate to ourselves continuously. We continuously experience our own thoughts and feelings. We each have an ongoing two-way conversation taking place within us. The next time you are on a busy street, watch the faces of the passers-by. Many will be deep in thought, concentrating on whatever thoughts are in their minds. Others will be visibly immersed in conversation with themselves. This self-relationship is often ignored, receiving little attention and even less nurturing.

Between work, school and other activities and the demands of life in the twenty-first century, family members and loved ones may spend only a few hours a day together, if that. You spend far more time with yourself than you do with even the most important people in your life. You are the only person that you are always with. You can never get away from yourself, although some people try to do so using various means such as alcohol, drugs, and various forms of escapism. These diversions may seem to be temporarily successful, but generally not for long. Such avoidance strategies often end up being seriously counter-productive, causing far more problems than they solve.

Your relationship with yourself is a key issue in your life. It deserves and needs time, attention and nurturing, as does any important relationship. The quality of the relationships we form with others springs from and mirrors the quality of the relationship we have with ourselves. A key feature of healthy selfhood is a gentle, self-supporting, self-validating, predominantly peaceful relationship with yourself. You can create and foster this by paying greater attention to your relationship with yourself, and by practical and sustained application of the ideas and actions in this book.

ACTIONS

1. Accept the reality that you have a relationship with yourself
Accept the reality that the relationship you have with yourself is your most important relationship, the cog around which your life and your world revolves. It may not seem easy to accept this reality, since you may initially become aware of what a difficult and painful relationship you have with yourself. Nevertheless, it is a fact, and the difficult emotions you may experience initially will pass.

2. Identify the current state of your relationship with yourself
Resolve to become more aware of the quality of the relationship you have with yourself. You do this by deliberately paying attention to the various ways in which you relate to and treat yourself, including your thoughts, words, feelings and actions. Are the conversations you have with yourself and your flow of thoughts and feelings toward yourself generally supportive and kind, or are they filled with self-criticism and self-undermining?

3. Commit to improving your relationship with yourself
Become a great deal more mindful of how you relate to and treat yourself. Commit to ensuring that the quality of your relationship with yourself reflects the fact that it is your most important relationship. Develop a low-grade, ever-present awareness of how you continually relate to yourself. Become practised at noticing how you talk to yourself, the feelings you experience toward yourself, your thought patterns including the thoughts you direct at yourself, and how you generally behave toward yourself. Developing this low-grade ever-present awareness will enable you to quietly observe yourself, and to quickly spot the moments when you relate badly to yourself. Each time this happens, gently state to yourself that you no longer relate to yourself in this way, that you now relate to yourself with love, kindness, friendliness and respect. Gradually this new way of relating to yourself takes hold within you.

4. Mirror work

People with a very low sense of self tend to be at one extreme or the other in terms of their visibility. Some have a desperate need to be seen, regularly seeking the limelight in an attempt to obtain affirmation from others that in reality only they can provide for themselves. They frequently look at themselves in the mirror, usually from the perspective of either great self-doubt or a frantic need to appear perfect. Others will go to great lengths to avoid being the centre of attention, sometimes even avoiding being included in a group photograph. Most studiously avoid looking at themselves in mirrors, being particularly reluctant to observe their own face, their own eyes. I believe that there is a definite reason for this avoidance, and it is linked to a recurring theme in this book, the avoidance of contact with ourselves. It is said that our eyes are the windows to our soul. Whether or not that is true, it certainly is true that making good eye contact brings us into closer contact, both with the other person and with ourselves, than not making eye contact. Looking into our own eyes, silently and unhurriedly, we make real contact with ourselves, something we might prefer not to do given the emotions this might bring up.

At least once a day, sit down and, using a hand-held mirror, devote a few minutes to looking at yourself. Hold the mirror about twelve inches from your face, ensuring that you can see all of your face in the mirror. Gently scan all aspects of your face, before settling on your eyes. Notice your reaction. You may feel an urge to look away immediately. You may quickly conclude that this is a silly waste of time. This reaction is an attempt to persuade you to stop: don't be seduced. You are now looking into your own eyes, the gateway into yourself. You are now making intimate contact with yourself. Your resistance to this reflects your reluctance to make direct contact with yourself and your emotions, including what you have been trying to hide from yourself, perhaps for years. Your immediate reaction may be 'I hate what I see'. This apparent self-hatred is a defence designed by you to deflect you from the hurts you hold inside you. Stay with this contact with yourself. Stay looking into your own eyes. Let whatever emotional reaction comes up to do so, no matter how intense it feels. If you find yourself wanting to break the contact, try to stay. If you do break the contact, go back to it in a moment. If you can't manage this, then do so later, or the next day. As the days and weeks pass, you will notice that how you see yourself when you look in the mirror changes for the better.

5. Reflection

During your reflection times, consider how you have conducted your relationship with yourself during the preceding hours. Renew your efforts to improve the quality of your relationship with yourself.

6. Affirmation

'My relationship with myself is the most important relationship in my life, and I relate to myself accordingly.'

Self-love

Many people find the concept of loving oneself to be vague and unattainable. As a client once said to me, it is difficult to feel the same sense of love and feeling for oneself that one might feel for another person. Perhaps it depends on what we mean by self-love. Think of self-love as the love one might feel for a very good friend, and loving oneself becomes more real and attainable. Being a good friend to yourself is all the more important in today's complicated world, where we are confronted with so much choice, change and uncertainty.

Very good friends are dependable, respectful, caring, compassionate and understanding. They are there for you, sensitive to you, sincere, genuine, supportive, considerate and loyal. They are empathic, affectionate, non-judgemental, patient but firm and honest too. They are forgiving, helpful, trustworthy and open. They believe in you. They listen well, and communicate well with you. They like you for who you are. They have integrity. Their friendship and companionship is unconditional. You know you matter to them. They are real with you. They are attentive, warm and encouraging, and want the best for you. They want you to be happy and for you to reach your full potential. A good friend is human, and won't get it right every time in their dealings with you. This is the type of healthy self-love and self-befriending that each of us can provide for ourselves.

ACTIONS

1. Clarify how you feel about yourself

Reflect on how you feel about yourself. Do you love yourself, hate yourself, or fall somewhere in between? Your feelings toward yourself are not as straightforward as you might initially think. For example, if your initial reaction was that you hate yourself, you may find that as you continue thinking about this issue, other feelings come into the picture, including sadness, anger, and at times, perhaps even a feeling of love for yourself. Convincing ourselves that we hate ourselves can be an effective way of distancing ourselves from emotions we would rather not feel. Many people feel this way about themselves, which is illustrated in Diagram 14. An accurate description of what the person is really feeling might be 'I hate feeling this way, and I hate how my life is'. However, as acknowledging this truth risks bringing up painful emotions, we may instead choose to change this to 'I hate me, therefore get away from me'.

2.   Where are you on the spectrum of self-befriending? See Diagram 15.
What kind of friend are you to yourself? Are you your own best friend, your own worst enemy, or somewhere in between? Resolve to be mindful of how you treat yourself in terms of friendship during the day.

3.   Affirm your right to love yourself
Every day, remind yourself that you are indeed deserving of your own

DISTANCING OURSELVES FROM OURSELVES

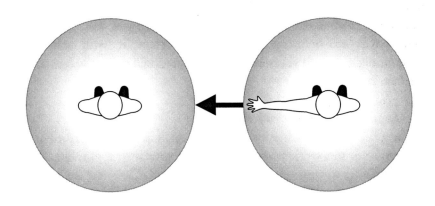

**I HATE MYSELF
GET AWAY FROM ME**

Diagram 14

SPECTRUM OF SELF - BEFRIENDING

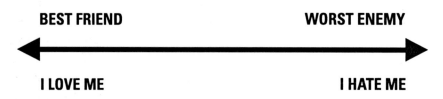

BEST FRIEND　　　　　　　　　**WORST ENEMY**

I LOVE ME　　　　　　　　　　**I HATE ME**

Diagram 15

love and friendship, because you are a unique, priceless human being. You are fundamentally a good person, who has experienced considerable loss, distress and struggle. Remind yourself of this at every reflection time.

4.　Notice when self-hatred arises within you, and gently counter it
When you notice yourself treating yourself with self-hatred, gently bring a different language into your mind, the language and feeling of friendship and kindness. You may find his difficult. There may be many times when your self-hatred surfaces quickly and powerfully, especially in the early stages. When the strong feeling of anger or hatred toward yourself has passed, gently reassure yourself. You treat yourself in this way because it is what you are used to, but in future you will increasingly notice this self-berating pattern, and replace it with self-loving communication with yourself. Your self-hatred will gradually lessen, and in time, it will cease.

5.　List the qualities of friendship
Make a list of the qualities of friendship, such as those described at the beginning of this section on self-love. Add your own if you like. Apply these qualities to your relationship with yourself. Carry the list with you in your pocket, wallet or handbag. Read through this list several times every day, including your reflection times. Gently notice when you deviate from treating yourself like a true friend, and replace that with the qualities of friendship.

6. Make a commitment to befriend yourself, and put your commitment
   into practice

From this moment on, commit to befriending yourself, to communicating with yourself as a best friend would. Let this be your standard of friendship with yourself that you will accept in future. You may need to force it a little at the beginning. You are ploughing through new soil, so expect considerable resistance within yourself in the initial stages. Keep it up and it will not be long before you see that you are making progress. Changing how you relate to yourself in this manner may at times in the early stages be accompanied by emotion, such as sadness and tearfulness. This is natural, since fear of experiencing your sadness and grief may well have been the reason you developed such a self-critical and self-hating relationship with yourself in the first place. You have been trying to distance yourself from these emotions by hating yourself and pushing yourself away from yourself, thereby attempting to push those emotions away from yourself also. Allow these emotions to come up and be released. They will not harm you, and their release will help to heal you.

7. Cupid's arrow to self exercise

Sit comfortably, your back well supported. Place one hand on your heart and the other on your tummy. Close your eyes. Gently bring your attention to your breathing. Take nice, deep, slow breaths, in and out. Place your attention on your heart. Send a cupid's arrow from you to your heart. In your mind's eye, watch the arrow approaching and entering your heart, carrying with it your love, filling you heart with your own love. As you do so, say 'I love myself'. Continue breathing gently and deeply. Gently notice how you feel, how your heart feels. Repeat the cupid's arrow exercise several times, each time noticing how your heart feels. Bring your attention back to your breathing for a few moments, and then open your eyes. Do this exercise every day.

8. Reflection

During your reflection times, consider the degree to which you have been loving and friendly toward yourself since your last self-reflection. Notice both the times when you were a good friend to yourself, and those when you could perhaps have been a better friend to yourself. Renew your commitment to living the rest of your life in a loving 'best-friend' mode, knowing that it will take you some time to master this.

9. Affirmation
'I love myself, and I am my own best friend.'

Self-empathy

Listed as one of the qualities of friendship above, self-empathy is sufficiently important to merit individual attention. Empathy is the capacity to understand and connect with the state of mind, emotion and experience of others, the ability to put oneself into another's shoes. Self-empathy therefore means cultivating this approach to yourself based on compassion, understanding and kindness.

Being willing to understand what someone else is going through is an important quality, when balanced with healthy self-empathy and self-centredness. This helps us lend support, understanding, help and empathy to our fellow human beings, without repeatedly being overwhelmed by the other person's situation. Many people have a major empathy imbalance. Some have endless empathy for other people, yet direct little compassion or kindness toward themselves. Other people have enormous empathy for themselves and little for others. Beware of excessive empathy: it can cause you to lose sight of your own needs in a given situation, and can create major problems for you.

Perhaps you are at the opposite end of the scale, having little empathy for others, and excessive levels of empathy for yourself. One example is the strongly held view that 'no one cares', or 'no one understands me'. While this view is sometimes correct, I have worked with several people who would not accept that their parents, partner or family loved them at all, or that friends cared, even though it was patently obvious that they did.

This reaction reflects the often excruciating degree of distress the person is experiencing, but it can place a major barrier between the person and those who love them. Parents and loved ones are often left scratching their heads, wondering how on earth they can get it through to the person that they love them, and are distraught at seeing them in such distress. It can be convenient to convince ourselves that no one cares. We can maintain a state of anger, thereby keeping our sadness at bay, or isolate ourselves so that we don't have to risk rejection, whereas acknowledging that people care may provoke within us contact with our grief and sadness that we may prefer to avoid.

Everything about you is valid. Your thoughts, feelings, the way you see and experience the world, your actions all make sense at some level within you, although you may not always be able to make this connection. When things do not work out the way you had hoped, this does invalidate your intention or action. Your distressing emotions are valid, as are your reactions to them, though because they are painful and difficult, you may invalidate both your emotions and your reactions to them.

Whatever side of the self-empathy scale you are on, you can work toward a more flexible and balanced place on the spectrum, taking action to balance the scales. By becoming kinder to yourself, you may risk experiencing feelings of sadness, loss and grief, which you may prefer to keep at bay but may actually need to release.

ACTION

1. Where are you on the empathy spectrum?
The spectrum of self-empathy and empathy for others is contained in Diagram 16. Where are you on this spectrum? The place to aim for is around the middle of each diagram, where you have a strong sense of empathy for yourself and for others.

SPECTRUM OF SELF - EMPATHY

EMPATHY FOR SELF

HIGH   LOW

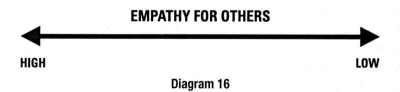

EMPATHY FOR OTHERS

HIGH   LOW

Diagram 16

2. *Toward balanced self-empathy*

Balancing self-empathy is attained through mindfulness and self-awareness. This involves noticing your habits and patterns regarding empathy for yourself and others, and gently working to correct any significant imbalance. If you tend to feel considerable empathy for others and little for yourself, remind yourself that you deserve an equal share. Bring self-empathy into your thinking, gently asserting to yourself your right to be empathic with yourself. Initially, you may find yourself resisting this, but if you stick at it you will notice that you are becoming more self-empathic. It is like any other habit: it takes attention, work, discipline and persistence to change it.

3. *'As if'*

If you find it very difficult to be kind to yourself, act 'as if'. You know the qualities of kindness. The chances are that there are some people (or animals perhaps) to whom you relate with kindness. At some stage of your life, it is likely that you have been kind to some person or some thing. If you are struggling with being gentle and kind to yourself because you currently remain convinced that you do not deserve this, relate to yourself as if you deserved kindness. You can use the 'as if' method in your work with any of the components of selfhood.

4. *Reflection*

During your daily reflection times, consider the degree to which you were empathic toward yourself since your last reflection time. Commit to being aware of the issue of self-empathy between now and your next reflection.

5. *Affirmation*

'I empathise with myself and others in a balanced fashion.'

Needs and need-meeting

There is a direct link between the level of a person's sense of selfhood and how effectively they get their needs met. We generally meet what we decide are our most prominent needs. Functional need-meeting means taking appropriate action to meet our needs effectively. Dysfunctional need-meeting refers to initiatives that may indirectly meet a few of our needs, but create more problems for us in the process. For example, regularly withdrawing in the face of challenges may satisfy the desire to avoid feeling the anxiety experienced as a result of taking on a particular challenge. The habitual avoidance of challenge undermines self-confidence and self-empowerment, the felt sense of having power. Problematic areas of one's life remain unresolved, and further difficulties are often created. Dysfunctional need-meeting is therefore quite limited in its potential to deliver contentment and fulfilment.

The American psychologist Abraham Maslow developed the five-level hierarchy of needs model. These levels are:

1. Biological and physiological needs, such as air, food, drink, warmth, sleep.
2. Safety needs, such as protection from the elements, security, order, limits, stability.
3. Belonging and love needs, such as family, relationships and peer groups.
4. Esteem needs, such as self-esteem, achievement, mastery, independence and status.
5. Self-actualisation needs, such as realising personal potential, self-fulfilment, seeking personal growth and peak experiences.

Maslow believed that people satisfy their needs in a sequence, hence the title 'hierarchy of needs'. He maintained that the higher level of needs does not become the dominant one until such time as the next lowest level of needs is met to the individual's satisfaction. In my experience, this is not always the case. For example, some people make the decision that their need to end the excruciating emotional pain they are experiencing is more important to them than staying alive. People who choose to stop eating lose weight to the point where they put their life in serious danger through starvation. These are distressing examples of people giving their emotional needs a higher priority than their biological needs and their physiological needs.

A person with a healthy sense of selfhood will instinctively maintain a healthy balance between their various needs. Feelings are related to needs. If your needs are fulfilled then you are likely to feel pretty good most of the time. If your needs are generally not met, you will experience a considerable degree of unhappiness. Whenever you deny your feelings, you are to a degree denying the fact that you have needs, since our feelings are such an important aspect of who we are. This often leads to considerable unhappiness, undermining our mental wellness. At any given time, we may have some needs that appear to be in conflict with, or in opposition to, each other. For example, you may feel a strong need to be in a relationship, but you may also feel a need to avoid risking entering a relationship out of fear the emotions that this might bring up in you, such as anxiety, fear, hurt, and worst of all, rejection if it does not work out.

Many people do not know what their needs are. Years of needs not being a priority, either to ourselves or others, may result in us becoming unaware of our needs. There is a certain convenience to this. If I am unaware of my needs, or even of the fact that I have needs, then I feel no responsibility to take the actions necessary to have my needs met. Paradoxically, this may suit me. If my level of selfhood is low, I may not have sufficient confidence in my ability to get my needs met, so it may suit me to not be aware of the challenging subject of my needs.

ACTIONS

1. Where are you on the need-meeting spectrum?
Consider the degree to which you are aware of and attend to your needs and the needs of others, as portrayed in Diagram 17. Do you think of

NEED - MEETING SPECTRUM

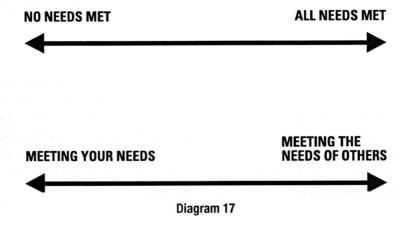

NO NEEDS MET   **ALL NEEDS MET**

MEETING YOUR NEEDS   **MEETING THE NEEDS OF OTHERS**

Diagram 17

other people's needs to the exclusion of yours, or perhaps the other way around? Meeting your needs is primarily your responsibility. If your needs are all you think about, then consider becoming more aware of other people's needs, and what you can do to help other people. This will have a beneficial effect on you, improving the contact you make with others. If you tend not to prioritise your own needs, your goal is to gradually increase the degree to which your needs are met, to the point where the majority of your needs are met on a regular basis. With regard to other people's needs, the aim is toward a balanced approach, where you are happy to meet other people's needs as appropriate, provided you are doing so without regularly over-extending yourself and repeatedly neglecting your own needs. There are of course some exceptions to this, depending on personal circumstances. For example, people may be very happy to regularly over-extend themselves in circumstances where a loved one is going through a serious illness or other major stress. Even in these circumstances however, over-extending yourself for long periods is likely to have a detrimental effect on your own health and wellbeing.

2. Identifying your needs

If you are not used to paying attention to your needs, it may take you some time to become aware of your needs, so be gentle with yourself. You have needs across a range of aspects – physical, emotional, psychological, social, relational, sexual and spiritual. By focusing on your needs across these aspects, you will gradually become more aware of them. Are you aware of your needs in each of these areas? Each of these aspects should be alive and functioning freely and effectively. Are they alive in your life, or are some far more developed than others?

3. Write out your needs

In your journal, make a list of headings of your aspects – physical, emotional, psychological, social, relational, sexual, and spiritual – one page for each. In time, you can expand this to include all of the components of selfhood. Each day this week, consider your needs under these headings, and write down the needs that you become aware of. Use Maslow's list of needs as outlined on page 169 to prompt you if you wish. Be playful: you don't have to be exact or precise.

4. Selfhood needs

You have needs relating to all of the aspects of selfhood that are discussed throughout this book. Are you aware of these needs? To what degree are you ensuring that as much as is possible and practicable, these needs are being met? You have needs regarding how effectively you deal with the world. Are you aware of these needs? Do they require greater attention than you are currently giving them?

5. Important questions to ask yourself

Regard the meeting of your needs as a fundamental right. Ask yourself questions, such as 'What really are my needs? What are my needs in this situation? What are my options? What needs of mine might I not have considered in this situation? Am I being honest with myself about my real needs here, or am I preoccupied with needs that ultimately lead nowhere and do not resolve any of my real problems or challenges in the long run and are therefore fundamentally dysfunctional? How effectively am I meeting my real needs?'

6. Become aware of your patterns of need-meeting

Cultivate the attitude of gently observing your patterns of need-meeting as you go through your day. Notice the degree to which you become aware of your needs as they arise and how you choose to deal with your needs. Do you tend to meet your needs directly and proactively, or indirectly and passively? Meeting our needs indirectly generally involves creating a complicated and convoluted scenario. Directly meeting our needs is much more straightforward and less complicated, though initially more intimidating. Doing everything for another, in the hope that they will in return meet your need for love and not leave you, is an example of indirect need-meeting. Do you express your needs to yourself? To the important people in your life?

7. How functional or dysfunctional are your habits and patterns of need-meeting?

Cultivate awareness of your habits in relation to your needs. Are there particular types of needs that you repeatedly give priority to at the expense of other important needs? For example, the need to be safe, to avoid risk, to avoid connection with yourself or other people? Are you prioritising needs that ultimately diminish your experience of yourself or of life itself?

If this is the case, then you need to address this imbalance. What needs are you actually meeting, your need to protect yourself in everything you do, or your need to live a full life?

8. To what degree do you ensure that your needs are met?
The meeting of your needs is fundamentally your responsibility. Handing over responsibility for your need-meeting to others may feel less risky, but you are giving away your power. You are left hoping that others will meet your needs, feeling hurt and resentful when they don't, even when you have not expressed your needs. Others cannot read your mind for you. This is often a recurring pattern in relationships and can lead to confusion and resentment between partners. The section on actions earlier in the book contains many ideas regarding possible steps you might take toward meeting your needs. Remember the importance of taking one step at a time. Identify your needs and steps you can take that edge you toward meeting your needs.

9. Reflection
During your daily reflection times, consider your needs, and the degree to which you took steps to have your needs met since your last reflection time. Renew your commitment to prioritise your needs.

10. Affirmation
'My needs matter. My needs are fundamentally my responsibility. I ensure that, as much as possible, my needs are met.'

Self-support
To support means to bear the weight of an object or person, especially from beneath, to hold something or someone in position so as to keep them from falling, sinking or slipping. Support has the effect of strengthening whatever it is that is being supported, keeping it from failing or weakening. To support also means to promote ideas and interests, to encourage and reassure, to provide for, maintain and to advocate. Self-support means applying these qualities and attributes to one's self.

People with a strong sense of selfhood instinctively support themselves. They do so effortlessly, usually without noticing that they are doing so. People with a low sense of self tend not to support themselves much, if at all. The idea of supporting themselves doesn't generally strike them, and if it does, their level of self-doubt is such that they have little faith in their ability to support themselves. They rarely reassure themselves as they go about their day. A person with a low sense of selfhood may feel a great deal of fear and anxiety about an activity they need to carry out frequently. The range of these activities is personal to the individual, and many people will have several such examples in their daily lives. Examples people have recounted to me include sitting in a public library, attending lectures, and being amongst people in various social settings.

Many of these are situations the person has been in many times. Each time they engage with that particular activity is like ground-hog day. They experience the same level of anxiety, the same fear-filled thoughts and feelings. They do not practise self-support or self-reassurance in their daily lives. They do not learn from their experiences, and they rarely become aware of the realities of the situation, since they are so preoccupied with the story and the experience they recreate each time. The bottom keeps falling out of their world, since they are not supporting themselves on an ongoing basis.

For example, Betty told me that she much preferred studying in her own room. I briefly mentioned this client on page 142 in the section on self-contact. Whenever she attempted to study in the college reading rooms, she became very self-conscious, believing that others in the room were repeatedly looking at her, criticising and judging her. Having gone to the reading rooms on five occasions and felt the same feelings, she decided that in future she would study in her own room. While this decision may be understandable and appear harmless, in taking this action Betty is confirming to herself that she cannot overcome this fear. This has a significant affect on her perception of herself, further decreasing her sense of selfhood and the level of confidence she will have regarding other attempts to overcome her fears. At no stage did she think of supporting or reassuring herself in the situation. I encouraged her to seek out ways of supporting and reassuring herself, both in this situation and in her life generally. I suggested that she commit to sticking to the facts and repeatedly bring her attention back to the facts when her mind wandered from them.

The facts strongly supported the view that there was no actual threat to Betty in the reading room. She had been there five times previously, and no one had threatened, criticised or judged her in any way. She acknowledged that the other students in the room paid little attention to her, they were getting on with their own work, what mattered to them. I suggested that she make a point of reassuring herself about this, before, during and after. I recommended that as she was approaching the reading room in future, she would repeatedly reassure herself that she had been here several times previously and experienced no actual threat of any description from anyone. While in the reading room, I suggested that she intermittently reassure herself that there was no threat to her, to look around occasionally at the other students, and to use what she sees (the other students deep in their own worlds) to reassure herself that she is safe and under no threat. I recommended that after she has left the reading room, she again reassure herself that even though she felt nervous and anxious in the reading room, nothing untoward happened to her either this time or any other time, therefore future visits were also likely to be without real threat to her.

Advocacy is a form of support, and therefore self-advocacy is an aspect of self-support. Self-advocacy means taking action on your own behalf, including speaking up for yourself and for the things that matter to you, including your needs, ideas, thoughts and feelings. Self-advocacy involves knowing your rights and responsibilities, standing up for your rights if necessary, and taking the decisions and actions you decide are appropriate. Balanced self-advocacy includes reaching out to others when you need their help and support. The growth of advocacy services in mental health reflects the growing awareness that many people who attend mental health services have lost their own voice.

Cultivating self-support in your everyday life will contribute significantly to raising your overall sense of selfhood. By becoming increasingly self-supporting, we feel less threatened by the opposing or critical views of others. We will be more open to communicating with and learning from others.

ACTIONS

1. Identify how supportive (or unsupportive) you are of yourself
Pay attention to how well you support and reassure yourself as you go about your day. You will soon become aware of how self-supportive and self-reassuring you are to yourself.

2.   Make self-support and self-reassurance your norm
Speak to yourself using words and sentences that are kind, self-supporting
and self-reassuring. This may initially feel and sound alien to you. This
practise will take some time to become automatic, but it will do so as
long as you keep it up. Provide self-support by validating everything about
yourself within reason and staying honest with yourself.

3.   Reassure yourself before, during and after
Get into the daily habit of reassuring yourself before, during and after
situations and interactions in which you feel threatened. As the time of
the situation is approaching, reassure yourself that you have come through
many similar situations before, and you will come through this. Think
of similar situations where you felt very anxious, and remind yourself that
although you felt threatened, nothing untoward happened to you. During
the situation, remind yourself that there is no real threat to you here.
Look around you. You will see that other people are doing their own
thing, getting their own business done. Afterwards, reassure yourself that
you came through the situation, that although you felt frightened and
under threat, the fact that nothing happened to you, this time and
previous times, strongly supports the view that there was no threat to you
this time. The likelihood is that there will be no threat to you the next
time either.

4.   Keep it up
As you make the practise of self-support a regular aspect of your day, you
will gradually notice it making its presence felt, often when you least
expect it.

5.   Reflection
At each reflection time, gently consider the degree to which you
supported and reassured yourself since your last reflection time. Remind
yourself that you are not alone, because you are always there with and for
yourself, to reassure and support yourself. Reassure yourself that you are
not powerless, that even when your worst fears do materialise, you
generally handle them much better than you might think.

Without using judgement or criticism, reflect on all of the occasions
during that day when you either did or did not support or reassure
yourself. The purpose of this reflection process is to learn, not to judge,

but to become more aware. At each reflection time, commit to being self-supportive and self-reassuring.

At your night-time reflection time, reassure yourself that even though you may have experienced much anxiety and fear today, you came through the day. Remind yourself that you will be there for you tomorrow, to comfort and reassure yourself. Assure yourself that whatever way you feel in the morning when you wake up, you will be okay. Many people go to bed hoping and praying that they will not feel a certain way tomorrow (anxious, frightened, depressed, for example). They are extremely disappointed if they do feel that way the following morning. Thinking of it this way often only increases the chances that you will feel the way you don't want to feel. If I say to you, no matter what you think about right now, do not think about a pink elephant, what do you find yourself thinking about? It is better to be flexible regarding how you may feel in the morning, and reassure yourself that whatever way you feel, you will be okay, that you will come through however you feel in the morning. You always do come through how you feel in the morning. What you are stating here is a fact. Resolve to support yourself in the various situations you encounter each day.

6. Affirmation
'I support myself in everything that I do. I provide my own reassurance.'

Self-regulation
To regulate means to maintain at the desired level, and it involves being able to take corrective action to restore equilibrium as and when this is necessary. Your body has an innate tendency toward self-regulation. If you drink a lot of fluids, your urine production will increase correspondingly, in an effort to maintain a balance of fluids within your body. If you become dehydrated, your urine output will decrease significantly. If you become too hot, you sweat, if you become too cold, you shiver, the body's way of generating heat from within, in order to maintain your body at optimum temperature. If you are suddenly exposed to bright lights, you immediately react by closing your eyes and turning away from the bright light. These are just a few examples of the process of self-regulation that your body continually engages in. It is as if your body instinctively knows the vital importance of self-

regulation. In our lives, it is equally important that we practise healthy self-regulation.

The domino effect is a useful way to describe self-regulation. We may find ourselves in situations that unnerve us, that throw us off track. This is similar to the effect of the first few dominoes falling. People who self-regulate well generally get themselves back on track quickly, because their level of selfhood is sufficiently high for them to do so. They notice when the first few dominoes begin to fall. They take good care of themselves, and take whatever action is required to stop things escalating further. They then take whatever action is necessary to get themselves back to a state of equilibrium.

Balance is important. Functional self-regulation is the goal. Dysfunctional self-regulation means employing methods of self-regulation that do not work effectively and cause further problems for us. Methods of self-regulation that are dysfunctional can be obvious to the person and their loved ones, or they can be subtle, going unnoticed by all, including the individual concerned. Under-regulation, over-regulation, and swinging between both of these are examples of dysfunctional self-regulation. Under-regulation is a common characteristic of many people, including many diagnosed as having bipolar disorder. Regarding many people diagnosed with bipolar disorder, either the person doesn't notice the first few dominoes falling, or if they do, they don't pay sufficient attention to this occurrence, and as a result don't take appropriate corrective action at an early stage. Often, they do not know how to take corrective action, or what corrective action to take. They may further exacerbate the derailing process, sometimes by giving in to the alluring and seductive power of a 'high', particularly if they feel overwhelmed, or overcome by a powerful emotion they might prefer to avoid. The rate at which the dominoes fall gathers pace, and they are soon on the road to a major derailment of themselves and their lives. During what is called the depressive phase of bipolar disorder, the person generally over-regulates. They live a dysfunctional rebalancing act, swinging from one pole to the other, bypassing the middle ground, rather than exercising balanced self-regulation.

Many people do not reach the level of deregulation that people diagnosed with bipolar disorder experience. However, regular lower levels of deregulation can cause a great deal of chaos and distress in our lives.

Many people diagnosed as having schizophrenia over-regulate themselves. Preoccupied with intense fear and powerlessness, they are in an almost constant state of over-regulation, repeatedly taking 'corrective action' to deal with the threats they perceive on an almost constant basis. This over-regulation is dysfunctional. It meets the immediate need for safety, but does nothing to resolve their deeper needs while repeatedly reinforcing their belief that they are powerless. Prolonged and exaggerated self-regulation may result in a build-up of inner tension that, like a pressure cooker, may explode outwards. This results in expressions of emotion that seem inappropriate to the situation but make perfect sense when the totality of the person's experience of life is taken into account.

Many of us do certain things to quite an excessive degree for a while, often for much longer than is good for us. We then hit a wall of exhaustion, often because of unrealistic hopes and expectations in the first place, and swing to over-regulation, perhaps withdrawing from others and taking to the bed. Developing the skill of living in balanced self-regulation is a key feature of mental wellness. The experience of bulimia involves considerable under-regulation that follows periods of over-regulation. The person reaches the point where the over-regulation becomes too much. Needing to release built-up tension, they switch from over-control into a frenzy of indulgence, over-eating to a great degree, often followed by self-induced vomiting to bring all the food back up. By the time this major consumption of energy is over, they are exhausted. Because the internal pressure is released, they are now ready to begin the dysfunctional cycle, entering the phase of over-regulation once again. One of the challenges faced by the person is to master functional, balanced self-regulation, thus eliminating the dysfunctional cycle of swinging from one extreme to the other.

ACTIONS

1. Identify the degree to which you self-regulate
Become familiar with your habits and patterns regarding self-regulation. If your sense of selfhood is low, it is likely that your self-regulation is either generally excessive, insufficient, or regularly swinging from one extreme to the other.

2. Develop a quiet continuous awareness of self-regulation
Having identified your patterns of self-regulation, resolve to work on them. The first few dominoes generally fall subtly, often going unnoticed. Develop a quiet, continuous awareness of self-regulation within your life, and a subtle ongoing awareness of when the first few dominoes begin to fall. Whenever you experience a cascade of thoughts, feelings, worries, fear or other powerful emotions, several dominoes may already have fallen.

3. Risk doing things differently
Take charge of the situation yourself. Keep working away at the issue of self-regulation. You will come to master it in time, through increasing self-knowledge and consistently taking action that is appropriate to the situation. Initially, it may seem impossible to stop thoughts and feelings popping into your head, that begin to throw you off balance. However, you can do something about them. See this as akin to the warning lights on the dashboard of a car, that light up to alert you when there is a problem. Stay aware of what is happening rather than slip into the sliding cascade. Consider the choices that are available to you to minimise the falling of the dominoes. You can separate from the thought, reassuring yourself that it is not you, that it is fantasy, since these thoughts are usually future-focused, and we can only live in the present. You can reassure yourself that they are just thoughts, and let these thoughts cross the horizon of your mind like clouds crossing the sky: they come, and they go. You can take action to get you out of the moment. Any simple action will usually suffice, as long as you deliberately keep your focus and attention on the unfolding detail of the action you have decided to take. Examples include a five-minute walk, ironing a shirt, feeding the cat, writing for five minutes regarding how you are, or sitting down for a few minutes and doing some simple breathing exercises, gently focusing on your breathing as you are doing so.

4. Reflection
During your daily reflection time, consider the issue of self-regulation, and how you have handled this since your last reflection period. If nothing in particular comes to mind, that is fine.

5. Affirmation
'I regulate myself as necessary, to bring myself back into balance.'

Self-comforting

We regularly encounter situations where we may feel afraid, unsure or distressed. Developing methods of receiving comfort and solace is important, so that we can soothe the hurts we experience. When young children are hurt or afraid, their first instinct is to run to a parent or other trusted person for a hug. A greatly upset child is often transformed into a happy one in minutes, such is the power of comforting and soothing actions. Since your relationship with yourself is your key relationship, developing the pattern of comforting yourself in times of distress enhances your ability to look after yourself.

People with a low sense of selfhood may venture away from balanced, functional self-soothing toward either extreme. Rather than self-soothing, they may repeatedly punish themselves. Others may exclude inputs from others that could help relieve their distress and aloneness, becoming preoccupied with self-soothing whilst simultaneously avoiding much engagement with life. This may be one reason why some people become heavy cigarette smokers. Spending several hours a day smoking may indeed feel soothing. Smoking can become a way of escaping from one's feelings, from distress and from the challenges of life. Smoking provides a smokescreen behind which one can hide away, from the challenges involved in making good contact with ourselves and other people when we feel vulnerable. Others use alcohol, other substances, practises and rituals to soothe themselves. We need to recognise the difference between healthy, balanced self-comforting, and unbalanced self-soothing that spills over into avoidance, isolation and escapism from living and from the challenges of everyday life, or which in the case of smoking and other drugs can cause us considerable harm.

Because we are social beings, we benefit not only from regularly comforting ourselves, but also from comforting others. This helps us to feel connected to others. We benefit from feeling that we are contributing to their wellbeing.

Gentleness and kindness toward yourself is an important aspect of selfhood and mental wellness, the sort of gentleness you might feel for someone you love or care greatly for, someone who is important to you. Life can be tough: we face many challenges along the way. These challenges are easier to deal with when we are gentle with ourselves. You can gradually cultivate an attitude of kindness toward yourself. Most people who give themselves a hard time are conscientious, sincere people doing their best. Self-gentleness does not give us a licence to avoid responsibility or to avoid taking appropriate action. It is not a dispensation to give up activities prematurely. It simply means that as you go through your day and your life, you value the importance of comforting yourself in a balanced way.

ACTIONS

1. Accept that you have the right to self-soothe
Babies quickly learn various methods of comforting themselves, thumb-sucking being the most obvious example. At times this can be a difficult world in which to live. You too have the right to soothe yourself.

2. Identify the degree to which you comfort yourself
Maintain a gentle surveillance regarding the degree to which you comfort yourself, and punish yourself, and the methods of self-soothing you use.

3. Cultivate ways of self-soothing that meet your need without causing further problems
A client of mine discovered that rubbing her left thumb gently along her right thumb and hand really soothes her, as did gently stroking her face. Whenever she feels overwhelmed with emotional distress and pain, she strokes herself gently, lovingly, usually with a positive outcome. She feels loved, held and cared for as a consequence of comforting herself in this way.

If you have no idea how to begin, experiment. The range of possible self-soothing actions is wide, including physical acts such as touching yourself as my client did, hugging yourself tightly, listening to uplifting music, either around the house or while lying down or sitting, being in nature and the fresh air, swimming, carrying a comforting or inspiring photograph or quotation in your handbag or wallet and accessing it regularly.

4. Balanced self-soothing
Some people might be tempted to self-comfort excessively. Doing so is not balanced, and has some drawbacks. The excessive self-comforting

does provide some brief comfort, but it also serves to block the person's experience of the painful feelings or the challenge they may be avoiding, which therefore remains unresolved. Afterwards, the person generally feels worse than before they took the comforting action, filled with guilt or self-hatred. The repeated and excessive use of a comforting act may have consequences, for example weight gain with comfort eating, alcohol-related problems with excessive drinking. Excessive use of self-comforting can be a way of avoiding contact with ourselves, our difficult feelings and challenges, other people and the world. This can leave us feeling increasingly isolated, often by choice, but this choice comes with a big price, since we are removing ourselves from vital aspects of life.

Initially, focusing solely on self-comforting may be entirely appropriate for you, particularly if you are in great distress. Try also to balance self-comforting with an openness to receive soothing and comforting from others, including animals, and a willingness to comfort others when appropriate.

5. Wrap yourself in a duvet for fifteen minutes a day
Wrapping yourself in a duvet for fifteen minutes a day is a simple, effective way of comforting yourself. As you are doing this, don't fight with your thoughts, or frantically try to remove worries from your mind. Gently and repeatedly bring your attention back to the present, to what you are doing, to the feel of the duvet around you, the snug and cosy feeling it gives you. If you have more time at your disposal, feel free to extend this beyond fifteen minutes. Be disciplined, though. If necessary, set an alarm to alert you that the period is over. Try to do it at roughly the same time every day. Whatever time of day works for you is fine.

6. How gentle are you on yourself?
Your aim is to be gentle with yourself most of the time, a healthy mix of self-gentleness coupled with self-honesty.

7. Make a decision today that you will be gentle with yourself
You may be intolerant of yourself, sometimes to the point of viciousness. You may set impossible standards for yourself, seeing any slip as an intolerable failure, resulting in an avalanche of self-punishment. You can change this pattern, gradually cultivating an attitude of gentleness toward yourself.

Deep inside yourself, you do know that fundamentally you are a good, conscientious person, doing your best, having taken many knocks in a difficult and challenging world. You deserve your own gentleness. Commit to noticing when you are being hard on yourself, and replace this with kindness. If this does not seem possible initially, do it anyway. Notice when you are being hard on yourself, and afterwards, do something that soothes and comforts you.

8. Declaration of kindness toward myself
Several times each day, remind yourself of the following facts about yourself:

> 'I am not a machine. I am a human being, therefore perfection is not an option for me. I am a sincere human being, and in general I do the best that I feel I can. I deserve comfort, gentleness and kindness from myself as I journey through this often difficult and challenging, sometimes terrifying but ultimately enriching experience we call life'.

9. Reflection
At your reflection times, consider whether you have been self-comforting and gentle toward yourself since your last reflection. You may have had no need to self-soothe during the previous few hours. The intention of this reflection is to increase your awareness of the importance of self-gentleness, of self-comforting, and of your habits and patterns regarding self-soothing.

During your reflection times, revisit those moments when you were harsh to yourself, when they have passed and the intensity of the situation is no longer present. Ask yourself if you really needed to be so hard on yourself. Resolve that in future similar situations, you will be kinder to yourself. Keep this up, and you will notice that you are becoming increasingly gentle with yourself.

10. Affirmation
'I comfort and soothe myself. I am gentle with myself. I am capable of soothing myself in times of crisis or distress. I sense when I need comforting and I take the time to do so.'

Case histories

Incorporating aspects of caring for themselves and practising this in their everyday life is a key theme in the following two case histories of clients who have attended me.

The following case history illustrates the pain we experience when self-love and self-befriending is replaced by self-loathing, and the benefits of recovering self-love and self-befriending. Ellen began attending me in her late thirties. Extremely intolerant of herself, Ellen experienced self-hatred virtually constantly, always putting her needs last in line. As she saw it, why should she, a worthless being, deserve any care and attention, least of all from herself?

In our work together, I repeatedly stated her immense value as a unique person, her need and right to take good care of herself and, in time, to love herself. In the past, Ellen had been in several relationships where she was not appreciated. It was second nature for her to believe that she was not deserving of love, rather than to see that she was indeed deserving of love, and feel the grief, hurt and losses she had experienced through not being loved with respect and dignity. By blocking the full expression of these painful emotions, Ellen had blocked their full completion and healing.

Ellen's partner died in his mid-forties. They had been deeply in love. Her self-hatred was at least partially related to not having fully grieved for her partner. Becoming preoccupied with self-hatred, Ellen succeeded in distancing herself from the full impact of her enormous grief. Many of our meetings revolved around that loss, and frequently involved her crying inconsolably. This went on for several months, with the result that she finally managed to work through her grief. She was then able to begin to see herself in a different light, as a young woman, worthy of her own friendship and love, while simultaneously profoundly missing her partner. By repeatedly telling Ellen that I was struck by her loss, grief, strength, integrity, dignity, and determination, I helped her to develop compassion and love for herself. Ellen began to see that she was a person worthy of her own love. This did not replace the great void in her life, but it did provide her with a platform from which to move forward, whereas previously she had felt completely stuck for several years. Ellen currently reports being much happier than at any time since her partner's death. Indeed, she says that her sense of self is stronger than at any previous time in her life.

Sam's story is an example of how difficult life can become when, through loss of selfhood, we do not have the ability to support and reassure ourselves. By the time Sam was in his early twenties, he had lost his sense of selfhood to a great degree. A major cause of this loss was his experience of significant bullying and ostracisation at school. He eventually reached a point of such overwhelm that it was thought best that he be admitted to a psychiatric hospital.

He began attending me shortly after being discharged from hospital. The enormity of his loss of selfhood and considerable emotional distress were painfully evident to me. I was particularly struck by his almost total inability to support himself, to stand on his own two feet. For the first few months after he began attending me, he spent all his time at home with his parents. His older three siblings had all progressed with their lives and were living away from home. Six months after our first session, Sam began a college course. He found being in a college environment very challenging, and he experienced a great deal of anxiety during his first few months there. He drove home every day to find some sanctuary from the huge struggle, even though it meant a round trip of eighty miles, five times a week.

All through that first year in college, he undermined himself continually. When walking from one lecture to another, he would frantically check the eyes of other students, desperately seeking to find out what they were thinking about him. Did they think he was an idiot? A waste of space? These were the thoughts that Sam had toward himself. Unwittingly, he was projecting his fears and self-doubt onto passersby, which immediately boomeranged right back at him in the form of his own thoughts, disguised as those of others.

Sam's loss of selfhood is major. He had just returned to begin his third year in college. Sam passed his second year college exams, and had coped well with his second year at college, although he had been slow to partake in activities involving contact with others. On the few occasions he did, Sam did not persist. The happiest and most relaxed I saw Sam during his second year was two days after he performed in an open mike song contest. For years, Sam had a strong desire to perform music in public, practising for several hours at home most nights, but he had never before mustered up the courage to actually do it. His feeling good was no coincidence, coming as it did so soon after taking what for him was such a giant leap. Unfortunately, through a combination of giving in to his own hesitancy to perform again, and some bad luck regarding the staging of subsequent open mike shows, Sam did not repeat or build upon his one performance. Choosing to take little or no action in the areas he needed to, his confidence gradually ebbed away again.

This situation was not helped by the choices Sam tended to make. For example, he chose to spend his four-month summer break from college in isolation, not making any contact with peers or indeed anyone outside of his home. This avoidance only served to heighten his anxiety, making it considerably more difficult to face his college colleagues again, and to deal with the presence of over ten thousand people on the college campus grounds. His tendency to withdraw from challenge and people continued when the next college year commenced. He did not go to college for the majority of the first two weeks, though he told his parents and me that he was indeed attending college. This attempt to deceive the people who were trying to help him was another unfortunate choice. A key issue for Sam is whether he is prepared to do whatever it takes to break through his anxiety, and to work hard at providing his own support. Whether he will cross this bridge remains to be seen, and depends on the choices he makes, including whether he addresses the challenges he faces one by one, or continues withdrawing and avoiding these challenges.

4. Attitudes toward yourself

In this section, we consider the components of selfhood that relate to our attitudes toward ourselves and how we choose to live. The components we focus on are self-perception, self-respect, self-discipline, self-ownership, self-honesty, self-revelation, self-acceptance, and self-forgiveness.

Self-perception

Self-identity, self-worth and self-esteem are included within this section on self-perception, since they are each aspects of how we perceive ourselves. Each of us has an image, a perception of ourselves. How we perceive ourselves goes far beyond our physical image of ourselves. We come to conclusions regarding who we are, how we perceive and feel about ourselves and our external environment, and how we believe others see, experience and feel about us. We tend to presume that other people perceive us the way we see ourselves. Our self-perception includes our image of ourselves across all aspects of our being and our life, built up over many years of interaction with others and with the world. It includes the collection of facts, judgements, beliefs and conclusions we have come to about ourselves, our lovability, our capability, what we believe we can or cannot do in relation to life, other people, situations and challenges.

Self-perception thoughts often begin with 'I' or 'I'm'. People with a low sense of selfhood will frequently have thoughts such as 'I'm no good at…', 'I couldn't possibly…', 'I always…', 'I'm useless', 'I'm unlovable', 'I'm never good enough', 'I'm such a loser that no one would want to be my friend', 'if people really knew me, they'd want nothing to do with me'.

Our self-perception is fundamental to the life we create for ourselves. We take what we *believe* about ourselves to be the *truth* about ourselves. People with a solid sense of selfhood have a healthy self-image. They have little difficulty in social situations and in dealing with change and new challenges. They have few doubts about their lovability, acceptability, capability, their capacity to belong, their ability to adapt to change. They generally do not experience severe anxiety, because they rarely have major doubts about themselves across the spectrum of interactions and relationships with others.

It is sometimes said that 'you can if you think you can'. The implication of this adage is that by changing your thinking, you can change both your attitudes and your ability to do more in your life. While there is some truth to this, it is difficult to change your thinking without appropriate follow-through action. We need to honour and fully take into account the level of fear we have around doing what terrifies us, and address this fear through graded, step-wise action. By doing so, we change our self-perception, and we experience a ripple effect, the unexpected benefits that accrue when we set about raising our sense of selfhood through appropriate action. Generally, I believe that it is important for people to know that 'you usually can, even when you believe you can't'.

Self-identity is an aspect of our self-perception. 'Who am I?' is a fundamental question. Our sense of identity changes during our life, particularly during our teenage years. Only one decade of life can begin to compare with adolescence regarding the degree of change undergone, the first decade from newborn baby to ten-year-old child. However, the first decade is not characterised by the degree of self-consciousness, awareness and sensitivity often experienced to a major degree by teenagers.

Our sense of identity gives us meaning, purpose and structure. We often extend our sense of identity beyond ourselves, to our home and locality, our important relationships, the values, principles and things that matter to us. This often includes our occupation, interests, our world view, our hopes and dreams, and all that we live by and construct our life around. If these structures are undermined, it can cause us enormous distress, particularly if our level of selfhood is low. We may have become dependent on who and what is in our life, and have little confidence in our ability to live without these supports. We may greatly doubt our ability to create new channels of identity, meaning, and fulfilment if we lose existing ones. Many of us have tied our identity to material possessions, appearances, reputation and status. We risk chaining ourselves to these external things, impairing our freedom to live in the full expression of our selfhood.

People with a solid sense of selfhood have a correspondingly solid and balanced sense of their identity. People with a low sense of selfhood lack certainty and confidence regarding their identity and where they fit in. Or, they may have a rigid sense of identity, tied to activities or beliefs to which they cling, believing that without these, they have no identity or existence.

Developing expertise and competence in one field or other certainly enhances our sense of identity. However, our level of selfhood benefits from the cultivation of an identity that transcends what we do. Linking our sense of identity to an activity, role or relationship is risky. Any alteration in our connection to that activity may then prove terrifying and overwhelming. We may be left ungrounded and uprooted, frantically wondering who we are and how to cope with this enormous change. We may repeatedly seek to bring contact and conversations with others back to the good old days, so we can re-live them and feel alive again, and ultimately become quite depressed. By living in the past, we are wasting the present. It is more prudent to look instead at our current life, and make whatever changes and adjustments are appropriate. Life can only truly be lived in the present. It is an individual's sense of their own identity that matters, not other people's sense of their identity.

Our sense of self-worth is an aspect of our self-perception. Anything that is unique is priceless, and cannot be replaced. Billions of people have walked on this planet, yet each human being is unique. It is therefore a fact that you are unique, and you have the absolute right to regard yourself as such. Because you are unique, you have immense worth. If you have trouble believing this, remember that to those who know and care about you, you are irreplaceable. This fact is sadly confirmed at funerals of people of all ages, particularly of young people who have died in tragic circumstances including suicide. Believing you have no worth can be a protective mechanism, making it easier for you to settle for the way things are. For example, if you are unhappy, your relationships are not enriching, or your life seems to be going nowhere, you can convince yourself that there is no point taking action to change things if you believe you have no worth, that you are not deserving. Believing that you have no worth allows you to remain stuck, to avoid important but challenging questions regarding your life, how you live, and what you need to do in order to emerge from the stagnation. If you choose to remain stuck in unsatisfactory situations long term, this is likely to have major consequences for both your spirit and your mental health.

The promotion of self-worth and self-appreciation has been gaining increasing support in society. This change is reflected in the way children are taught in school. Balanced self-appreciation means that we do not depreciate the value of other people. We appreciate the uniqueness of others, just as we accept and appreciate our own uniqueness. Balanced self-appreciation enhances mental wellness. It is right and proper that you should appreciate yourself. If you do not value yourself independently of your achievements, you will not truly value your achievements.

Self-esteem is the quality of having esteem, regard and respect for oneself. The word 'regard' is derived from the French verb 'regarder', which means 'to look at'. The esteem or regard we have for ourselves is an important aspect of how we look at ourselves. It is important that you hold yourself in high esteem, and you have every right to do so. A person with a solid sense of selfhood generally has a corresponding level of self-esteem. People with a low sense of selfhood have little regard for themselves. They are excessively focused on seeking esteem from others. I therefore call this 'other-esteem', the polar opposite of self-esteem.

As depicted in the water-tank analogy on page 14, the pursuit of other-esteem is a waste of time. It is far better to cultivate esteem for yourself. The more you lack self-esteem, the more vulnerable you are to external influence. When your reference point for esteem is centred within yourself, you live predominantly in a state of peace and security, rather than the ever-present dread and insecurity that accompanies the never-ending fruitless search for esteem from others. Having low self-esteem can be a way of protecting yourself from risk and from the unknown, minimising your chances of exposing yourself to anxiety, overwhelm, rejection and failure.

ACTIONS

1. What is your current self-perception?
How do you currently see yourself? Identify your current sense of identity. Write about this in detail. Start a fresh page of your journal with each of the following: I'm, I'm not, I can, and I cannot. Develop each page with examples of how you perceive yourself. If your level of selfhood is low, your sense of identity is likely to be correspondingly low, confused, and linked to all sorts of things and people. Notice your current level of self-worth and self-appreciation. Reflect on the level of esteem and regard that *you* have for *you.*

2. Your self-perception: what's in it for you?
If your sense of selfhood is low, having a positive perception of yourself may feel scary, risky, impossible. You may fear that if you had a positive self-perception, you would feel pressurised to behave in ways you feel are beyond you, that would feel terrifying such as asserting yourself or risking disapproval. Having a perception of yourself that is filled with self-doubt and self-criticism may appear to work in your favour, as it gives you a reason to do what you most want to do when your sense of selfhood is low: to avoid taking risks.

3. Risk believing that you are who you are, not what you do or what you have
Gently and repeatedly remind yourself that no person or thing has the right to take away your identity, who you are, and that your identity as a

unique human being is not defined by what you do, what you possess or your external appearance.

4. Stick with the facts

In reflecting on your self-concept, become clear regarding what is fact and what is not. Stick with the facts about yourself, not your opinions about yourself, or other people's judgements about you, real or presumed. A regular question to ask yourself might be, 'what evidence do I have to support this belief about myself?'

5. Facing your fears

Taking appropriate action to change your self-perception involves risking doing what scares you, one step at a time. As a general rule, there is solid ground on the other side of the risk, not the abyss we fear. With repetition, we realise that we can do it, leading to a major surge in our level of selfhood. In time, our self-perception is transformed, leaving us feeling freer, thrilled with ourselves and energised.

6. Cultivate a strong sense of self-worth and self-appreciation

As you go through your day, tell yourself repeatedly that your self-worth is a given, non-negotiable, incontrovertible. You do not have to believe all this initially. It will sink in gradually, as long as you maintain the practise of repeating this statement about your own worth to yourself. Risk accepting the reality that you are unique, that there is not and there never has been a human being exactly like you. Risk accepting the reality that because you are unique, you are priceless. You therefore have a right to your place in this world. You do not have to apologise for, explain or justify your existence, your beliefs, your needs, or your opinions. Every human being is a remarkable creation, including you. Risk appreciating yourself as a unique human being, never replicated in the entire history of the world.

7. Declaration of self-worth: I am who I am. I am not what I do.

Read the following declaration of self-worth out loud to yourself every day:

> 'Who I am and what I do is not the same thing. I do not take criticism personally any more. Nothing and no one outside

of myself determines my worth. I am priceless because I am unique. My worth is a given, always there, dependent on nothing. My worth is rock-solid, unquestionable, because I am a unique human being. I appreciate myself for being the person that I am.'

8. Identify the sources of your esteem

Identify who or what you look to for your esteem. Likely sources include the important people in your life, your work, your roles and interests. Resolve to let go of this pattern of esteem-seeking. Shift the momentum in the opposite direction, as you commit to becoming the provider of your own esteem.

9. Become mindful regarding your sources of esteem

When you notice yourself seeking esteem from any outside source, involvement or activity, gently remind yourself that the real esteem you need is your own. Bring your attention back inside your boundary, into your own space. Reassure yourself that from now on, you are the creator and provider of your own esteem. While it is a pleasant experience when other people show you that they hold you in high esteem, the only esteem that really endures is the esteem that originates from within.

10. What others think of you is none of your business

At first glance, this may seem like an unbelievable statement. There are many situations where it is appropriate for us to respect the rights and expectations of others. For example, if you turn up for an important job interview looking unkempt and untidy, don't be surprised if this counts against you in the interview process. In an interview situation, you do not have to become agitated that you are dressing to please the interview board. You do not have to see it as an issue at all, unless you choose to.

In general, what others think of you is generally only important to you if you let it be important by letting their opinions cross your boundary into your personal space. You have then allowed others to dictate to you, rather than come to your own conclusions. Remind yourself several times a day that what others think of you really is none of your business. What *you* think of *you* is what really matters.

11. Commit to being the creator and provider of your own esteem
This involves the cultivation of a new habit: ensuring that your awareness is within your own space, and that from *within your own personal space* you risk cultivating esteem and regard for yourself.

12. Jog rather than sprint
In the early stages of this work, expect a feeling of emptiness as you bring your attention back to yourself and your own space. With repetition and practise, you will gradually tap into the well of selfhood that exists within you, including your esteem for yourself. You will then fully realise and experience that you are indeed the creator and provider of your own esteem.

13. Working on other aspects of selfhood raises the quality of your self-perception
For example, making your personal boundary and personal space a reality is an important step toward developing a healthy sense of identity. Having a healthy sense of identity is difficult, if your attention is predominantly focused outside of your own personal space, beyond your boundary.

14. Reward yourself, as a token of appreciation for yourself
Cultivate a balanced approach to self-rewarding. Make it a regular feature in your life, but not so regular that it loses its beneficial effect or becomes a dysfunctional pattern of self-comforting.

15. Reflection
During your reflection times, consider your perception of yourself. A brief reflection on your perception of yourself at reflection times will help you keep this important issue within your awareness. Consider whether how you handled the previous hours since your last reflection helped to reinforce your old perception of yourself, or sowed some seeds toward a new, more expanded perception of yourself. Reflect briefly on your sense of identity, and whether this surfaced as an issue since your last reflection time. Consider the degree to which you valued yourself as a unique, priceless human being during the preceding hours. Remind yourself that nothing can add to or take away from your immense worth. Commit to be mindful of appreciating yourself during your day. Consider how your sense of self-esteem was since your last reflection time.

16. Affirmation
'I am me. I see myself as the capable, loving and lovable person that I am. My identity is not dependent on anything or anyone. I am a unique, priceless, worthy human being. I appreciate myself. I hold myself in high regard. I am the provider of my esteem for myself.'

Self-respect
If your level of selfhood is low, you may be preoccupied with a strong desire for others to respect you. It is far more important that you respect yourself. People with a strong sense of self feel little or no need to seek respect from others, as they practise self-respect on an ongoing basis, often without realising they are doing so. Repeatedly seeking the respect of others involves enormous effort, and it does not work, as any positive effect on your wellbeing is very transient, particularly if you have little respect for yourself. If you have respect for yourself, you are also more likely to take good care of yourself, and generally refrain from activities that involve you being disrespected or abused.

If we respect ourselves, people will tend to respect us in return. If we do not respect ourselves, we will often find that others do not respect us either, and that may hurt us greatly. By generating our own self-respect, the opinions that others hold about us matter little, thus leaving us much freer. Employing self-respect as a principle is not a licence to deceive yourself. If you are behaving in ways that are disrespectful to yourself or others, be honest with yourself. See your behaviour for what it is. Do what you can to end this practise, to make amends, to ameliorate the situation if appropriate. We are all human, we all transgress and make mistakes in our lives. Learn from the experience and move on.

Self-honouring flows naturally from self-respect. If you respect yourself, you will naturally tend to honour yourself in your various interactions and activities. Self-honouring means listening to and honouring your thoughts, feelings, reactions and needs. The opposite of self-honouring is self-dishonouring, or self-betrayal. This is often accompanied by excessive other-honouring, always putting others first, predominantly honouring the needs and desires of others, and repetitive people-pleasing. Many people derive great satisfaction from honouring the needs of others. People whose work and activities entail meeting the needs of others may derive immense fulfilment from their efforts. These people are honouring themselves too, choosing to involve themselves in these activities because they want to, though it is important that they balance honouring others with honouring themselves.

Assertiveness is an aspect of self-respect. Definitions of assertiveness include being self-assured, stating a fact or belief confidently to others, behaving or speaking in a confident or forceful manner, and being emphatic and definite in one's communication with others. All this can sound quite intimidating when your sense of selfhood is low and you have no confidence in your ability to behave in this fashion. In practise, asserting yourself can be done in a gentle, quiet manner, particularly in the early stages. With practise, you will gain confidence in your ability to be assertive. Many assertive people go about their business quietly, with few words, rarely feeling the need to raise their voice. You will seldom find assertive people shouting at others. People who are assertive do not resort to aggressive or passive tactics. Being assertive entails tuning into what you need, and then taking appropriate action. Being assertive does not involve forcing your opinions, views or needs down other people's throats. Assertiveness means that you consider and attend to your needs in the various situations in which you find yourself.

The beauty of assertiveness is that it can be done subtly. It does not require a major battle. The process can be initiated quietly, beginning with the simplest and tiniest of steps. The task of becoming assertive is an inner commitment that you make to yourself. Do not begin by explaining and justifying to others what you are setting out to do, in the hope that they will give you a green light to proceed. Such a move merely serves to diminish what little sense of inner power you feel you have. A wiser and better strategy is to simply go ahead and do it, with the minimum of discussion and fuss. Adopting this approach is often made considerably easier by the fact that many of our fears of being assertive are our own creation, are in our own minds, the product of great self-doubt. As you embark on the process of becoming assertive, you will find that many of your fears regarding how others will react do not materialise. Other people are unlikely to notice the changes you have made in terms of your new-found assertiveness to anything like the extent that you feared they might.

The following scenario illustrates the importance of assertiveness. You need to make a challenging phone call. If your level of selfhood is low, you may think incessantly about making the call, agonising about it for hours. Your anxiety escalates. You may procrastinate, coming up with various convincing excuses regarding why now is not the right time to make that call. Reluctantly, you eventually make the call without having checked with yourself regarding what you want to achieve and how you will handle the conversation. You allow the other person to dictate. The conversation heads in directions you neither intended nor wanted. You dishonour yourself, agreeing to things you do not want to, your self-confidence dented, fear and anxiety increased. You feel even more powerless than ever. Afterwards, you agonise about the call for hours.

Let us look at the same situation, this time employing assertiveness. Before you dial the number, you identify how you will handle the phone call. You clarify your parameters, your reasons for making the call, your aims and objectives, and how far you are prepared to go. You notice when the conversation drifts in directions you did not intend. You keep your parameters and terms in focus. You listen respectfully to the other person. As often as necessary, you bring the conversation back to your agenda, your reason for making the call. You agree to things you want to agree to. You honour yourself, so that you end up with your sense of selfhood increased, your fear and anxiety reduced. You experience a little more inner power than before. Assertiveness has pervaded the entire conversation.

Some people fear that by becoming assertive they risk losing important people in their lives. In practise, this rarely occurs. People who truly care about you, and want you to be happy and fulfilled, will be delighted to see you becoming more assertive. Others, through fear of what they might lose (including you), may not support you as much as you hoped. They may attempt to undermine your journey toward assertiveness. When these people realise that they can cope with you being more assertive, that you being more assertive can actually enhance their relationship with you, they may feel safer about the process. If you lose someone as a result of you committing to becoming assertive, their loss speaks volumes about the quality of the relationship that you had with them.

It is important for our mental health and wellbeing that we are assertive. This is a challenging time to be alive. Family members, peers, friends, people and situations may have a serious impact on the rights, needs and desires of others. The diversity of such impact-creating scenarios can be immense. It may range from bullying to peer pressure to drink alcohol, smoke, take drugs, or engage in sexual activity before the person feels ready. It may be pressure to perform extremely well in examinations or follow a particular career path because others think it is a good idea.

A person who does not feel they can assert themselves will end up doing things they do not want to do, regularly saying 'yes' when they really want to say 'no', in an effort to avoid conflict, to gain approval and acceptance. They will neither champion nor advocate for themselves. They do not feel confident enough to make their own choices or to state that they do not want to engage in a particular activity. They are afraid to risk liberating themselves from acquiescing to the demands and expectations of others.

Saying 'no' is healthy when it is balanced. Some people who have lost their sense of selfhood say 'no' far more frequently than 'yes'. Constantly saying 'no' gives them a vague semblance of autonomy, power and control. They are protecting themselves from further hurt, humiliation and risk, and from feeling painful emotions such as anxiety, sadness and fear. Saying 'no' almost becomes automatic, something they do without thinking about it. It seems a better alternative to remain in their own, small, relatively safe world than to say 'yes', and risk experiencing a range of difficult emotions including anxiety, uncertainty, and fear of failure.

Sometimes, people who do not feel they can assert themselves stray beyond assertiveness into aggression. They are over-compensating, attempting to use their aggression and loudness to camouflage their feelings of inadequacy and get what they want. Passive-aggressive tendencies are common among people who do not exercise assertiveness in their lives. Failing to assert themselves, they passively go along with what other people want them to do, but inside they are angry, and translate this anger into various and often disguised expressions of aggression. People who are not accustomed to being assertive may fear that there will be a major backlash from others if they do assert themselves. Occasionally, there may be some truth in this. In some relationships, many aspects of the communication process may be unbalanced. Assertiveness, or the lack of it, is one such example. Certain relationships seem to be characterised by one person being passive in response to the other person's aggression. The passive person may fear an aggressive backlash if they become assertive.

In general, the people who are most admired in life are those who do not seek to be admired. They are people who assertively do what they believe to be right, irrespective of the views of others.

ACTIONS

1. To what degree do you respect, honour and assert yourself?
Reflect on the level of respect you have for yourself. What do your behaviour patterns and your way of living reveal about your level of self-respect? Identify the degree to which you honour and dishonour yourself. Observing your thoughts, feelings, actions, behaviours and interactions will help you to identify the degree to which you honour and dishonour yourself. If you are primarily motivated by a desire to please others, you repeatedly run the risk of not honouring yourself, of always putting other people's ideas, wishes, needs and desires before their own. How assertive are you? By observing yourself in your interactions with people, you will get a clear and honest picture of how assertive you are.

2. Consider the apparent benefits of not respecting yourself
Disrespecting yourself allows you to continue to berate yourself, a convenient though painful way of distancing yourself from your deep emotional hurts and painful emotions. Risking feeling respect for yourself may result in stirring up considerable emotion you might prefer to avoid, such as sadness, loss, grief and tears. Disrespecting yourself also allows you to avoid taking risks that scare you. By not having respect for yourself, you will not stand up to or challenge others if they disrespect you. This may suit you, because the very thought of standing up for yourself feels extremely intimidating if your level of selfhood is very low.

3. Commit to respecting yourself
You have every right to respect yourself. You have encountered many difficulties and challenges in your life, and you have coped with them as best you could. You deserve your own respect for that. Base your self-respect on the same principles as those upon which you base your self-worth, the fact that you are a unique, priceless human being. This alone is sufficient reason for you to respect yourself. Identify three reasons why you deserve your self-respect. If you find yourself resisting this practise, it is probably for the reasons outlined in action 2 above. Allow whatever feelings that well up inside you to come to the surface.

For Hilda, a hairdresser, one reason for creating self-respect was her conscientiousness, skill and experience in her work. She risked increasing her fees to the average price range for hairdressing services. She informed clients in the habit of not attending appointments, or of giving inadequate or no notice that they would not be attending, that in future a charge would apply. Hilda had learned that self-respect was more important that placating her clients at the cost of disrespecting herself. These clients soon changed their behaviour and respected her more, mirroring Hilda's increased respect for herself. Confucius was correct when he said 'respect yourself and others will respect you'.

4.   *Let go of other-respect, habitually seeking respect from others*
Set a mental warning light to go off whenever you slip into the old habit of seeking respect from others. Notice when you do this. Bring your focus and attention back into your own personal space. Gently tell yourself that you are the provider of your own respect. Through repetition of this action, you make it a new habit in your life. Be patient. Focus on the work rather than the outcome. You may not notice much change initially, since you are new to this approach and you don't yet believe in it. Persist with this action, and you will increasingly notice that you are indeed becoming the provider of your own respect for yourself.

5.   *Keep a check on your patterns of self-honouring*
If your level of selfhood is low, the chances are that you tend to seek to honour others far more than you honour yourself. As you become aware of this, you may feel a tinge of sadness, that is quite normal and it will pass. Commit to increase the degree to which you honour yourself. Do not announce this to the world. Implement it quietly, without a word of explanation, justification or approval-seeking. It is you who needs to become convinced of the rightness of self-honouring, not others.

6.   *Experiment with self-honouring in different situations, beginning with the least threatening*
The achievement of little successes will gradually demonstrate to you that you can actually honour yourself without the world coming to an end. Success breeds success, though there will be slippages, and success may in the early stages generate fear, as you do not yet believe in yourself or your ability to carry this through. Before long, you will have built up quite a repository of experience of successful self-honouring within you, that you can use as your foundation for continuing this process for the rest of your life.

7. Striking a balance

Self-honouring is not a licence to dishonour others. Compromise and negotiation are important aspects of relationships. The healthiest approach is one where there is flexibility, where you honour yourself and the rights of those around you, including their right to honour themselves.

8. Become more aware of situations where you need to be assertive

This may take some work. When we have a low sense of selfhood, we may not notice many of the situations where we need to be assertive. This is often a defence mechanism. By not seeing the situations, we feel no pressure to be assertive, we avoid the fear we would experience if we risked being assertive, and we may feel less guilt, but the downside is that we remain stuck. Keep mindful of the degree to which you are assertive as you go through your day, and you will become more aware of the situations that arise where you might consider being more assertive.

Since being assertive need not involve explaining, justifying or challenging other people, experiment with being more assertive, without anyone else being aware of what you are doing. Every day, choose a few situations that are on the least threatening end of the scale in terms of self-assertion. Many of these situations will involve either saying little or nothing in order to assert yourself. You will generally find, to your surprise, that people's reactions are far less threatening than you had presumed they would be. They may not even notice that you are being more assertive, as most people are far more preoccupied with themselves than with you.

For example, one small significant step for Irene was to be more assertive with customers. Irene owned a corner shop, and was often mistreated by her customers, some of whom took advantage of her generosity and her lack of assertiveness. One day, a customer expressed dissatisfaction regarding the bill. Irene and I had been working on assertiveness, so she knew exactly how to handle this. Previously in such situations, she would have become flustered and upset, apologising profusely, virtually refunding money before she even checked the receipt. This time, Irene remained strong, firm, self-centred within her own personal space. She checked the customer's receipt. It transpired that the customer had been charged the proper amount. Irene informed the customer of this, and the exchange ended there. Irene did not agonise over this encounter, as she would have previously, for hours.

9. Decide what assertive actions to take
This does not have to be major actions, or ones involving confrontation
or major explanation, as Irene's example above demonstrates. That whole
interaction lasted less than a minute, but it was a significant step on the
path toward assertiveness for her.

10. Persist with the process
The process of becoming assertive takes time, but will yield some results
quite early in the process if you stick with it. Because this process is likely
to be both new and intimidating, you may feel awkward, stumbling your
way through your initial attempts to be assertive. You may feel that this
awkwardness is further proof that you will never succeed in becoming
assertive. Clumsiness is par for the course at the beginning, and does not
at all signify failure. Expect this, and when it happens, remind yourself
that the more you practise, the better you become at being assertive.
Maintain a daily routine of asserting yourself, and within weeks you will
be in the process of building up a foundation of successful assertiveness.
As you get more comfortable with this concept through practise, you can
experiment with asserting yourself in situations that are a little more
challenging. Keep up this practise and it won't be long before being
naturally assertive is an aspect of yourself that you can tap into and use
whenever you need to.

11. Reflection
During your reflection times, think about how you have been toward
yourself in relation to self-respect, self-honouring and assertiveness. Note
the occasions when you respected yourself, and praise yourself for this.
Note also the times when you disrespected yourself, consider what other
options you had in that situation, and gently resolve to act from a place
of self-respect next time. Reflect upon the extent to which you honoured
yourself in your various interactions and activities. Commit to honour
yourself between now and your next reflection. As you go about your day,
keep the following question gently within your awareness: 'Am I
honouring myself in this situation, in this moment?' Did you maintain
an attitude of self-respect and self-honouring toward yourself since your
last reflection time? If there were times when you didn't, be gentle with
yourself about this. Learn from the experience, and increase your resolve
to respect and honour yourself in future situations. Consider whether

you have been as assertive as appropriate since your last reflection. There may not have been any situations where you needed to assert yourself and that is absolutely fine. The point of considering assertiveness at each reflection is to help you become increasingly mindful of assertiveness in your everyday life.

12. Affirmation
'I respect myself at all times. I honour myself in my everyday life. I assert myself as necessary and appropriate.'

Self-discipline
Discipline is fundamentally a positive concept. Discipline refers to work and training that is intended to produce a specific character or pattern of behaviour, especially training that produces moral or mental improvement. Discipline refers to activity, exercise or a routine that develops or improves skills and behaviour. It often involves employing a system of rules of conduct, designed to bring about a state of control, order and improvement.

Self-discipline is the practise of training and establishing control over oneself and one's conduct, especially for personal improvement. It often involves training ourselves to incorporate a useful code of behaviour into our lives, in a controlled and habitual way, in a balanced fashion without excessive control. It is the ability and the determination to do what is necessary or sensible without needing to be continually prompted by others, the ability and conviction to pursue what one believes is right despite temptations to abandon it. Self-discipline is the ability to control ourselves and to make ourselves work hard or behave in a particular way. It involves the cultivation of firmness of purpose and will, the correction and regulation of ourselves for the sake of improving ourselves. Through practising self-discipline, we learn healthy balanced self-control, we recognise important limits, and we learn when to stop. Self-discipline does not involve exerting ongoing control over our feelings by banishing them from our experience. The healthy management of emotions is discussed earlier in the book.

Self-discipline issues are frequently an aspect of mental health problems and unhappiness. Becoming self-disciplined is a core part of the recovery of selfhood and mental wellness. Because of its beneficial effects, many spiritual and religious groups recommend self-discipline. Being self-disciplined means attending to important yet often ordinary everyday things, such as getting up in the morning on time, making things happen when they are supposed to happen, getting into healthy routines, making sure you begin tasks, including those you do not like, in sufficient time to complete them properly. It means not putting things off, and instead dealing with them, seeing them through to completion, thus giving yourself a sense of achievement and confidence.

I recommend cultivating self-discipline as a way of life, and applying this attitude across the wide range of activities and interactions you experience. For example, we benefit from having a self-disciplined and balanced approach to eating, consuming alcohol or other drugs. Our spending, our level of exercise, how we take care of ourselves, all need to be carried out with gentle, but when necessary firm, self-discipline. The practise of self-discipline applies many times every day, though we may not be aware of this. Making things happen when they need to happen, even when we do not feel like doing so, or when we are faced with distractions or other more appealing options, is an important aspect of self-discipline. It can be a challenge to ensure that, as best we can, we honour our priorities and our needs in the face of the demands and priorities of other people, of work and other activities. Self-discipline is necessary to ensure that we fulfil the goals we set for ourselves, ensuring that we complete the steps involved in achieving our goals, whether they be little or major ones.

Self-discipline is most effective when there is room for flexibility. There will be times when we do not attain the standards we have set for ourselves. The important thing is to gently get back on track without undue delay. When applied in combination with action, persistence and mindfulness, self-discipline produces results. This is true irrespective of the types of tasks and challenges that we might have to deal with in life.

Frequently, it is not the one-off major occurrences that destroy lives, relationships or lead to the collapse of businesses, but the accumulation of small things that go unnoticed, unresolved, gathering momentum over time. Being self-disciplined, we deal with the little things, preventing this process of escalation.

The following story from my own life illustrates the beneficial effects I experienced through developing balanced self-discipline. I did quite poorly in my final year school exams. My level of selfhood at the time was pretty low. I was unhappy and lonely, with few real supports in my life. I entered my teens quite happy and confident in myself, but this confidence became greatly eroded as I struggled through boarding school. I became one of those quiet, frightened teenagers who people feel are doing fine because they are not causing trouble or drawing attention to themselves. If fact, they are generally doing everything in their power to ensure that they do not attract attention. My poor results were directly linked to my low level of selfhood and my deep unhappiness. My heart was not really in my studies because I was in considerable emotional distress. I had to repeat the final year exams in order to get into university.

This was a major turning point. The approach I adopted was *the* critical factor in making that year a great success. From the outset, I undertook to work hard. I became self-disciplined and determined, approaching my workload for the year methodically, strategically. I did not focus on the results I needed. I concentrated on working the hardest and the smartest that I could, happy to let the results look after themselves.

That was a wonderful year for me. I quickly got into a good routine, with a healthy mixture of hard work, self-care, and a necessarily limited but good social life. As the year progressed, I could see that my work was bearing fruit. I was doing well in school, and I was much happier than at any previous time in my teens. My level of selfhood increased greatly that year. My results were enough to secure entry to medical school. The satisfaction of reaping the success of a year of hard work was sweet, and served to further enhance my level of selfhood. The key factor was the balanced self-discipline I had decided to make the foundation stone of that year. I did not have a high sense of selfhood when I went to the new school, but I was still able to become self-disciplined and take responsibility for myself. I was aware that the outcome depended principally on me, on my attitude, my actions, on staying focused, pacing myself and taking good care of myself, and sticking at it even when I did not feel like it.

I was also kind to myself, taking regular breaks when I needed them, while never losing sight of my goals. My self-discipline and determination were catalysts for the considerable growth of selfhood I experienced that year, a period I still recall with great affection. By the end of the year, I had internalised a regime of self-discipline, commitment and hard work. I knew that if I could do it once, I could do it again. That was a great feeling. Since then, self-discipline has been a great ally in my life. We need to integrate and maintain self-discipline within ourselves and within our lives. In time, healthy self-discipline enhances our level of selfhood and our sense of freedom and self-empowerment.

There is the world of difference between seeing the importance of self-discipline and actually integrating it as a way of life. When I spoke about self-discipline to a client recently, he quickly replied that this was an obvious 'no-brainer'. Yet, self-discipline was a recurring challenge for him. For example, although I had previously advised him to continuously bring his attention back to the present, he acknowledged that he was spending about half an hour a day at most truly living in the present.

A good example of the importance of self-discipline surfaced recently with a client. A man in his mid-fifties, he was a successful businessman and a very nice person. Like many people in business in Ireland in 2011, he was experiencing financial worry and pressure. However, how he was dealing with these pressures escalated his distress considerably. In particular, he was not employing self-discipline in his attempts to deal with the situation. He was allowing his focus to continually drift from the present into either the future or the past. He spent most of his spare time passively looking at television or lying on the couch, deliberately withdrawing from his family, who loved him dearly and whom he loved very much. He turned down many offers from family and friends to do things together, to spend some time together. These actions, though understandable, were highly dysfunctional, in that they were diametrically opposite to the actions he needed to take in order to nurture himself. Unwittingly through his actions, *he was starving himself of the love and support that would sustain him through these difficult times.*

I encouraged him to discipline himself, to take action toward making better contact with his family and friends. I suggested that he say 'yes' when people contact him with requests to meet for a chat. I asked him to initiate contact with friends and family, people whom he knew cared greatly about him. I told him that he needed to take these actions even though his first impulse would likely be to withdraw from all contact. I suggested that he gently work on disciplining himself to live in the present. I recommended to him that when his tendency to fly off into the future and what catastrophe might face him at some point in the future surfaced, he should repeatedly bring his attention back to the present to what is real *right now* in his life. I suggested a similar approach when his attention raced into the past, berating himself for decisions he had made. I reminded him that he made every decision in good faith, given the information at his disposal at that time, therefore any criticism of himself based on information which was not available to him at that time was inappropriate, and entirely unfair to him. Overcoming this impasse depended on the degree to which he was prepared to become truly self-disciplined, as we had discussed. Two weeks later, I received a text from him, in which he told me that he was taking the actions I recommended, and that he felt much better.

ACTIONS

1. Identify how self-disciplined you are. Be honest with yourself.
How self-disciplined are you? Is there much evidence of self-indiscipline all around you, clutter, mess, disorganisation, for example? How disciplined are you about living in the present moment, and about where you choose to focus your time, energy and attention? How disciplined are your routines, your days? Does your indiscipline include taking on too many projects, having fingers in too many pies and not completing them, leaving many loose ends in your life? How disciplined and balanced are you in your everyday activities, such as eating, alcohol and drug consumption, in taking care of yourself? Do you ensure that you generally see your plans, goals and responsibilities through to completion?

2. If you are not sufficiently self-disciplined, commit to the task of raising your level of self-discipline without putting pressure on yourself to achieve rapid results
Make a commitment to yourself that you are going to foster and develop the attitude of self-discipline across the various aspects of your life. Remind yourself several times every day of this commitment you have made to yourself.

3. Baby steps
Take greater control of your time, your day. Do the little things well. Finish tasks. If your level of self-discipline is low, then completing even the smallest tasks may feel like an enormous challenge. Get them done,

one at a time. Come back to each task several times if you have to. Do whatever it takes to get it done. You will gradually feel a sense of achievement, and a healthy level of self-discipline will take shape within your life. If not living in the present is a habit of yours, commit to bringing your focus and attention back to the present as often as necessary. Notice when your mind is wandering into either the present or the future. Gently bring your attention back to the present, a thousand times a day if necessary.

If your pattern has been to be excessively self-disciplined, your challenge is to take actions that involve gradually letting go of control. Again, small steps, one step at a time is the way to go.

4.   *Being in the present: exercise one*

It is particularly important that you discipline yourself to live in the present, in the now, since the present is the only time in which you actually live and can achieve anything. Several times a day, for example during your reflection times, take a moment to do the following simple exercise. Sit for a moment. Look around you, and say to yourself that you are now here, in this place. Name everything you see. For example, if you are in your kitchen, look around the kitchen, naming what you see. Wherever you are, that is your present, your current reality. As you are doing this exercise, if your mind wanders to the future or the past, gently bring your attention back to the present, to where you are and what you are doing. Practicing this exercise every day will gradually help you to become more self-disciplined about living in the present.

5.   *Being in the present: exercise two*

I have a client to thank for this one. It is an exercise he used to use, one that helped him (and can help you) become more accustomed to living consciously in the present. If you drive, and when you are driving on your own, imagine there is a passenger in the car with you, to whom you are going to describe what you see on your journey. Describe out loud what you see as you drive by, the people, buildings, trees, fields, the weather, for example. For obvious reasons, do not let this interfere with your focus and concentration on your driving. While you are in theory describing what you see for the benefit of your supposed passenger, you benefit, because you are focusing your attention on and connecting with the reality of what is around you now, in the present moment. The client who mentioned this to me observed that time passed much more quickly when he engaged in this exercise, and he enjoyed driving a lot more when doing so. This is not surprising, as we generally feel more alive when we are making good contact with ourselves in the present. If you don't drive, or even if you do, you can do this exercise in many situations, for example, whenever you go for a walk.

6. *Reflection*
At your reflection times, briefly consider how you have dealt with the preceding few hours from a self-discipline point of view, and renew your intention to be self-disciplined.

7. *Affirmation*
'I practise a gentle and consistent self-discipline in my life.'

Self-ownership
Self-ownership means taking ownership of and responsibility for yourself. It means acknowledging the fact that you are the primary decision-maker in your life. It is important that you take ownership and responsibility for yourself, but doing so can seem daunting when you have lost your sense of selfhood and you are filled with self-doubt. Taking ownership of yourself helps you realise that you are the author of your own destiny, that you are continually the choice-maker, and that you can work your way through change, challenge and the unexpected.

Take the word 'responsibility', reconstruct the spelling and it becomes 'the ability to respond'. It is only when we are prepared to take responsibility for ourselves that we can respond effectively to life's challenges. Taking ownership of ourselves, our choices and our life is challenging, but it gives us power. If we do not take ownership, we surrender our power within and over our life.

Some of us may have lost our sense of selfhood at an early age and consequently, choose to respond to life, people and situations in defensive ways. When we refuse to take ownership of the aspects of ourselves that we do not like, or feel we cannot handle, we are literally disowning ourselves. We cannot change, reconcile or heal these aspects of ourselves and move beyond them unless and until we own and take responsibility for them.

By committing to practise self-ownership and self-responsibility in your life, you will be better able to deal with both the expected and the unexpected. You no longer blame others or circumstances for your predicaments. Always bring the seat of power back to yourself, and carefully assess what options you have in any given situation. When we regularly apportion blame, we alienate others, and we remain stuck in a rut, convinced that we are powerless to do anything to improve the situation for ourselves. Self-ownership and self-responsibility mean being prepared to acknowledge our role, learning from the experience, taking appropriate action, and moving on.

Fear, and how we choose to deal with fear, is often at the root of our refusal to take ownership and responsibility for ourselves. If you have little experience of taking responsibility for yourself, you may greatly doubt your ability to take ownership of and responsibility for yourself. Taking responsibility may initially bring up fear, sadness and guilt, as you become aware of the times when you did not take ownership and responsibility, and the consequent loss of time and opportunity. This passes, as long as you persist with the work. American psychiatrist Dr William Glasser is the founder of Reality Therapy and the author of many books, including *Choice Theory*. Dr Glasser believes that we can heal ourselves by becoming more aware of our choices and decisions, and by owning and taking responsibility for them and for ourselves, and making better choices and decisions. I agree.

ACTIONS

1. Where are you on the spectrum of self-ownership and self-responsibility?
Look at Diagram 18. Consider where you are currently on the spectrum of self-ownership and self-responsibility. Some people refuse to take ownership of and responsibility for anything. Others take ownership and responsibility for everything, including that which is not their responsibility at all. Identify where you stand.

2. Commit to developing the mind-set where you take ownership and
   responsibility for yourself
Commit to owning and taking responsibility for everything about yourself, including your thoughts, feelings, actions, choices and decisions. You have the power to make your current life more peaceful and

meaningful. Take ownership of your part in the current situation in your life. Initially, you may well find yourself resisting this. Part of you might prefer to continue the old, disowning ways. This is understandable, since it has felt good to pass the buck to others. Be gentle with yourself. It will take you time to change, and you can expect old habits to re-surface many times. From now on, your challenge is to take note of this pattern, each time replacing the old pattern with self-ownership and self-responsibility. They are your thoughts, feelings, actions, reactions, choices and decisions.

3. Balanced self-ownership and self-responsibility is the key
You do not have to overburden yourself with responsibilities that in reality belong to others. If this is a habit of yours, gently resolve to hand back responsibility to others for themselves. You don't have to tell them you are doing this: make a commitment to this within yourself.

4. Reflection
At your daily reflection times, reflect upon the degree to which you did (or did not) take responsibility for and ownership of yourself since your last reflection. The aim is not to find reasons to berate yourself, but to become more aware of the subtle and not so subtle ways you handle self-

SPECTRUM OF SELF-OWNERSHIP

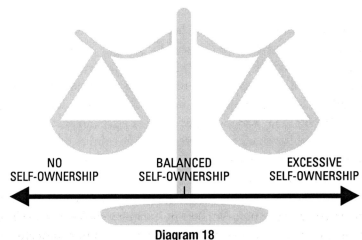

| NO SELF-OWNERSHIP | BALANCED SELF-OWNERSHIP | EXCESSIVE SELF-OWNERSHIP |

Diagram 18

ownership and self-responsibility. Over time, you will learn a great deal about yourself. Commit to be gently mindful of how you handle self-ownership and self-responsibility over the next few hours, until your next reflection time.

5. *Affirmation*
'I own everything about myself and my actions. I take responsibility for myself.'

Self-honesty
Being honest with yourself means tuning in to how you really are, and acknowledging the realities of yourself, of others and of life. Employing self-honesty enables you to live in harmony with the world as it really is, rather than living a fantasy life of sorts. In time, developing the practise of self-honesty will strengthen your sense of selfhood, and the belief that you can live a fulfilling life, enabling you to deal more effectively with problems and with life's challenges.

Self-honesty can seem too threatening, too unpalatable. It may appear easier to avoid certain truths and realities, out of fear that we could not cope with full acknowledgement of them. We might prefer the distorted image that we have of ourselves, and perhaps of others, rather than taking the full truth on board. Letting go of strongly held beliefs can be scary and can create considerable sadness initially, feelings we might prefer to avoid. We feel the magnitude of the hurt, loss, pain and fear that we were seeking to avoid by believing in the fantasy. We may experience the recognition of what we have lost, including time and possibilities, by continuing to believe in these fantasies for years.

This understandable pattern of avoidance is sometimes necessary, as a defence mechanism when the truth really is too unpalatable for us to bear. If this pattern of self-dishonesty is not worked through later, our losses may remain within us, a block of unprocessed grief and pain. This weighs us down and holds us back from living a full life, compounded by ongoing self-dishonesty that continues to create more problems for us unless we tackle this pattern. As Richard Bach, author of *Jonathan Livingston Seagull* said, 'the worst lies are the lies we tell ourselves. We live in denial of what we do, even what we think. We do this because we are afraid'. It is often said that one lie begets a thousand lies. When we lie to ourselves, we have to create many more lies and deceits in order to maintain the self-deception, to keep the real truth at bay, outside our awareness.

'I can't' is a common form of self-delusion, particularly in the context of doing something that generates fear within us. What we usually mean is 'I'm too afraid so I won't', but we say 'I can't' because we like the certainty and control it gives us, minimising our guilt for choosing to say no. We feel it is less risky that telling the truth, and risks less challenge from others. It can be a convenient way to avoid direct contact with ourselves and with our painful emotions. Audrey, who was twenty years old, had unfinished emotional business regarding the deaths of members of her extended family. I suggested that she write a letter to an aunt who had died, with whom she had a very close relationship but had not grieved for her death. As she read this letter to me the following week, one of the first lines in her letter was 'I can't do this'. But she did do it. She wrote the letter, brought it to her next appointment with me, read it out loud in my presence, crying and sobbing. She was reluctant to write the letter, as doing so would bring her into direct contact with her grief, which she had been previously avoiding. Another early sentence in her letter referred to her feeling numb as she wrote. Becoming numb, anesthetising herself, was another sign of her reluctance to feel her emotions. In reading the letter out loud in my presence, she certainly was not numb, far from it. She came into direct contact with her previously suppressed emotions, crying intensely, doing important healing work in the process. Afterwards, she felt lighter, unburdened, relieved.

The avoidance of self-honesty is a slippery slope, often creating chaos and stagnancy both in our lives and in the lives of those around us. It corrodes self-confidence, self-empowerment and many other key aspects of mental health and wellbeing. You cannot heal or change what you are not prepared to acknowledge. There are understandable reasons why people choose habits that are the polar opposite of self-honesty, such as self-delusion and other distorted interpretations of their world, themselves and others. These reasons generally involve significant loss of selfhood, the experience of considerable hurt, heartbreak, disappointment and broken dreams, great self-doubt, fear, terror, lack of self-belief and self-confidence. As with any pattern, self-honesty can be cultivated and developed into a real skill through mindfulness, persistence, discipline, and working on this gently but firmly. It is important to accept that this will take some time, so that rigid deadlines are not set.

ACTIONS

1. *Identify your level of self-honesty*

This can be a bit tricky. If you have a tendency to delude yourself, you may find it much easier to delude yourself on this one than to be truly honest with yourself. Consider your level of honesty regarding your reasons for doing or not doing things. You may be surprised at how frequently you tell yourself little white lies, and some that are not so little. Perhaps you conclude an alternative reason for an action or decision, when the real reason is one you would rather not be aware of. Our underlying motivation is often fear, or the desire to avoid feeling painful emotions such as sadness, grief and guilt. Notice and observe your patterns of criticism and blaming, both toward yourself and others. By being honest with yourself, you may realise that there is a more balanced and less judgemental way of looking at the situation.

2. *Honesty is the best policy*

Becoming aware of what you might prefer to remain unaware of might make you feel uncomfortable initially. Doing so offers you the opportunity to address important issues which, if not dealt with, will continue to cause problems for you and possibly also for those around you. Make a commitment to be honest with yourself. Resolve to take note of your blind spots when they surface, and they will surface from time to time. Become aware of your behaviour patterns in relation to being dishonest with yourself. Be truthful with yourself about how you handle emotions. Do you deal with the core emotion as it occurs, or do you translate some core emotions, such as hurt or sadness, into other emotions such as anger, depression, numbness, for example? Do you use some emotions as a way of avoiding taking necessary but challenging actions, or perhaps project your emotions outwards, becoming angry with others when the real issue lies within yourself?

3. *Bring it back home*

If you regularly blame others for the difficulties you experience, bring your consideration of these situations back to yourself. Ask yourself what part if any you may be playing in the continuation of the problem, and what possible contribution you could make toward its resolution. Do some reality testing: consider the beliefs and opinions you have regarding difficult situations in your life, and honestly consider what factual evidence there is to support these. Be prepared to risk changing your beliefs, opinions and conclusions accordingly.

4. Reflection

During your daily reflections, consider how honest you have been with yourself since your last reflection time. Notice the occasions when you have not been fully honest with yourself, and re-commit to self-honesty as a philosophy of living. Reflect accurately on the various situations that occur during your day. Include situations that you found difficult, intimidating or hurtful. See and take ownership of your role if any in these situations, not in a blaming, judgemental way, but in an open-minded, self-supportive way. Having taken ownership of your role, you can consider what options and choices you may have, both now and in future situations.

5. Affirmation

'It is safe to be honest with myself. I commit to self-honesty, knowing that this will help to foster my personal growth.'

Self-revelation

People with a solid sense of selfhood reveal much of themselves as they go through their life. They will be themselves, their own person, wherever they are. People with a low sense of selfhood generally hide a great deal of themselves and what they experience. This may cause them great sadness and loneliness. Young people who have experienced bullying or considerable criticism may clam up, surviving by saying the minimum to as few people as possible in order to minimise further hurt and humiliation. Some people may appear to be communicating and interacting well with others, and to an extent they are, but they may not be revealing who they really are and what they are experiencing. Many people use humour as a way of attempting to belong, get attention, be accepted and hide how they are really feeling. They do not feel they can truly be themselves. We live in a society where it is often not okay or safe to reveal everything about ourselves. Some degree of holding back who we are is natural and healthy, but the greater the degree of masking, the more likely the person is to feel sad and lonely, even when surrounded by people.

Sometimes, when a person takes their own life, people who knew them say they had everything to live for. They seemed so happy, always messing and joking. They may not realise that the person may have had major aspects of themselves that they felt they just could not reveal to others. The intense loneliness that this creates can be enough to spur some people to choose to end their life. Anything considered by society or the person's peer group to be off limits may result in considerable isolation and ostracisation for those who are experiencing what is frowned upon or rejected by wider society. Feeling, expressing or displaying distressing emotions, self-doubt, fear and lack of confidence, especially for men, is just one example.

In many countries, the subtle, pervasive censorship of the expression of emotion continues. We have become so accustomed to this censorship that we may not notice it, accepting and subscribing to it without thought or protest. I was reminded of this censorship while watching the news on a major international television network on 4 March 2009. One of the news items concerned a model. Apparently, she had tears in her eyes as she walked the catwalk. The news presenter informed the world that the model then changed her outfit and returned to the catwalk, crying all the while. A spokesperson for the model assured the press after the fashion show that the model had most definitely not been crying. The newsreader reassured the public that if they received any further updates, they would broadcast them without delay.

All this fuss over a few tears. That model sure had guts to allow herself to be seen crying in public, if indeed she was crying. I do hope she did not lose her job. The clear message from the news report was that to cry publicly in such circumstances is both wrong and highly newsworthy. This interpretation is corroborated by the model's spokesperson's immediate statement that she had not been crying. Had the model been laughing, it is unlikely that she would have hit the headlines. I see examples of this censorship every day in my work as a psychotherapist. I often wonder if there would be such a demand for counselling, psychotherapy and medication if we had a more rounded, tolerant and mature attitude to the expression of emotions and of diversity.

Sadness and tears are particularly poorly tolerated. When we are moved to tears by an event, this is often considered acceptable and often welcomed by others. Men who cry when their beloved team wins a major sporting event are warmly supported in their tears by friends and fellow supporters. Tears of sorrow are a different kettle of fish. Witnessing other people's grief and sadness makes many of us feel uncomfortable, and we do not like to feel uncomfortable. We may accept other people's tears as long as we know why they are crying, but only if from *our* perspective the reasons justify their tears and sorrow. Even when a person has an obvious reason to be sad, such as following a bereavement, our tolerance for their tears often runs out quickly, usually long before the person's grieving process has reached its conclusion. 'Shouldn't they be over it by now?' is a common reaction. Losses of any kind can generate sadness and grief. Both the experience and the duration of grief are deeply personal to the individual and to their relationship to the source of their grief.

As with any form of prohibition, the lives of many people are affected by this veto on emotions, so great is the scale to which this ban has been accepted and integrated into everyday life. The people who are most affected are those who experience a great deal of grief and sadness, including those who feel suicidal.

Several organisations provide an excellent listening and support service for people in great distress. The very fact that people have to turn to such organisations when in crisis highlights the lack of acceptance, tolerance and understanding of these emotions and experiences in everyday life. Such organisations and their good work tend to be somewhat removed from everyday life, a further reflection of the censorship and distancing of emotional distress that pervades modern life. People experiencing great sadness and tearfulness may consequently feel the need to withdraw from society, feeling there is no place for them in it any more. Fearing judgment and rejection, they may cut contact with friends and activities. Already isolated by the intensity of their distress, their isolation is augmented by their belief and experience that they no longer fit in. Society's reaction to their distress can actually increase their suicidal feelings.

Anxiety is another emotion that is generally not received well in public. Fear and anxiety are natural reactions to change. The lower a person's level of selfhood, the greater the degree of anxiety and fear they experience in the face of change, challenge and the unknown. Censorship and societal disapproval of anxiety leaves people who experience it in a difficult position. They are terrified that others will see their nervousness and judge them for it. They may feel they have little option but to avoid situations that provoke anxiety, creating major limitations to their life. Four young people with whom I am currently working all share the same experience: enormous self-doubt and great anxiety when attending school or college. They are each terrified that this will be noticed, and that they will be severely judged for it. If we were more accepting of painful and difficult human emotions and experiences, the life of these four young people and millions of others would be a great deal easier.

Many young people go through their day keeping themselves to themselves. This is fine as long as it is truly how they want to be. The issue is whether the person is living and communicating in the way they wish, or as they feel they have to. The level of peer pressure that exists in youth culture is considerable. Parents and other older adults sometimes presume that because young people have more choices and more freedom than ever before, life is wonderful and easy for them. This may be true for young people with a strong sense of selfhood, but for those with a low sense of selfhood it is usually quite the opposite. There is an enormous amount of peer competition and peer pressure to conform, be cool, accepted, sexy, attractive and successful. Many young people decide to hide who they really are rather than risk exposure, humiliation, ridicule, and rejection by the most important group in their world in their eyes, their peers. Their fears of reprisal are often not nearly as justified as they anticipate, their real fear sometimes being experiencing their own painful emotions.

We wear masks in an attempt to get approval from others, to avoid risking rejection. In doing so, we become increasingly alienated from ourselves.

ACTIONS

1. Identify the degree to which you hide aspects of yourself from yourself
Commit to noticing what aspects of yourself and your experience of life you hide away from yourself. There may be important aspects of yourself that you hide from yourself, that you have decided you should not feel or experience, so you try to banish them from your experience. Keep this issue in your mind, and you will gradually become aware of aspects of yourself that you mask from yourself. Most commonly, we hide away our sadness, losses, fears, grief, loneliness, our vulnerability, hurt, difficult emotions, and aspects of ourselves and of life around which we are very scared. Reveal yourself to yourself in your daily journalling, and generally during your day.

2.   *Make a real commitment to yourself to be who you are*
This will take some time, so don't put yourself under undue pressure. Make the commitment, and then take one step at a time.

3.   *Gradually, reveal more of who you are, to yourself*
Consider in detail the aspects of yourself that you have hidden away from yourself. For example, if your level of selfhood is low, you are likely to have experienced more fear, hurt and loss than perhaps you realise. Explore this in detail. For example, think about how much fear you *really* experience in your life, or would experience if you risked living a more full life. Think about it, and write about it, honestly. You may find that your level of fear is much greater than you had thought, that it is holding you back greatly in your life, and that you really need to address this.

You may have some good qualities, such as kindness, gentleness, courage and integrity, that you do not give yourself credit for, dismissing them as nothing. It is time that you acknowledged fully your many good qualities. Refusing to acknowledge these is a form of hiding important aspects of yourself from yourself.

4.   *Gradually, reveal more of who you are to others*
Risk taking small steps toward being yourself with others. Risk being true to yourself more. Gradually, reveal aspects of yourself to the people with whom you are most comfortable and safe. Small and regular actions generally work better than large and occasional steps. A good time to do it is when you are getting on well together, when things are good between you and the people you might risk revealing more of yourself to. Revealing yourself gradually to trusted others helps you to express the truths about yourself about which you feel vulnerable and fragile. Having these witnessed, held, understood and respected by someone you trust and care about and who cares about you can be deeply moving and healing. If you have no one in your life with whom you can safely reveal yourself to, consider attending a good counsellor, or contacting mental health support lines. The people who man these phones are generally well trained in the art and skill of listening. They know how to create a safe space for you to talk freely about yourself, without judgement, criticism or rejection.

In time, risk revealing aspects of yourself to others in your everyday exchanges with people. It is not necessary for you to reveal everything about yourself. Indeed, there are times when it is entirely appropriate not to reveal aspects of yourself to others, depending on the situation. Start small, as this may well be a terrifying concept to you.

5. *Reflection*
At each reflection time, consider how the issue of self-revelation might have been relevant in your life since your last reflection. Commit to being mindful of this issue between now and your next reflection time.

6. *Affirmation*
'I reveal myself to myself, all of who I am, what I feel and experience. I reveal myself to others as feels appropriate for me.'

Self-acceptance
When we do not accept ourselves, we reject ourselves. This is like embarking on a journey, but insisting that we should be starting from somewhere else. When we do not accept ourselves and our current life situation as our starting point, we remain stuck in the moment, feeling and situation. Do not confuse acceptance with resignation. Acceptance of our current reality is a necessary first step toward initiating change. Resignation means concluding that there is nothing we can do to initiate or create change, a very different thing.

Accepting yourself, including what you perceive as your imperfections, in time liberates you. It disentangles you from the scourge of constant self-criticism and its accompanying paralysis, distress and inaction. Accepting yourself does not mean trying to convince yourself to like everything about you and your life right now. How and where you are now is the point from which you take the actions and make the changes required to increase your happiness and contentment. It is an internal acceptance, and has nothing to do with the viewpoints of others, or striving to convince others to accept you, a practise that is a waste of your precious time and energy. The more we resist or reject how we are and our current reality, the more obstacles we put in our way. The importance of acceptance is highlighted by its central role in the grieving process, a process of adjustment to major loss or important change in one's life. If acceptance doesn't happen, the entire grieving process becomes stuck, put on hold.

ACTIONS

1.   Identify where you are on the spectrum of self-acceptance
Do you generally accept yourself and your current reality? Or do you reject much of who you are, your emotions, various aspects of your life situation? Take your time with this one. Your immediate reaction might be 'of course I accept myself and my current reality', whereas on reflection you may find that you do not accept quite a few things about yourself and your life.

2.   Get a clearer sense of what you do not accept about yourself
Possibilities include your thoughts, feelings, body image, your life circumstances and experiences, your self-perception, including what you perceive (or have been told) about your intelligence, skills and abilities. Welcome them back into the fold. Explore the parts of you that you feel vulnerable about, that you reject. Accept and work with them, and you will become more fully whole. Do some reality testing. For example, if you feel that your appearance is totally unacceptable, ask yourself if you get similar feedback from others. I recently worked with a woman who utterly rejected her facial appearance. Yet, at regular intervals, men asked her out, and women commented on how well she looked. As discussed in the next action, her self-rejection served a purpose for her.

3.   Consider how not fully accepting yourself and your current reality
     might have helped you
I have worked with several clients for whom self-rejection was in part a protective mechanism. For example, if I become preoccupied with my appearance, and become convinced that I cannot leave my house because of my appearance, there are pay-offs. My preoccupation with my appearance means I do not have to be aware of and deal with more core issues such as grief, loss and fear. I now have a reason to stay at home and minimise my risk-taking in life, including risking entering relationships. Ask yourself if there might be certain payoffs for your lack of self-acceptance.

4.   Accept yourself and your current reality
Pledge that from this point onwards you will accept yourself, who you are and everything about yourself, including your thoughts, feelings and your life circumstances. You do not have to like your current reality but

you do need to accept it, as the starting point on your journey toward recovering your sense of selfhood, toward making the changes you need to make. Once you accept where you are now, you can begin to address what needs to be addressed.

5. Implementing self-acceptance in your daily life

Be mindful of self-acceptance as you go though your day. Gently remind yourself many times each day that you accept everything about yourself. You may resist this initially. Do not engage in battle with the part of you that resists this. Keep it simple. Just keep gently reminding yourself that from now on, you accept yourself.

6. Avoid comparisons

Sitting back in a state of inaction and comparing ourselves, either to others or to how we used to be, does not help. We are each on our own personal life journey, the twists and turns of which are individual and personal to each of us. When your attention drifts to other people and the ways in which you feel their lives are better than yours, bring your attention back to yourself, within your own space. You are where you are in your life, right now. This is your starting point. Consider what actions you can take to progress things just a little for yourself. This approach helps you to foster resilience, which will help you to recover your sense of selfhood and move on with your life.

7. Reflection

During your daily reflection times, consider whether you have practised self-acceptance during the previous few hours. Notice both the moments of self-acceptance and self-rejection. At night, say to yourself that you will accept everything about yourself and your current reality in the morning, including your feelings, as the starting point for your day.

8. Affirmation

'I accept myself, my current reality, and all of my feelings and experiences.'

Self-forgiveness

To expect that we could live without ever hurting anyone is expecting the impossible. We may become bitter and frustrated with ourselves, others and life, particularly if many of our hopes and dreams have not materialised. The forgiveness we most need is often forgiveness from ourselves. It is likely that on many of these occasions we did cause hurt to others, we did not intend to or realise that we were doing so. We may have felt very distressed and overwhelmed at the time. While this may not excuse our actions, it puts them in some context. The guilt that arises when we do not forgive ourselves can cause great distress, often leading to people becoming severely depressed, and tragically, sometimes to the point of suicide.

Guilt serves a purpose. It gets us thinking about our transgressions, our regrets and how best to come to peace with others and within ourselves. It is likely that we were doing the best we could at the time, given the information at our disposal, the state of our life and how we were emotionally. Of course, there are occasions when we do not do our best. This too is understandable, and deserving of our self-forgiveness because we are human beings, not machines. It is not possible to do or be at our best every minute of every day. No one can know all the outcomes of their actions in advance. If we remain preoccupied with guilt, we immobilise ourselves, resulting in further inaction. Guilt can be a very effective way of keeping ourselves stuck in the past and and preventing us from taking ownership or responsibility for both our present and future. We are wasting time we could instead spend either repairing some of the damage we have caused, making amends in some way, or steering our lives in more productive directions.

ACTIONS

1. Consider how self-forgiveness might apply to you
Do you have a pattern of self-recrimination, blaming yourself for what is happening in your life or in the lives of others? If this is the case, you may well need forgiveness from yourself.

2. Reflect honestly and fairly
Reflect on what you have said or done in your life. You will realise that you were generally doing the best you could, given how you were, how your life was for you, and the knowledge and information you had at your disposal at the time.

3. *Forgive yourself*

You are a human being, not a machine. You make mistakes. We all do. Learn the lessons from your mistakes, let them go, and wish all of the people involved well. Commit to doing your best in future. Be gentle with yourself. Apologise if that is appropriate. Make your peace with yourself, and if it is possible and practical, with those affected by your actions. If there is little you can do to make amends, own up to yourself about your behaviour and your actions. Accept responsibility for them, but forgive yourself. Perhaps at the time you were in considerable emotional distress and pain yourself, and therefore perhaps you were doing the best you could in the circumstances. Make peace with your god, if that is important to you.

4. *Seek support from people you trust*

Getting such support can be very helpful, though be careful. Many people do not know how to listen very well, often prematurely giving advice from their own standpoint, which is often not what you need.

5. *Reflection*

At your daily reflection times, consider self-forgiveness and how it might apply to you. Commit to being aware of the importance of self-forgiveness.

6. *Affirmation*

'I forgive myself for the mistakes I have made in the past. I now give myself permission to move forward with my life.'

Case histories

Here are two stories of individuals I have worked with, for whom aspects of their attitudes to themselves were central to their problems. The two individuals chose very different ways of dealing with the challenge that faced them, and therefore the outcomes could hardly have been more contrasting.

Wallace's story typifies the key role of our self-concept within our overall level of selfhood. Wallace began attending me when he was twenty years old. His sense of selfhood had never been high in his childhood and teenage years. He dealt with his low level of selfhood and major self-doubt by playing safe, slipping quietly through life without attracting any attention, generally keeping his opinions and his thoughts to himself. Always reluctant to make decisions and take risks, he relied heavily on his parents, preferring them to make his decisions for him.

Wallace was not happy, but he got by. It is not possible to be happy when your level of selfhood is low, and you don't feel sufficiently confident and self-assured to live a full life. When he went to college, he struggled greatly. Previously, he had not really been tested in terms of his ability to live effectively in the adult world, always playing safe, refusing and avoiding the hurdles of life including change, risk, the unknown and decision-making.

The image of himself that Wallace had constructed during his teenage years was a direct reflection of how he had chosen to live during those years. It was filled with self-doubt, with far more 'I can't' than 'I can'.

This way of living left him unprepared for college life, with all its challenges and opportunities. Wallace could not see himself being able to cope with college life. His self-perception was 'I cannot do this. Being in college is far too terrifying. It is impossible for me'. He attended college for a month, experiencing high anxiety, attending only the occasional lecture. He fell behind in his subjects, and having become overwhelmed, pulled out of college. This confirmed his negative perception of himself: 'I knew I couldn't do it. Why did I put myself through all that, when I knew from the start that I would have to pull out? This just proves how stupid I am'. Future attempts to go to college or to create positive change in his life would prove even more intimidating.

Deeply affected by this experience, Wallace retreated into his shell. For a few months, he worked part-time in a boring, unchallenging but safe job that involved little risk-taking, which suited Wallace. He decided to attend a different college in a city quite a distance from home the following year. As this second college course approached, his level of anxiety increased significantly, reaching fever pitch the week he was to register for the course. He attended me two days before the date of registration. He only needed to attend college for less than an hour to register, but to Wallace, walking to the North Pole in his bare feet in a blizzard would have seemed a more attractive option. He was restless, agitated, speaking and breathing rapidly and erratically. His heightened anxiety was closely connected to his self-perception, which was being challenged by what he was about to do. 'I am about to do something I am convinced I cannot do' was the dilemma he faced. Going to live in a different city in itself was extremely challenging for him. He had always been a real home bird, another manifestation of his low level of selfhood. He had an overwhelming need to feel safe and to minimise his risk-taking. He genuinely could not see himself going to college and sticking at it.

I offered to stay in close contact with him during this period of transition, several times a day if necessary. I often do this when people are at a critical point in their lives, a point that involves the threshold between what they feel safe with and what they don't.

I felt that if Wallace handled his crisis well, he would experience a major breakthrough. His self-perception would be radically transformed from 'I can't' to 'I can', with major positive ripple-effects spilling over into all areas of his life. I was therefore fully prepared and willing to be in daily contact with him to help him to cross this crucial threshold.

When we spoke on the phone the day before he was due to travel to register for his course, Wallace was panic-stricken, coming up with a hundred reasons why it was impossible for him to go. I listened patiently, validating the rightness of his anxiety given his low sense of selfhood and his previous experience at college, while gently expressing my belief that he was well able to do it, even though he was feeling very anxious. He did indeed register at the college, experiencing a great deal of anxiety in the process. I had prepared him to expect this.

On the day he was due to take up his new accommodation in college, his anxiety reached new heights. He sent a text to me early that day, convinced that he could not go through with it. I suggested he go ahead anyway, and that he contact me later in the day when he had arrived there. This he duly did, still full of anxiety and trepidation about what lay ahead for him, his self-perception still insisting that he could not possibly go through with the challenge. Again, I reassured him that he could do this, one step at a time. In the weeks leading up to the beginning of his college course, we had discussed in detail what he could expect, in terms of his anxiety and his reactions. This reassured him that he was not 'going crazy'. It also increased his confidence in me, since what I suggested might happen generally did happen, conveying the message to Wallace that I really did understand what he was going through, and how things would work out for him. I had warned him in advance that the few days before college were going to be filled with a rollercoaster of thoughts and feelings including panic, terror, a strong urge to pull out altogether and not attend college. Being advised of this in advance meant that I could now concentrate on helping him get through one day at a time. Once he got through the initial weeks, an internal track record of success would be created within him, an inner knowing based on the fact that he was attending college and his lectures.

As is usually the case when our level of selfhood is low, situations seem to get complicated. Prior to going to college, Wallace worried about every possible aspect of the scenario facing him. He wanted his anxiety to disappear within a few days, to settle fully and comfortably into his new life away from home for the first time, to make friends and fit in, all within the first few days. I explained to Wallace that while it was understandable that he would want this, he was being completely unrealistic. I advised him that this would take several weeks, and initially he should create a small number of goals, and focus on attaining these goals.

I suggested three goals: that he travel to his new college city every Sunday, go to the college every day no matter how much he felt like not doing so, and he attend as many lectures as he possibly could, without feeling pressure to attend every single lecture. The first week in college was very tough for him. Getting on the bus to college every morning was itself a harrowing experience, largely because the bus was taking him right into the lion's den. He experienced huge anxiety before and during lectures. He went to most of his lectures that week, but he could not manage some, such was the level of his anxiety at times. Wallace was filled with fear and self-doubt, wanting everything including socialising to work perfectly, and for his distress to end immediately. Finding the whole situation quite overwhelming, he became preoccupied with big issues, such as 'I knew I would never be able for college', 'this anxiety will never go away', and 'I will never be able to have a proper life'. I had anticipated this reaction, and had forewarned him that this was precisely how he would find himself thinking. On the phone, I listened intently, honouring his experience, and then reminded him of some of the key topics we had been working on. Focus on three goals, no more: forget the huge questions for now. I suggested that he repeatedly bring himself back to the present, to what was his current reality and the next thing to be addressed, rather than succumb to the temptation to race ahead of himself into tomorrow, next week, next year. I recommended that he should not engage in analysis of the situation. This is a time for doing, for *action*, not for analysing. It was far too early for that.

During his first week at college, Wallace attended around 60 per cent of his lectures, quite an achievement for someone who was convinced he could not even go to the college, never mind sit through lectures. When we met at the end of his first week, Wallace was preoccupied with what he had *not* achieved, including the lectures he had not attended. I praised him for sticking with the process even though he felt he could not. I reassured him that things were going according to plan. I advised him that while the rollercoaster wasn't over yet, he could feel proud of himself and what he was doing.

The following Sunday, Wallace again experienced considerable anxiety about leaving home for college. He conveyed his self-doubt to me by text message. I advised him to stick to our plan, to do rather than analyse, to focus on the three goals we had agreed. We remained in contact most days during his second week of college, a week he found easier although there were many moments of heightened anxiety. As I reminded him many times that week, directly experiencing and challenging that which we are terrified of is quite a rollercoaster ride in the early stages.

When we met at the end of the second week, he described his experience in precisely those terms: a rollercoaster ride. There was a hint of excitement and achievement creeping into his demeanour. He could not believe he had actually been in college now for two weeks and had stayed for 70 to 80 per cent of his lectures. I focused on this in order to emphasise the point about self-perception. Because his self-perception all along had been 'I simply cannot do it', he was amazed that he now had done what he had previously perceived as impossible. To his astonishment, his perception of himself was changing before his eyes. Because he had not yet experienced a sufficiently long track record of success at college, he was not ready to trust in himself, to believe in a new, more expanded self-image. He was between two worlds, gobsmacked at the new world he had dared to enter, surprised at how his perception of himself was visibly changing after just two weeks. He could not deny this new reality. He had incontrovertible evidence: *He had done it*! He was quite amazed at himself, almost in a state of shock and happy disbelief.

Two months on, each week was getting progressively easier, although he still had some tough days. His need to be in contact with me had decreased significantly, as he was gradually finding his feet. Life was still quite a rollercoaster ride, but his new perception of himself ('I *can* do it') was slowly taking hold, built on the solid, trustworthy reality of action, of *doing*. This created a real felt sense of knowing within himself that he was able to do it. Previously, he would frantically seek external reassurance from others that he could do things. This rarely worked, and certainly not in a sustained way, because it was not originating from within himself, and it did not give him a felt sense of self-belief or achievement.

To maximise the supports available to him during this difficult time, I had encouraged him to make contact with the college counselling service during his first week. Since then, he had met with a counsellor every five or six weeks. At the second session, the counsellor suggested that he consider taking antidepressants. This interpretation of difficult experiences such as Wallace was going through is not uncommon, unfortunately. Doctors often recommend these substances in such situations, and it is not the first time that I have heard of a counsellor suggesting to such clients that they were suffering from clinical depression and perhaps needed antidepressant drugs. In reality, Wallace was experiencing a great deal of anxiety because he was confronting his fears, terrors, and his previously very limited self-perception. In outlining the pros and cons of taking antidepressants, the counsellor omitted one important consequence of taking medication: the effect on Wallace's self-perception. He already had a tendency to develop dependencies, usually on other people. Had he taken the medication and managed to continue in college, Wallace may quickly have become psychologically dependent on the drugs, which would have had a major counter-productive effect on his self-perception. He would have concluded that 'I was only able to do this because I was taking medication', which would have reinforced his already heightened self-doubt. He would then have had a big decision to face: 'do I continue taking the medication and, if so, for how long? Can I cope without them?' Had he taken medication, it is not likely that he would have experienced the transformation in his self-perception and the raising of his sense of selfhood.

This was precisely the practical lesson Wallace learned, a lesson that liberated him, and from which he will reap major benefits for a long time to come. Wallace need not rush to sort out his other concerns, such as social life and friendship. Indeed, to his surprise and delight, four months after the start of his course, many of these have already improved considerably. He settled in well with his course colleagues, he soon felt that he belonged within this group, and that many fellow students already seem to like him. Now, two years since Wallace began his second college course, his self-perception has changed greatly, as he now has a two-year track record of staying at college and dealing effectively with all of the challenges inherent in college life.

The following story is an example of the stark consequences that can follow our decision to refuse taking ownership and responsibility for ourselves. When she first attended me in her early twenties, Martha exuded anger and aggression. Martha blamed many people, including her parents and former teachers, for all of her current problems. I believe that she dreaded taking corrective action herself, although that was not how she saw it. She was not prepared to take any ownership of where she found herself in her life, or any responsibility for her journey toward recovery of selfhood. Her aggression and blaming were coping strategies, dysfunctional attempts to exert power and control. She chose to use her apparent bravado to mask her major self-doubt and insecurity.

I listened carefully to Martha's story, empathising with the distress she had experienced in her life, but refusing to join her in a blame game. Martha enjoyed the self-righteous indulgence of blaming. She would not countenance the fact that, whatever about the past, her future depended greatly on herself, her choices, her actions, the paths in life she chose to carve out for herself. Martha stopped attending me after four sessions. I believe that Martha was not hearing what she wanted to hear from me, and therefore chose to end our meetings.

From phone calls from Martha and her family over the following twelve months, it was clear that nothing had changed. Martha continued to create chaos in her own life and in the lives of many of her family, completely and conveniently blind to her own contribution to that chaos. Co-incidentally, eight years later, I was contacted by a mental health carer, asking for advice regarding Martha. The carer worked in a residential mental health service where Martha was now living. From my conversation with the carer, it was apparent that Martha had not changed her ways in the intervening eight years. She continued to blame others for everything, resisting all attempts to help her take ownership and responsibility for herself. Martha was even more entrenched in her seriously dysfunctional ways of living than when she had attended me, which is always what happens when we continue to avoid addressing key issues in our life. Martha's possibilities of living a fuller, more fulfilled life were slowly but inexorably slipping away, due mainly to her determined refusal to take ownership and responsibility for herself in her life. When we refuse to take ownership and responsibility for ourselves, the destructive patterns in our lives escalate, and the possibilities for our recovery of selfhood remain very limited.

5. Self-efficacy

Self-efficacy means having an inner knowing that you can succeed in a given situation, execute whatever action is necessary to manage the situation effectively for yourself, and bring it to a resolution that is satisfactory for you. You are more likely to tackle challenges if you believe that you can succeed.

People with a solid sense of selfhood have a strong sense of self-efficacy. They see challenging problems and situations as tasks to be dealt with effectively. Motivated people, they generally become deeply interested in and strongly committed to the undertakings in which they become involved. They bounce back quickly from setbacks and disappointments. People with a low sense of self-efficacy tend to avoid challenges. They believe that coping with difficult situations and tasks is beyond them. They focus primarily on what they see as personal failings and negative outcomes.

When we do not tackle what we fear yet need to encounter if we are to live a full life, our sense of selfhood deteriorates. We reduce our options, experiencing increased fear, anxiety, despair, hopelessness, sadness and depression. We raise our level of self-efficacy by *doing*, by building up experience in doing, in small incremental steps.

The components of selfhood discussed in this section relate to self-efficacy, and include self-will, self-generated security, self-confidence, self-belief, self-empowerment, self-expression, self-actualisation and creativity.

Self-will
Self-reliance, self-referral and self-directedness are also considered within this section, as they are aspects of self-will. We can develop the quality of

self-will by becoming self-reliant, and by cultivating self-referral and self-directness.

Self-will is often considered as synonymous with a range of undesirable traits including stubbornness, obstinacy and intransigence. Yet, many of the people who have had a profound impact in the world, such as Nelson Mandela, Martin Luther King, Mahatma Gandhi, Mother Theresa and Bob Geldof, have necessarily been strongly self-willed. Self-willed people carve out their own pathways in life, forging through resistances and blocks, resistances often placed out of greed, fear or ignorance.

The quality of self-will is both revered and feared. The human herd instinct often encourages and sometimes seems to demand sameness, subordination, repression and suppression of our true selves. Self-will is the opposite of this. People who embody self-will often provoke envy and jealousy, perhaps because they remind us (sometimes intentionally, often unintentionally) of our own potential that we may not yet have developed and realised.

People who have a strong sense of self-will tend to be autonomous and self-determined. They are guided in their lives primarily from within themselves. They may take the views and advice of others on board, but in the end they make their own decisions. Autonomy means being self-governed, having free will, coupled with the ability to identify, confront and solve problems. Self-determination means determining a course of action yourself, being the main shaper, driver and decision-maker in your own life.

Self-reliance is the characteristic of relying on oneself, one's own powers, efforts, capabilities, judgement or resources, rather than on other people. It means possessing the ability to manage one's own affairs and provide for oneself. Self-reliance is an inner knowing that you can effectively deal with the challenges life throws at you, looking principally to yourself for guidance and direction.

As a general rule, young people have an inner desire and need to become self-reliant. This desire is at the heart of the 'terrible twos', when the two-year-old embarks on the adventure of repeatedly saying 'no'. It is also at the centre of the conflict that often occurs between teenagers and their parents. If they can rely on themselves, a young person will be better prepared to deal with life, with challenges and changes, with the unexpected, and with the joys and losses that come their way. A balanced sense of self-reliance has a beneficial impact on our mental health and wellbeing. We all benefit from knowing that there is a delicate balance between self-reliance and being able to rely and depend on others when necessary. Self-reliance can be taken to unhealthy extremes, where the person never risks relying on anyone.

The decisions we make shape our experiences. We make hundreds of choices and decisions every day. Our methods and patterns of decision-making become second nature to us, and we generally take no notice of them. If our decision-making patterns cause us problems, we need to become aware of, understand and review these patterns.

There is a key instant in the decision-making process, the moment when we refer the decision for assessment and consideration. People with a strong sense of selfhood automatically check with themselves and then decide what is the best option. They refer the matter to *themselves*. People with a low sense of selfhood seriously doubt their ability to self-refer. They often want someone else to make the decision for them, to tell them what to do. They wonder what others might think, what decisions others might make in this situation. I call this 'other-referral', as the decisions they make are dictated primarily by what they think others might want and expect them to do, what others would consider to be the right thing to do in that situation. They are checking not with themselves, but with the real or presumed opinions, judgements and expectations of others.

Healthy self-referral is the pattern of referring the questions, issues and challenges you encounter in your day to yourself as the principle choice-maker in your life, which you are anyway, whether you accept this fact or not. It is important to develop this pattern of self-referral, since other-referral is a recipe for chaos. Its consequences include great unhappiness, stress, distress, powerlessness and repeated disappointment. Other-referral eats away at your mental wellness and wellbeing, and is a common feature of mental health problems such as anxiety, depression, eating disorders, obsessive-compulsive disorder, bipolar disorder and schizophrenia. Working to change your pattern of referral from others to yourself will also help to raise your sense of selfhood.

Every behaviour pattern has its rewards, as perceived by the individual who chooses that behaviour, otherwise the person would not choose it. Using other-referral minimises the perceived risk-taking involved in self-referral, including the risk of making 'wrong' decisions, or that other people may disapprove of your choices. It is impossible to have a solid sense of selfhood if you constantly other-refer.

The habit of other-referral rarely provides more than a momentary feeling of relief. It is invariably followed by yet another surge of anxiety and self-doubt as its impact quickly evaporates. While choosing to seek advice from other people has its place, be firm with yourself that any action you undertake ultimately originates from self-referral. Weigh up the advice you receive, and you then decide what course of action to take, if any.

There needs to be a balance between giving and receiving, a sharing of responsibility and workload. Healthy self-referral does not mean that you always do what you want to do, irrespective of the needs of others. A person who is practising healthy self-referral will generally be more than willing to do their fair share. They know that they will be mindful of their own needs. They will be there for others in a balanced, effective way, but not at the expense of habitually negating their own needs, as people who practise other-referral regularly do, often at great cost to themselves.

People with a healthy sense of self-referral and selfhood will not be over-sensitive regarding how other people perceive them. They are therefore less likely to be easily hurt. By regularly practising self-referral, you develop confidence in your own decisions, values, priorities, opinions and reference points. You become happy in your own skin, content in the knowledge that you are in the driving seat of your own life. The more other-referring you do, the more chaotic your life will be.

Self-directedness, the quality of being directed from within yourself in your decisions and actions, follows from self-referral, just as exhaling naturally follows inhaling. You cannot become self-directed unless you also self-refer. Having first referred a decision or challenge to yourself, you are then directed from within yourself regarding the decisions and actions you take to deal effectively with the decision or challenge. People who habitually refer their decisions and challenges to others for their opinion and advice will also habitually turn to others for direction regarding what to do about the situation. People who are self-directed are the constructive navigators of their own life journey. There is quite a difference between functional and dysfunctional self-directedness. The latter leads to counter-productive ways of living, such as cutting off from other people and becoming very isolated within one's world. This is particularly likely when the person is totally directed from within themselves, never considering anyone or any other perspective apart from their own. Functional self-directedness involves a balance between being the shaper of one's life, while being prepared to listen to the views, wisdom and experience of other people when appropriate. It is about not being ruled in your decision-making by what others feel you should do. At times it means following your own direction even if no one else agrees with your course of action.

We can develop the quality of functional self-directedness. Adopting the opposite position (other-directedness) is akin to a driver handing the keys to the front seat passenger, and then waiting for them to drive the car from the passenger seat. This is your life. You, and only you, are the pilot of your life. Others can certainly help you, and be there to support you. But it is you who need to take action to get your life back on track and keep it on track.

We each have the power and the ability to direct and determine our own lives, whether we realise it or not. Jugglers know that they need to be in control of their process of juggling. We are all jugglers, often having many balls in the air. When we are not self-willed, we lose control of our juggling process, with so many balls in the air that they all fall down all around us. We may then decide to stop juggling altogether, or to over-control the amount of juggling we do, out of fear that we will again lose control.

The absence of self-will leads to considerable problems. A person who has little sense of being able to self-govern is caught in an unproductive spiral. This will increasingly lead to the erosion of any remaining sense of self-confidence that they can live effectively and authentically in this world.

ACTIONS

1. Identify your level of self-will

Reflect on the degree to which you are self-willed. There are two extremes: being pseudo-independent (an apparent state of independence, but which is really a rejection and an avoidance of contact), or completely dependent, never making your own decisions. If you feel you are very independent, ask yourself whether this is true independence or self-isolation through fear.

2. How self-reliant are you?

Become familiar with your habits and patterns regarding self-reliance. How self-reliant are you? Identify your current level of self-referral, the degree to which you check with yourself and others before making decisions and coming to conclusions. Become aware of your patterns of directedness. Are you primarily directed from within yourself or by others?

3. Your 'should's', 'must's', and 'ought to's'

Think and write about your 'shoulds', 'musts', 'ought to's', important aspects of your rules of living. Reflect upon whether each of these originated from yourself or others. Identify which of these you want to keep, and which you want to let go. Be mindful of the rules of living you have decided to let go, notice them when they surface, and each time gently remind yourself that you are not beholden to that rule any more.

4. Commit to becoming self-reliant

Your goal is to become fundamentally self-reliant, while simultaneously being prepared to rely on others when necessary and appropriate. Aim to inch forward slowly rather than try to change your self-reliance habits quickly. Every day, rely on yourself in a few situations where you would usually rely on others. Focus on the next small step rather than on the entire issue or ten steps down the line. Work toward self-referral. The optimum pattern is one where you predominantly refer to yourself, take into account the opinions of others when appropriate, and ultimately decide yourself regarding the most appropriate decision for you. When you notice yourself thinking about other people's possible opinions, bring your attention back to yourself, what you think and feel about it. Having referred the situation to yourself, follow through with action directed from within yourself.

5. Commit to forging your own pathway

Make a commitment to yourself that you will risk taking more charge of your life and of how you spend your day. You are the architect, the decision-maker in your life.

6. One step at a time

If you tend to avoid being self-willed and self-determined, think about some steps you might take. You may be keen to do so, or resist the idea out of fear, or both. Do it anyway, one step at a time. Resist making that phone call seeking approval, advice or affirmation, if so doing is a major recurring counter-productive pattern of yours. Provide for yourself what you seek from others. Practise taking little initiatives, small tasks, making them happen despite your resistance, and seeing them through to completion. Keep this up and you become more practised and confident in being self-willed and autonomous. If your pattern is one of being completely independent, consider what little steps you might make toward reconnecting with others. Take small steps, and keep taking them.

7. *Carry on regardless*
Initially, you may find that emotions such as anxiety, fear or sadness may surface as you work toward becoming more self-reliant. This is understandable, and can occur whenever we make significant changes in our lives. We become aware of emotions that we may have been blocking, and we may grieve for what we have lost as a consequence of living this way. Press on regardless.

8. *Practise referring back to yourself*
Always refer the situation back to yourself regarding both the *problems* and the *solutions*. Consider what *you* can do about it, what baby step possibilities exist for you. Stick primarily to your perspective, your gut feeling, what *you* believe to be right, proper and appropriate. Work gently and consistently to separate yourself from the opinions and beliefs of others, and develop your own values, priorities, opinions, and reference points. You develop these by *doing*. With practise you integrate them within yourself.

9. *Employ self-directedness in your life*
Practise being directed from within yourself regarding the choices and decisions you make. Initially this may generate considerable anxiety in you. This is to be expected, since you are taking a step into what for you is the unknown, the unfamiliar. This anxiety will pass. Allow yourself to feel whatever anxiety surfaces within you. Begin with the least challenging decisions you face. Risk making your own decision, and follow through on it, directed from within *you*. Maintain this practise daily, and you will become more accustomed to being self-directed. You will find that the backlash and overwhelm that you feared would happen rarely occurs in reality. The temptation to seek direction from outside of yourself will remain strong for some time. Expect this, and you are less likely to feel

disappointed when it happens. It is part of the process. Deliberately and consciously as you go through your day, risk making decisions for yourself, having first referred the matter to yourself for consideration rather than to others. Gradually, your confidence in your ability to be self-directed will grow.

10. Reflection
During your reflection times, consider the degree to which you exercised your will and autonomy since your last reflection time. Reaffirm your commitment to become increasingly self-willed in your life. Consider the degree to which you were self-reliant since your last reflection. Renew your commitment to being self-reliant, to noticing your patterns of self- and other-reliance. Consider the degree to which you self-referred and other-referred. Were there times when you could have self-referred more? If your pattern is to never refer to others, bear this in mind, and experiment with referring more to others. Reflect also on the many times you did actually refer to yourself during the preceding hours. Reflect on the degree to which you were self-directed and other-directed since your last reflection time. A quick review will do. With practise, you will quickly become aware of these moments during your reflection times. Resolve to remain focused on self-directedness, and to notice when you pass the buck, when you seek direction from others. It is okay to seek direction from others at times. It is your overall pattern that matters.

11. Affirmation
'I am my own person, self-willed in my thoughts, feelings and interactions. I rely on me. I refer everything primarily to myself, and in my everyday life I am directed from within myself.'

Self-generated security
We see the world not as it is but as we are. For example, during his second consultation with me, a person diagnosed as suffering from schizophrenia became visibly terrified in my office. I asked what he was thinking and feeling. He replied that he was wondering if he could get out of my office alive. Objectively, he was under no threat. I was the only other person in the room. But subjectively, because he had no

confidence in his ability to generate his own security (to make himself feel safe), he genuinely felt terrified. Through working with me over a period of several years, he has made a full recovery, and he is off medication for three years. I discuss this man's story in more detail in a case history at the end of this section.

Circumstances that would trigger no anxiety for a person with a solid sense of selfhood may feel overwhelming for a person with little sense of self, requiring major defensive and protective responses. A key challenge for us all is to protect ourselves in our everyday dealings with people and with life. The degree to which we feel unsafe and under threat parallels our level of selfhood. People with a solid sense of selfhood have a solid sense of safety and security. This inner knowing is so second nature to them that they are generally unaware of it.

People with a low sense of selfhood feel unsafe most of the time. Feeling constantly under threat, they may go to great lengths to create some vestige of safety in their lives. They are convinced that they cannot generate safety and security from within themselves. The only options they see are to minimise their exposure to perceived threat by controlling their environment as much as possible, or to become dependent on others, in order to maintain some semblance of safety and security. Perceiving situations as desperate, they may respond with desperate actions including avoidance, panic, or spending hours ruminating about the situation. They frantically plan strategies they hope will help but in which they have little confidence. They repeatedly miss out on many of life's opportunities, causing them great sadness, which they may seek to diminish through distractions of various kinds.

Not feeling able to protect oneself is a common characteristic of people diagnosed with mental health problems, including eating disorders, depression, obsessive-compulsive disorder, bipolar disorder and schizophrenia. Feeling constantly unprotected and unsafe is a major contributor to the extreme withdrawal that is a central characteristic of schizophrenia, a condition characterised by a catastrophic level of loss of selfhood.

People who know they can generally make themselves safe rarely think about it. People who have little or no confidence that they can protect themselves are constantly aware of this painful reality. The lengths to which we will go in order to protect ourselves parallels how unsafe we feel and our level of loss of selfhood.

ACTIONS

1. Identify your level of self-protection and self-generated security
Do you generally feel safe and secure, or do you experience a pervasive sense of dread and threat, feeling unsafe most of the time? Identifying where you currently are in terms of self-protection and self-generated security is the first step toward working on it.

2. Fantasy-creating and mind-reading
Do you have a habit of writing your own version of events as they unfold? How often do you try to read the minds of other people, wondering what they are saying about you? Is this a pattern of yours? Does this pattern generally make you feel more unsafe, or less so?

3. Deal-making
People who habitually feel unsafe and unprotected tend to make deals with themselves, God, the world, or the individual situations in which they find themselves. They regularly make such deals in a frantic attempt to feel somewhat safe, to stay afloat and prevent them from drowning. Identify the degree to which you employ this strategy, and commit to gradually let go of this practise. These 'contracts' are only signed by one party: you. The other party has not signed up to the deal, so you risk being repeatedly disappointed. You are needlessly giving your power away every time you choose to engage in this practise.

4. Bringing it all back home
Whether your pattern is to create fantasies, mind-read, make deals or all three, the solution is the same. Commit to noticing this pattern whenever it surfaces. Bring your focus and attention back, from being outside your own space and on other people or situations, into your own personal space. Reassure yourself that although you may not *feel* safe, in fact you *are* safe, and that you can protect yourself and in time make yourself feel safe.

5. Link into boundary and personal space work, and self-reassurance
Improving your sense of self-protection and self-generated security is done in conjunction with work on your boundary and your personal space. Whenever you attempt to do something that usually makes you feel

unsafe, visualise your boundary around you. Keep your attention focused on your boundary, and how it keeps you protected as you walk down the street, or enter a shop, or whatever it is that provokes you to feel unsafe. It will take some time for this process to work, since you may have little or no experience of generating your own inner safety and protection. Keep up the work, and the previously unfamiliar (in this case, feeling safe) becomes the familiar, and the new habit gradually becomes the norm. If you regularly feel unsafe, and you have little faith in your ability to generate your own sense of security, you need to make self-reassurance a regular activity every day.

6. Safety reassurance

When you notice yourself becoming anxious or feeling unsafe, gently say to yourself that you are okay, that you are safe, that you have had these thoughts before and you have always come through the situation. Reassure yourself that there are plenty of actions you can take to protect yourself and make yourself safe if you really need to.

7. Creating a protection shield

Visualise that you have a beautiful, blue, fluorescent, bright shield all around you at arm's length. It is a powerful shield. This shield is there to protect you, to keep you safe. Hurtful things cannot get through this shield to you. It is strong and firm all around you, protecting you. This shield is especially strong in front of your tummy and your heart, protecting these areas from being hurt. You bring this shield with you everywhere. Whenever you feel unsafe, visualise this shield all around you. This shield will keep you safe. Keep this exercise with you, in your handbag, wallet or pocket. Read it, or visualise it, as you embark on anything that may increase your feeling of being unsafe.

8. My personal declaration of safety

Read this personal declaration of safety at least once a day.

> 'I am safe, right here, right now. Contact with others is generally safe for me. Although I frequently *feel* unsafe around people, I *am* generally much safer than I feel I am. This is because many of the threats I perceive do not actually exist in the real world. I feel these threats because I greatly doubt my ability to

make myself safe and to generate my own self-protection. These feelings are valid, as they reflect my felt sense of lack of safety. In reality, I am generally much safer that I feel I am. Although I may feel afraid, I will be okay. I can make myself safe and protect myself. I can take actions to make myself safe. Whenever the need arises, I reassure myself repeatedly that I am safe.'

9. Reflection: before, during and after
During your daily reflections, do a reality check regarding moments when you felt unsafe since your last reflection. Did what you feared actually occur? Were you really under threat? Reflect on the fact that you felt afraid beforehand, anxious and scared during, and afterwards felt either relief or immediately became preoccupied with the next possible threats. Reassure yourself that you were safer than you thought you were during that situation. Reassure yourself also that it is likely that you will be safe during the next few hours, until your next reflection time. Practise creating the safety shield and read your personal declaration of safety at each reflection time.

10. Affirmation
'I am safe. I can protect myself. I am the provider of my own protection, security and reassurance.'

Self-confidence
Being confident enough to adapt to changing, unexpected circumstances, and to deal effectively with the people we encounter is an essential ingredient of healthy selfhood and therefore of mental wellness. Your level of self-confidence is affected by how successful you have been at getting your needs met, how lovable, acceptable and capable you believe you are, and how safe and secure you feel within your world. All of the above are affected to a considerable extent by your previous experiences.

The idea that we learn by doing, considered by Maria Montessori as the most effective method of learning for children, applies to the recovery of selfhood, including the recovery of self-confidence. Your level of self-confidence may vary considerably across various aspects of your life. Even if your overall sense of selfhood is low, you have self-confidence in particular areas if you have an established track record of success in that field. I said recently to a person who frequently experiences low self-confidence that no matter how much I tried to persuade him that he could not drive, he would not believe me no matter how convincing I was. He would not believe me because he has been driving for years. He therefore has confidence in his ability to drive, he has an inner knowing that he could drive, a track record build up by doing. No amount of talk on my part was going to undermine his strongly-rooted confidence in his ability to drive.

By taking action, you increase your self-confidence. Fear decreases as self-confidence increases. We increase our self-confidence by taking actions that in time lead to the resolution of our fears and challenges. In areas where we lack self-confidence, it is not likely to return without appropriate action in that area of our life.

ACTIONS

1.   Identify your level of self-confidence
This may vary for different situations, relationships and activities.

2.   Identify how you handle your lack of self-confidence
If your level of selfhood is low, you probably live within a narrow comfort zone, rarely engaging in activities close to the edge of your comfort zone, since you have learned that doing so provokes considerable anxiety within you, and you don't like feeling anxious. This is understandable, but it is not possible to raise your self-confidence if you are always shying away from situations, activities and feelings about which you feel scared. Any avoidance strategies repeated often enough contribute to lowering your self-confidence. These avoidance strategies include procrastination, distractions, giving up easily, beginning but not finishing tasks, minimising risk-taking, and habitually sticking with the familiar.

3.   Confidence grows through taking action
Gaining confidence occurs through doing. You cannot talk or think your way to greater self-confidence unless you also take appropriate action. If you have not been doing so, attend to the little things in life to begin with. This might include organising your home, clearing clutter, creating healthy routines, and ceasing procrastinating. Becoming self-disciplined and developing persistence contribute considerably to raising self-confidence.

To raise your self-confidence, you also need to gradually address the tendency to always play safe. Some of us go to the other extreme, acting out with behaviour that is excessive and sometimes out of control, an attempt to bypass or to compensate for our lack of confidence.

4. *Small steps*

Give some thought to areas in your life that you would like to be different. Pick one or two areas that are the least threatening for you. Break these areas into very small steps to begin with. Accept the fact that you will feel increased anxiety. With repetition, this will pass, and you will feel glimpses of delight at your achievements and your consequently growing self-confidence.

5. *Reflection*

At each reflection time, consider how your self-confidence has been over the previous few hours. Areas where you felt less confident need more attention, gradually, one step at a time. You can use the areas you are already confident about to increase your confidence, so long as in doing so you do not confine yourself to the areas of yourself and of life about which you are confident, and ignore those about which you are not confident. This approach lacks balance, and will considerably limit your potential for growth.

6. *Affirmation*

'I have confidence in myself in several aspects of my life. I am working toward increasing my confidence in myself in the areas of life that I am less confident about.'

Self-belief

Self-belief and self-trust are considered in this section. Self-belief is an essential ingredient of mental wellness. People who do not believe in themselves experience a great deal of emotional pain, anguish, fear, anxiety and hurt. Self-belief fosters effective social interaction and the creation of a vibrant and diverse life, one where our needs are largely met. As is the case with the loss of other components of selfhood, loss of self-belief is both a result of loss of selfhood and a consequent parallel growth of self-doubt, and a cause of further loss of selfhood. Losing self-belief becomes a way of avoiding taking risks that might lead to further hurt, rejection and criticism, a damage limitation exercise. Lack of self-belief kicks in as a protection mechanism, as we opt for what feels familiar and safe. We thus avoid the uncomfortable feeling that often results from venturing into the unknown.

Not risking to believe in ourselves keeps us stuck in a narrow circle and experience of life. Much more is lost than is gained long term by choosing this way of living. Addressing our lack of self-belief involves expanding our comfort zone, and enduring the anxiety that inevitably occurs when we address our fears.

People with a solid sense of selfhood instinctively trust themselves. If you have a very low level of selfhood, you do not trust yourself, and you repeatedly question yourself, your opinions, thoughts, feelings, actions, relationships, and anything else that you do or are involved in. You feel pressurised in situations where something might be expected of you. Increasing your level of self-trust results in a parallel increase in selfhood.

ACTIONS

1.   Where are you on the spectrum of self-belief and self-trust?
A brief consideration of this question will yield your answer. If your level of selfhood is very low, you are likely to have very little self-belief. To what degree do you trust yourself?

2.   As a general principle of living, risk believing in yourself
You may find this quite difficult at first because it can feel safer and more familiar to not believe in yourself. If, for a period of several years, you have been focused on trying to get others to believe in you, then your attention has been predominantly focused outside your own space. Bring your attention back to yourself, within your own personal space, and risk believing in yourself.

3.   Pick three things about yourself you can believe in
Start small. Pick three things about yourself that are safe to believe in, the least threatening aspects of yourself that you can think of. As you become more familiar and comfortable with the ideas and practise of believing in yourself, take the risk of expanding what you believe in about

yourself to one or two other things. Stick with this level of self-belief for as long as it takes in order to become reasonably comfortable with the concept.

4. *Expand the concept a little more*
Risk believing in other things about yourself, based on your observations regarding aspects of yourself you can currently believe in, for example, situations you have handled well. You may have to jog your memory somewhat, as we tend to dismiss and minimise our achievements when our sense of selfhood is low. You will gradually become more comfortable with believing in yourself.

5. *Work toward trusting yourself*
If your level of selfhood is low, then initially this will present a frightening prospect. Carry on regardless. Make a decision that you will work toward trusting yourself, toward seeing yourself as being worthy of your own trust in yourself. You have done quite well for yourself in your own way, even if much of your energy has gone into protecting yourself as much as possible. You have been there for yourself much more that you may realise. You are worthy of your own trust in yourself.

6. *Start small, baby steps*
Begin by taking the risk of trusting in aspects of yourself that you find the least threatening, aspects that you can accept without too much difficulty, that you know to be true. If you think about it, you will find many examples of thoughts, feelings, decisions and actions that made sense and that worked for you, in which you can trust. Regard these as examples of your wisdom, intelligence and decision-making abilities. Initially, you may reject this because trusting yourself may seem too terrifying. Stick with it and, over time, you will come to trust in yourself.

7. *Reflection*
During your daily reflection times, consider the degree to which you believed in yourself since your last reflection time. Note the aspects of yourself you did believe in, including the most simple of tasks such as your ability to make a nice cup of tea, dress yourself, go for a walk, to drive or cycle, for example. The little things add up. Renew your commitment to believing in yourself until your next reflection time. Consider the degree

to which you trusted yourself since your last self-reflection. This need only take a minute. You may find that you trusted in yourself a lot more that you might have thought. If at times during your reflection nothing stands out, no problem. Renew your commitment to trust yourself.

8. Affirmation
'I believe in myself. I trust myself.'

Self-empowerment

A recurring theme among many people, including those who develop mental health problems, is the belief that they have little or no power. They generally feel powerless to make their own decisions, to make things happen in their lives, when and how they want them to. They are convinced that they do not possess inner power, and they live accordingly. In people who have been diagnosed with a mental health problem, this perceived loss of inner power parallels both the level of loss of selfhood and the level of the mental health problem, since all three are intimately linked to each other. Helping people to reconnect with their inner power promotes both the regaining of selfhood and the alleviation of the mental health problem.

We human beings have the ability to convince ourselves of many things. People who do not *believe* they have any power live as if this is a *fact*, which is not the case. They continually hand their power over to others. The people to whom this power is given frequently neither realise this is happening nor want this power. Others are quite happy to take the person's power when it is handed to them, and then manipulate situations to suit themselves. Some people realise they are continually giving away their power but feel powerless to stop doing so.

Self-empowerment is a quiet, strong, inner knowing that one has the power to make effective choices, take productive action, adjust and adapt to changing and unexpected life circumstances. People who do not have this sense of self-empowerment are at a distinct disadvantage. They are far more prone to anxiety, depression and other mental health problems. They are less able to adapt and adjust to the unexpected, the challenges, losses and changes that come their way. Self-empowerment is a key aim of counselling and psychotherapy. It means taking back the power we give away to others, training ourselves to live consciously inside our boundary, in our personal space, our true home, the seat of our own power, from where we exercise this power quietly on an ongoing basis.

The importance of changing the little things and the effect this can have, and the power dynamics that frequently develop within relationships, was illustrated in the experience of Alfred and Katie. Married for over twenty years, Katie had over the years gotten into the habit of repeatedly giving her power away. Alfred generally occupied the space of decision-maker within the relationship. One day, Katie decided to take charge of two situations. Katie's car had a slow puncture. Traditionally, she would always leave such matters to Alfred. On this occasion, she went into the garage herself, dealt with the staff, and got the puncture repaired without Alfred being involved at all. Later that evening, Katie rang the local pizza delivery store to arrange the delivery of their usual Friday night treat. For years, Alfred had made that call. Alfred was generally very encouraging of his wife's attempts to recover her sense of selfhood. Both were involved in this change. He had to pull out of the space of power, to leave that space for Katie to enter into. She had to be prepared to enter the space now vacated by Alfred, take that power and use it.

Alfred was delighted by these two events, as was Katie, who felt greatly empowered by her actions. Little things mean a lot, and this is certainly true of the process of increasing one's sense of selfhood. The next day, Katie took further action. Whenever they travelled in the car, Alfred always drove. She again took the initiative, and shared the driving with Alfred, reclaiming more power. Katie's challenge is to keep up this pattern, so that this felt sense of self-empowerment can in time become embedded and rooted within her.

Power is neither good nor bad. It is simply power. It is what we do with power that dictates whether it is used for good or for ill. If you regularly give your power away or rarely feel that you have any inner power, then you have much to gain by working on reclaiming it.

ACTIONS

1. Where are you on the spectrum of self-empowerment?
When our level of selfhood is low, we tend to live at one of two extremes regarding our inner power. Many people habitually give their power away

to others. They may not realise they are doing this, as through repetition over many years, it can become an unnoticed and regular practise. Others hold on to their power like a dog with a bone, regularly undermining others in order to maintain control over them. This too is a feature of low selfhood. The person clutches tightly to their power because they do not have sufficient confidence in their ability to hold onto it, particularly when in contact with others. Where are you on the spectrum of self-empowerment?

2. Notice what you do with your power
Becoming aware of how you handle your power is the first step toward making the gradual change toward living in an empowered way. You are powerful. You may choose not to be powerful as a way of protecting yourself. Notice when you feel a sense of power within yourself, and when you feel powerless. Become aware of the power dynamic that occurs between you and others. Become mindful of how your sense of power changes in the different situations you encounter. Is your sense of being in control different when alone compared to when you are with others? Notice what happens to your power when you are with family, friends, acquaintances, authority figures, and when you enter a shop or walk down the street, for example. Notice what you do with your power over your boundary and personal space, and your patterns of letting others invade your personal space. Risk living through your own power. Remind yourself to think regularly in this way, every day.

3. Cultivate the habit of bringing your attention back home
Keep bringing your attention back to yourself, to your own power, within your personal space, the seat of your power. Always refer the situations you encounter back to yourself, both the problems and the solutions. Ask yourself what *you* can do about it. This way you hold on to your inner power. When you are with others, stay mindful of the issue of power. Notice what you do and say to yourself regarding your power. Perhaps you repeatedly put yourself down, feel less than good enough or compare yourself to others, always unfavourably. Gently and repeatedly, remind yourself that you are working on holding on to your own power, rather than giving it away so easily and often. Cease all analysis of what others might be thinking of you. This is disempowering, and it is a total waste of time. Your attention needs to be on your own

power, within your own space. Gently remind yourself repeatedly during the day that you have power, that when you give it away you can also take it back. You have more choices regarding your power than you may have thought. Choosing not to choose is itself a choice, and every choice involves the exercising of your power. Even when you give your power away, you are being powerful. The outcome is exactly as you envisaged. Your power is given away because you, the powerful one in your life, chose to give it away.

4. Experiment. Start small, baby steps

As always, start small. If your loss of selfhood is at the upper end of the scale as is the case of a person diagnosed with schizophrenia, you may feel intimidated by pedestrians when walking on the street. If this is the case, before leaving home, say to yourself that you will try to hold on to more of your power today than you would usually do. Visualise your boundary before you leave home. Reassure yourself that your boundary is there to protect you, to keep you safe, to keep your power inside your own space. Do this every time you leave home. It will work better on some occasions than others. Do not analyse the process, just do it. Do not focus on the outcome. You will gradually swing the pendulum of power back to you. Experiment. Pick a few situations every day. Deal with these a little differently, holding on to your own power. This is your private experiment, no one else needs to know about it. You will be pleasantly surprised that (a) you were able to do it (b) others whom you thought would immediately notice and chastise you, neither noticed nor cared that you were taking slightly different actions. It won't work every time, nor does it have to. This is a process. Do the work and keep doing it, and the results will look after themselves. Gradually build on this as the days and weeks pass.

5. Boundary exercise

Exercise your power by becoming more adept at managing your boundary. Practise closing your boundary when doing so feels appropriate, and deliberately opening it when you feel safe enough to do so. Visualise your boundary closing fully around you, and stay with that thought for a moment. Then, visualise your boundary opening, allowing what you want to enter your space. Keep this up, and in time, you become masterful of your power regarding your boundary and your personal space.

6. Switch from being problem-focused to being solution-focused
This single change will lead to a considerable increase in your sense of self-empowerment, provided you keep it in mind and act accordingly as you go about your business. Initially, you may need to force yourself to think about possible solutions rather than the problem. With practise this new way of approaching challenges will embed itself within you and become increasingly more effortless.

7. Let people's comments in one ear and out the other
This is a powerful way of retaining your power within the various interactions of your day. You do not have power over what others say or do. You can however decide your own reaction to what others say and do. If people say potentially hurtful things, these words do not have the power to change how you feel unless you let them. You can decide not to give this power to other people's words. Once their words reach your boundary, your personal space, their impact depends primarily on how *you* decide to deal with them. Decide that from now on you do not allow potentially hurtful words to penetrate your boundary. Instead, you keep them outside your boundary.

8. Declaration of my own power
Say the following declaration of your own power at least once a day, out loud preferably:

> 'Over the years, I may have given my power away. I did so because I felt afraid, unsure and insecure. I now take back my power, and I make a commitment to myself to stop giving my power away. I take back my power in small, baby steps. In every decision and interaction I am involved in today, I consciously bear in mind what I am doing with my power. If I do give my power away in situations or interactions, I notice this, and I gently resolve to take my power back, back into myself'.

9. Reflection time
At each reflection time, consider what you did with your power since your last reflection time. Were there times when you relinquished your power, when there might have been other options available for you that you chose not to engage with out of fear?

10. Affirmation
'I hold on to my power in every interaction and situation I encounter.'

Self-expression
The word 'express', derived from Latin, means 'to bring out of'. When you express yourself, you bring out of yourself what you want to communicate, decreasing the pent-up pressure you feel inside when you are holding in your emotions and other strong experiences. By expressing them, you release them, and you express what is true for you. Young people need to express themselves and seek to do so in a variety of ways. This expression of self can occur through words, actions or behaviour, such as the clothes they choose to wear, the music they listen to, the company they keep. As we get older, many of us fall into habits and patterns of non-expression. This is unfortunate, since lack of self-expression contributes to the sadness, unhappiness and loneliness experienced by so many people. It is also a major contributor to the onset of the distress and overwhelm that becomes diagnosed as depression, manic depression, eating disorders, schizophrenia and other mental illnesses, and suicide. Suppression of a person's experience of reality may cause or contribute to that person's loss of selfhood. Self-expression helps ease, release and prevent problems.

The degree to which people need to express themselves varies, as do the methods of self-expression. There is no one right way that applies to everyone. Some people do not feel the need to express themselves to any great extent. Others may appear to be expressing themselves a great deal, and yet do not seem to be happy or contented. This may be because either the methods of expression or what is expressed do not truly reflect themselves or their needs. There may be other significant sources of discontent and unhappiness within themselves or their lives that are not being rectified.

Two groups deserve special mention. The first is the quiet young person who remains in the background, often seen as 'good as gold', 'never any trouble'. They rarely speak their mind. They give the reply they feel will satisfy others, keep them both out of trouble and out of the limelight. They have lost their voice. They rarely initiate conversation, especially dialogue that is of genuine interest and importance to them. Others struggle even to speak when spoken to. Many find it extremely difficult to ask for help or to acknowledge that they need or deserve help.

The second group is the joker, the person who always seems to be in great form, who rarely if ever shares with anyone how they really feel. They appear to laugh everything off, but inside many are lost, and hurting badly. Repetitive joke-telling and humorousness does not necessarily equate to inner contentment. It is striking how many supposedly happy people take their own lives.

As the experiences of Lydia, Ruth and Ivor demonstrate, expressing yourself can be an effective way of coming into contact with our emotions and expressing them, and getting our needs met. One of Lydia's patterns was to remain silent, to not express her feelings, to avoid contact with her own feelings. Lydia had been married for over twenty years. Many patterns had developed within her relationship with her husband. For example, every Christmas Eve, her husband went out with friends for drinks. Lydia was always left alone to wrap the presents and generally get the house ready for the arrival of Santa Claus. For years she hated Christmas, and Christmas Eve in particular. She had in the past tried to communicate this to her husband, but nothing changed. In expressing to me in great detail what Christmas Eve felt like for her, Lydia came into full contact with her own grief and sadness. She cried deeply. Mixed in with her grief were her own painful memories of childhood Christmases. Her mother died when Lydia was a child. She experienced great losses because of her mother's untimely death, losses that had not previously been properly honoured and grieved for. Her husband was a good, kind man, but he sometimes did not listen to her and unwittingly dismissed her requests. Having come into direct contact with the loneliness and sadness regarding Christmas Eve, she was more ready to communicate this to her husband, and to communicate her need for him to be there to share Christmas Eve with her.

Ruth was emerging from a very traumatic period in her life, which had seriously affected her level of selfhood. Self-expression was a key area for her, an area we particularly focused on in our work. Now in her forties, whenever Ruth visited her parent and siblings, she experienced a surge of powerful feelings including anxiety, trembling, and great restlessness in her body. These sensations were sufficiently strong for Ruth to avoid visiting her family for months on end, which saddened her greatly.

On one such occasion, while travelling with her husband to visit her parents, Ruth felt the usual build-up of fear, anxiety and restlessness. For the first time ever, she articulated what she was feeling. In the car she simply stated, loudly and definitely, 'I feel very anxious'. She talked briefly about how she was feeling with her husband. Within minutes, her anxiety turned into grief. She cried deeply, sobbing for several minutes, not knowing why, but she let it happen. She had learned from me that she did not have to know why she was crying. This feeling was then replaced by a feeling of lightness, ease and peace. Ruth felt that a burden had been lifted from her chest and shoulders. She would typically arrive at her parents' house feeling tense and hyped up, feeling that she had to leave within minutes and usually did. This time, she happily entered their house, chatted away to her family, stayed for over an hour, and enjoyed the experience.

For Ruth, anxiety was a secondary rather than a primary emotion. Expressing precisely how she was feeling, and staying with that feeling, opened the door to the primary emotions of grief and sadness that lay behind her anxiety. After just a few minutes of direct contact with her primary emotions, the wave had washed though her, and she felt lighter, unburdened, at peace. She experienced a very different outcome, because she had chosen a different action. This is an example of the healing power of healthy self-expression.

Twenty-year-old Ivor had a real problem expressing himself. He typically avoided any self-expression, particularly when doing so might express his vulnerability. Ivor routinely avoided contact with himself and others. Although I had emphasised to him the importance of expressing his true feelings, he would rarely go there, resulting in protracted emotional distress for both Ivor and those who loved him. For example, he had arranged to attend a concert with his sister. The day before the concert, he became restless and angry, cursing and swearing, throwing furniture around the house. He repeatedly criticised others, what they were doing but should not be doing, and weren't doing but should have been. He did not go to the concert. His whole weekend and that of his family was spent in turmoil. All the while, he would not articulate what he was *really* feeling. He attended me the following Monday with his mother. We had addressed his need for self-expression many times: Ivor was not new to the concept. Yet, it took him thirty minutes to acknowledge that he had felt too frightened to attend the concert, and to admit that his behaviour over the weekend was due to the fact that he was scared but did not express it to his family, choosing instead to be angry, irritated and difficult at home all weekend. Because he had not been prepared to articulate his core feeling, he did not experience the wave-like flow of emotions passing through him to ultimate completion experienced by Ruth above. Instead, because of his choices regarding how to handle his emotions, Ivor remained stuck in the secondary emotion of anger all weekend, causing much additional distress for himself and for his family who wanted so much for him to be at peace with himself. His family felt powerless to help him, as he was not prepared to help himself.

The components of selfhood work together in harmony with each other. For example, healthy self-expression will also fit in with other components of selfhood, such as self-containment. Continuous self-expression to others of every thought, feeling and idea we have contradicts healthy self-containment, and is therefore not a constructive goal to aim for.

ACTIONS

1. How self-expressive are you?
Wherever you are on the spectrum of self-expression, that is your starting point.

2. Journalling
There are many ways to cultivate self-expression. Writing is one way to express your inner world. Diary-keeping has been popular for centuries for this reason. Writing on a daily basis is a way of taking time to connect with yourself and to express what matters to you on paper. Begin by writing truthfully in the language of emotion. While it is okay to write about your experience of secondary emotions such as anxiety, numbness, depression, endeavour to write more fully about the primary emotions that lie beneath these, such as sadness, fear and grief.

3. Express yourself more accurately and fully to yourself
Observe how you communicate to yourself, your self-talk, discussed in detail on page 104. Do you communicate clearly and honestly with yourself? Resolve to become more familiar with the patterns of self-expression you adopt in your communications with yourself. Make this communication a channel for open communication, for free and honest self-expression.

4. Baby steps toward communicating more clearly with others
Take one step at a time, risks that to others might seem small, but to you may feel enormous. Begin speaking your truth, how you really are, what is really going on for you, in situations where there is not too much risk involved. Expressing yourself clearly to yourself and to others usually involves the regular use of 'I' rather than 'you'. Communicating in this way is more direct, and far less likely to result in the other person feeling threatened. For example, 'I felt very unsure, fragile, scared, lonely today when...' is a true statement to yourself and others regarding how you felt, helping you to connect with what you are feeling and need to express.

5. Practise clear communication
Practise becoming increasingly aware of how you are feeling and what is going on within you, and expressing this to yourself in simple, accurate language.

6. Reflection
At your reflection times, consider how you have handled the issue of self-expression during the hours since your last reflection time. Renew your commitment to be aware of the importance of self-expression in your life.

7. Affirmation
'I express my own truth, as I know and experience it, to myself and to others.'

Self-actualisation
Self-actualisation means reaching your full potential in life. This concept has at times been promoted as meaning that there are no limits to what we can do and achieve. This Utopian notion is not grounded in reality, leaving many subscribers to this idea disillusioned and disappointed. Inherent in every choice we make is the letting go of other options. We cannot be in two places at one time. We cannot have our cake and also eat it. There is a limit to what we can do. Perfect health throughout our lives does not turn out to be a reality for most people, and the ageing process in evitable, as is death. Accepting that there are limits, self-actualisation becomes an important concept, grounded in the realities of

life. Self-actualisation means developing one's potential to the full and giving things our best shot, whatever the outcome.

The consequences of a major lack of self-actualisation in our life include great sadness, low self-confidence, guilt, preoccupation with lost time and opportunity, making it feel even more difficult for you to move on in your life. Recovering the feeling and the experience of self-actualisation is a pleasant and selfhood-enhancing experience.

The four seasons provide a useful analogy to help us understand self-actualisation. Spring is the season of new growth, of renewal. Summer represents fruition, maturation and expression, the full development of the growth and potential initiated during springtime. Autumn is the transition between summer's full bloom and winter, a gradual slowing down, a process of retreat. Winter is the time of endings, trees are bare, sunlight hours are increasingly limited. This seasonal pattern is a cycle of balance, each season a necessary part of the cycle of life. Winter is as necessary a part of the cycle as spring. Winter brings closure, making space for the renewal that is just around the corner.

We human beings are at our happiest and most fulfilled when, as it were, all four seasons are evolving on parallel tracks. No matter what our chronological age, it is possible for us to regularly encounter and experience the key characteristics of each season. These are new growth (spring), potential reaching full bloom (summer), some things slowing down (autumn) and others ending (winter).

The lives of most unhappy people are seriously out of balance with regard to the four seasons. The commonest pattern is a great deal of stagnation (winter), with little new growth, stimulation and fruition (spring and summer). Other people live excessively in springtime mode, initiating many activities but rarely persisting with them, so they rarely experience the joy of fruition and the satisfaction of completion. This pattern causes intense frustration for themselves and others. Life gets extremely complicated, with loose ends everywhere. These people are often impatient. Forgetting that the seasons will not be rushed, they often become disheartened and disillusioned. Many people have this tendency, including many people diagnosed with bipolar disorder.

Our ability to self-actualise is enhanced when we are prepared to accept and work with what each season represents. This involves a balance between undertaking new challenges and experiences, working on and developing our skills and talents, carrying them through to fruition, and being prepared to let things go when the time is right. This may involve experiencing the emotions that accompany endings such as sadness and grief, thus creating space for new beginnings.

If we were to think of childhood in the context of the four seasons, we might presume that childhood is all about spring and summer, with no winter. The lives of young people are characterised by more endings than we might think. These include leaving home and starting playschool, leaving playschool to start primary school, leaving childhood behind to begin the turbulent years of adolescence, leaving a class or a teacher, the death of loved ones including pets, the ending of friendships and boyfriend/girlfriend relationships, the ending of career dreams or ambitions to be a great sportsperson. These are just some of the myriad changes, endings and closures that young people go through, the significance and impact of which may go unnoticed by others.

We might equally presume that the lives of older people would rightly be dominated by the endings, closures and stagnation of winter. Many ageing people themselves succumb to this belief. Ageing does bring with it closures and endings, including retirement, friends and family deaths, loss of health, degrees of loss of physical strength and agility, which may necessitate the gradual letting go of certain cherished activities. Nevertheless, there remains considerable scope for the new growth of spring and the coming to fruition of summer in the latter years of life. Many people have demonstrated this, such as Jimmy Carter and Nelson Mandela. Older people have accumulated much wisdom and life experience. Among some nations and tribes, the elders are revered for this reason.

Here are some examples of spring (new growth) and summer (fruition) among the more elderly in society. In the 1990s I was a member of Toastmasters, the international public speaking organisation. I recall being struck by a story and photograph in the monthly Toastmasters magazine. The article was about a woman over one hundred years of age who had just completed her icebreaker speech, the first speech a person makes as a new Toastmasters member. She was the oldest woman ever to have made an icebreaker speech in the history of toastmasters.

In September 2009, ninety-five-year-old Marguerite Faulkner from Tyrone in Northern Ireland won the Silver Surfer of the Year Award at the IMAGINE IT! Conference in Ireland. This conference was a celebration of older people and information technology, organised by Age Action as part of Positive Ageing Week. She won the award because she had developed considerable computer skills in recent years. Marguerite spent most of the day after receiving the award sending texts to family and friends to share her joy at receiving the award. Marguerite had some stiff competition, particularly from an eighty-seven-year-old female self-taught computer user, and a seventy-five-year-old who records his own songs on Garageband, a Mac editing software package. The previous year, Marguerite had her driving licence renewed for a further three years.

On a recent holiday, I was struck by a group of three people, as were many others in the resort. The group consisted of a husband and wife, and a sister. The man looked at least ninety years of age, the women slightly younger. One morning, I went to the beach before breakfast at 7.30 am. All three were emerging from the sea, having had their morning swim. They were constantly happy and contented-looking, regularly engaged in lively conversation with themselves and others, including the beach-pedlars whom most people did not entertain. Curious about life, they seemed interested in everything around them. Many people went to help them, but they gracefully declined help unless it was truly necessary, choosing instead to do things for themselves, remaining as independent as possible. They regularly showed affection to each other. It was obvious that they were here for a good time, that they did not see their age as a restriction to enjoying life. On one occasion, I overheard one of the women engaged in an animated and good-humoured debate about cricket with the hotel receptionist. There was an international cricket tournament on in the region at that time. These elderly people kept themselves open to possibilities, within the scope of what was possible for them. As a result, they experienced self-actualisation as a regular occurrence in their daily lives.

Coincidentally, on the day I was writing this, a client happened to tell me about her aunt, who was eagerly anticipating her impending marriage to a man she loved very much. Her aunt was eighty years old. These wonderful stories bring up important issues regarding stereotyping in society. It is very important that, like all of these individuals, we do not passively accept and buy into stereotypical notions, for example that there is no life after sixty-five.

Beginnings and endings are a normal part of life, the natural order of things. Our mental wellness is best served when we accept this reality, experience whatever emotions are appropriate to changing situations, and use our resources, including support from others as appropriate, to deal with the changes. This way, we integrate the various changes and their consequences, moving beyond them without incurring significant emotional scars, with the minimum of disruption to our wellbeing.

Many people choose to deal with life by protecting themselves from further risk and exposure to hurt. They reduce their contact with the outside world, take fewer and fewer risks, and they find themselves increasingly shut off from society. They may become depressed, which is often a protection mechanism to avoid feeling their sadness and pain and also to avoid further risk. The cycle of limitation is now well established. They experience little spring-like new growth. Since summer can only occur if there has first been new growth, they rarely experience fruition, their full potential. They rarely experience autumn, as the slowing down can only occur if there has been full fruition to begin with. Virtually every day of their lives is experienced as winter, bleak, bare, stagnant, lifeless and devoid of colour. Possibilities for self-actualisation become quite limited.

ACTIONS

1. Identify your current level of self-actualisation
Reflecting on your life, what is your current situation with regard to self-actualisation? This is your starting point. Identify where you are in the spectrum of the four seasons on Diagram 19. Use the diagram to identify were you are with regard to each season.

2. How balanced are the four seasons in your life?
Use Diagram 19 to identify the degree to which each season is alive within your life. Is there a healthy balance between the four seasons, all being active and flowing in your life? If your sense of selfhood is low, there may not be a balance between the four seasons in your experience of life.

3. Look for ways to balance the four seasons
For example, if there is too much winter and not enough spring in your life, look to balance this by initiating a small number of new actions, one step at a time, and seeing them through to fruition. In time you will experience satisfaction, competence and confidence as a result. See the

piece on action on page 52 for some ideas, or brainstorm and come up with your own ideas.

If you have too much spring and not enough winter in your life, address this by dealing with one task or project at a time, and seeing it through to fruition and where appropriate, to its completion and ending. Address the other loose ends in your life in the same fashion, one by one. Resolve to resist the attractive temptation to keep initiating new plans and then abandoning them all. Initiate fewer plans and see them through to completion. You will increasingly experience the pleasure, relief and increased confidence that accompanies regular completion of actions and tasks.

4. Small steps

Consider what small steps you might take toward expanding your world, toward greater self-actualisation. Begin where you are right now within your life and your world. Completing relatively simple tasks, such as

THE FOUR SEASONS

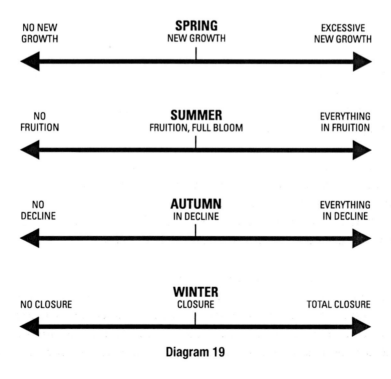

Diagram 19

cleaning your room, cooking a nice meal and cleaning up fully afterwards, addressing tasks you have been postponing, one by one, helps you to feel better and to begin experiencing brief flashes of self-actualisation. Each step you take may generate a sense of fear, since initially you may have little or no confidence in your ability to make things happen, to see them through. Begin with small steps, feel the anxiety, reassure yourself repeatedly, and persist. Once you have integrated these small steps within you, take further small steps. Continue this process, and you will find that you can gradually realise many of your hopes and dreams.

5. Respect and honour your losses

You may have experienced such a high degree of fear and self-doubt that you have felt unable to realise your dreams, to make your hopes and aspirations materialise. The sense of loss that usually accompanies this lack of self-actualisation can be enormous. You have possibly been unwittingly protecting yourself from feeling these losses for years by ensuring that you rarely think about self-actualisation and lost potential, and when you do, you quickly banish the thought from your mind using some form of distraction. Some unfulfilled aspects of your life may have passed their time of possibility, for example, a woman who only realises how much she wants to have a child when she is no longer able to conceive. Respect and honour your losses fully. Grieve as much as you need to, if and when that grief surfaces, and be open to channelling your energy into other areas of yourself and of life that may increase your sense of fulfilment and self-actualisation.

6. Reflection

During your reflection times, consider the degree to which self-actualisation emerged as an issue since your last reflection time. It may not have arisen, and that is perfectly okay. If it did, be gentle with yourself, note your reaction at the time, and consider other options regarding how to honour your need for self-actualisation in future similar situations. Briefly consider the four seasons, how developed they are in your life, and their relevance to you in your day today. Bringing this issue into your awareness during your reflection times will keep you mindful of it, and aware of the need to gently make changes and to create balance, when appropriate.

7. Affirmation
'I am working toward self-actualisation in my life. I have the capacity to realise my potential, one step at a time. I am moving gently toward a healthy balance between the four seasons of new growth, fruition, slowing down, and ending.'

Creativity

When we think of creativity, we may immediately think of the arts such as music, art and dance, and these avenues of creativity are very important. However, creativity reaches far beyond these into everyday living, actions, activities and interactions. We are all creative by nature. Through our creativity, we learn about the world and test ourselves within it: we explore and develop our mind, talents, thoughts, emotions and ideas. We creatively seek effective ways to express ourselves, to belong, to communicate and make contact with others, to make the most out of life. We get many of our needs met through our creativity. Creativity is so second nature to us that we are frequently unaware that we are in a virtually constant state of creativity. As Diagram 20 illustrates, our habits and patterns around creativity parallel and reflect our level of selfhood.

Let us look at the types of creativity engaged in by people at four different levels of selfhood, high (90%), moderate (50–60%), low (30%) and very low (10%). The range of the level of selfhood is a continuum: I use percentages here simply for illustration purposes.

A person with a high sense of selfhood will be creative in ways that express their already healthy sense of selfhood. They engage in forms of creativity as long as these are serving them well and are enhancing their experience of themselves and their world. They engage freely with the world as they choose. Their creativity flows easily and naturally. They have little need to channel their creativity into anxiety- and fear-infused survival or self-protection mode, since they do not experience life as a constant internal struggle. When one form of expression of creativity becomes no longer useful or possible, they move easily toward other modes of creativity.

A person with a moderate level of selfhood has considerable doubts about themselves, and their patterns of creativity reflect this. A certain amount of their creativity is accompanied by anxiety and fear, and is directed toward self-protection, particularly in situations where they feel

THE SPECTRUM OF CREATIVITY

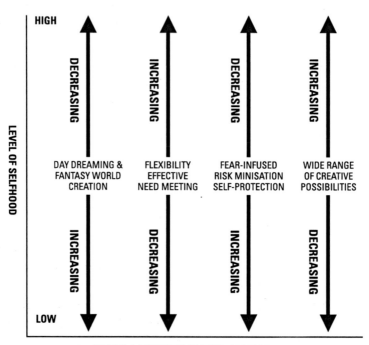

Diagram 20

under threat. They are more hesitant to express their creativity freely, but in many of the situations they encounter, they are still able to do so to a reasonable degree. As their level of selfhood is relatively solid, they use a considerable amount of their creativity effectively meeting their needs, including their need to interact with others and to deal relatively effectively with most of the situations they encounter. They have a sufficiently solid sense of selfhood to remain in good contact with the world and deal relatively effectively with challenge, though they are somewhat cautious in their outlook.

A person with a low sense of selfhood experiences a considerable degree of fear, anxiety, insecurity and self-doubt, all of which is reflected in their patterns of creativity. Their creativity is to a large extent taken up with survival and self-protection, and getting through the day with the least possible amount of upheaval. For example, people who have experienced a lot of bullying will constantly be thinking of ways of avoiding further bullying, sometimes going to great lengths to avoid any remote possibility of further hurt and humiliation. A young person who dreads reading in class may spend a lot of time trying to come up with creative ways of avoiding it.

People with a low sense of selfhood may find it very difficult to let go of a particular type of creativity even though it may no longer be serving them well. They doubt they will be able to successfully replace it, and they may have become dependent on their forms of creativity as a crutch, believing they cannot survive without them. People with a low sense of selfhood can generally still manage to use some of their creativity to get a number of their needs met, while maintaining some contact and involvement with the outside world, difficult as this is for them. In addition to channelling considerable amounts of energy into self-protection, they direct quite of a lot of their creativity into other ways of trying to get their needs met and escape from their distress, such as day-dreaming and creating imaginary fantasy worlds where they try to meet some of their unmet needs. For example, a young person who has no friends, who feels rejected by their peers, may direct some of their creativity into creating fantasy worlds and stories where they are popular, successful, the leader, where their wishes, hopes and dreams come true.

A person with a very low sense of selfhood, having major doubts about their ability to live in the real world and deal with its challenges, channels the vast majority of their creativity in two directions: self-protection and fantasy-world creation. Withdrawing from the world, into a very narrow band of experience of life that they control meticulously, living within rigid routines and rituals, takes care of most of the self-protection issues. The need to self-protect becomes a live issue whenever the person's routines are challenged or changed, when this need can become very strong.

They may create a parallel, make-believe world for themselves, one that functions and interacts in accordance with the individual's own personal wish list, but which has little connection with the reality of their life. In this make-believe world, they can imagine themselves having all sorts of adventures, without having to take any risks. Many of the features of schizophrenia are examples of creativity directed into fantasy because, having a virtually absent sense of selfhood, the person has no inner belief that they can be effectively creative and get their needs met in the real world. This parallel fantasy world may seem to work for the person on certain levels. It can become very alluring, and many people will prioritise time for their fantasy worlds above most other things in their life. However, living in fantasy worlds inevitably causes much angst and pain, because by definition it is not consistent with the world as it is, with reality. This can make it progressively more difficult over time for the person to live in the real world, connect with people, and the make and maintain friendships and relationships.

The lower a person's level of selfhood, the more likely they are to create a tunnel vision world, where they block from their awareness the many aspects of life that they find overwhelming. The aim of the exercise is to push what they do not want to contemplate out of their awareness. Much of their creativity is then taken up with creating and maintaining this tunnel of experience. Many people make the walls of this tunnel very thick, in an effort to minimise their risk of ever becoming aware of the aspects of life that lie outside of this tunnel. However, they cannot keep reality out forever, and from time to time reminders pierce through the tunnel and upset them greatly. Many react to this by withdrawing even further, and by reinforcing the walls of their tunnel to try to remove all possibility of further breaches. This cannot work forever, because reality will break though the tunnel into their life at regular intervals despite their best efforts to ensure that this does not happen. Difficult as it might be, it might be better for them to accept reality a little more, grieve for what is lost, and edge forward productively in their life.

ACTIONS

1. Get a sense of the ways in which you express your creativity
Take your time with this one, since expressing your creativity is so tied in with everything you do. You are being creative on an ongoing basis in your day. Even the most simple things involve using your creativity, such as making a sandwich, sweeping the floor and playing with ideas in your mind.

2. Is your creativity getting sufficient expression across the range of your life?
Consider whether your creativity is getting sufficient expression across the various aspects of your life, including work, leisure and relationships. Be mindful of the amount of passivity there is in your life. If, for example,

you spend several hours a day watching television, it is likely that you could do with more active, vibrant creativity in your life.

3. Consider other possible areas of creativity
If you feel there is not enough fulfilling creativity in your life, consider broadening your creativity horizons. Feel free to use the list of actions in the actions section outlined on page 58 to get you thinking of possible options. Put some thought into it. Is there any form of activity or creative pursuit that you have often felt like pursuing but never got around to? Why not have a go now. Working consistently with the contents of this book is an example of a healthy and productive way of utilising your creativity.

4. Consider your daydreaming
Everyone daydreams to one degree or another. Many people get their best ideas when they are daydreaming. Get a sense of how much you daydream, and the general content and patterns of your daydreaming. Identify the degree to which you use daydreaming as an escape from reality, as a way of avoiding taking action in the real world that might actually progress your situation.

5. Edge forward
If you use much of your creativity in passive ways, if your creativity has become somewhat deadened, or if you frequently use daydreaming as an escape from reality and from taking action, you need to make some changes. You need to become practised at taking more productive action. Any simple action that stops the cascading daydreaming and brings you back to reality will suffice, once you ensure that you are fully present in and aware of whatever it is you are doing.

6. Reflection
At your reflection times, consider briefly how you have exercised your creativity, the degree to which you have channelled it productively or passively. Reflect on your daydreaming, and consider whether you have more work to do to use your creativity more productively.

7. Affirmation
'I am a creative being. I channel my creativity in ways that are positive and enhancing in my life.'

Case histories

There follows two stories of people who have attended me, for whom aspects of self-efficacy were at the core of their problems.

Arthur's story illustrates the importance of self-actualisation. Now in his early thirties, Arthur's level of selfhood had been low for as long as he could remember, and it affected every aspect of his life. His low level of selfhood was a central factor in his being diagnosed ten years previously with bipolar disorder. When he first began attending me, he was very distressed. He was single, not by choice, but because he did not have sufficient self-confidence to risk being in a relationship. He had been on sick leave for the previous three months and could not envisage ever feeling confident enough to return to work. However, slowly, through his work with me, his level of selfhood increased. He did get back to his job as a teacher after six months on a part-time basis, later returning to full-time work after a further four months.

During the past school year, Arthur encountered many unexpected challenges. His school underwent a routine and thorough inspection by the Department of Education. Arthur had some challenging children in his class, resulting in quite intense contact with parents and the school principal. Because his level of selfhood had increased substantially, he was able to hold his ground and remain in his teaching job. Previously, his tendency would have been to run away from stress and pressure, as he had done twice previously in different schools. He now knew that running away did not solve anything, merely serving to enhance the stature of the challenge, feeding his fears and further eroding his level of selfhood. This time, he dealt with the issues that arose, one by one, without shirking them. This was the key to the increase in his sense of selfhood at this time.

As the school year drew to a close, Arthur was delighted with himself. It had been by far his best year at work since he graduated as a teacher. During the year, he had also made progress toward getting his needs met more effectively and taking more charge of different aspects of his life. For example, he joined a gym, and enjoyed a good physical workout several times a week. Arthur renewed contact with his old friends, made new friends, and created a better social life. As a consequence of his successful year at work, his summer holidays were the most relaxing and enjoyable he had experienced for years. This did not surprise me. Having had an excellent year at work, his level of selfhood had increased considerably, including his level of self-actualisation. The resulting feeling of wellbeing had a knock-on effect on other aspects of his sense of selfhood and therefore on how he experienced being on holidays.

His level of self-actualisation was higher now than at any previous time in his life. He felt content and quite proud of himself, a feeling he had not experienced for a very long time. As is generally the case when a person puts in the work to attain a high level of selfhood, they experience unexpected positive benefits, as did Arthur regarding the enjoyment he experienced during his holidays. This is in sharp contrast to the negative spirals and cycles experienced by people who have a low sense of selfhood and are not making progress. Provided he continues to persist with this way of living, as he has done in recent years, I expect that his level of selfhood will continue to increase, enabling him to reach ever-greater levels of self-actualisation and satisfaction.

The following is an illustration of the importance of self-generated security to a strong sense of selfhood and mental wellness. I referred briefly to Stephen's story on page 238 in the section on self-generated security. Prior to attending me in his late thirties, Stephen had been diagnosed five years previously as having paranoid schizophrenia. The level of loss of the components of selfhood, including the ability to make oneself feel safe, is at the extreme end of the scale in people diagnosed as suffering from schizophrenia. He attended me to explore possible avenues of recovery. I could see how Stephen was diagnosed as having paranoid schizophrenia. He saw threat and danger everywhere, when objectively there was none. Stephen's level of selfhood was at rock bottom, and this was a fundamental underlying reason for his problems. His paranoia was entirely understandable as seen from his perspective, given that one of his main experiences was that he constantly felt unsafe, unprotected and unable to generate any personal security for himself. This was borne out in his second session with me. As I mentioned briefly in the section on self-generated security, ten minutes into the session, Stephen looked terrified, and I asked him why. He replied 'I'm not sure I can get out of this place alive'. There were only the two of us in my office, and nobody in the waiting room. Objectively, there was no threat to Stephen, but he genuinely felt terrified for his life. He described the raw terror he felt almost constantly.

I focused on enabling Stephen to progressively raise his level of selfhood. In particular, I worked with him on self-protection and self-generated security, because his lack of these dominated his life, the reason for his fear-filled thinking. I reassured him many times that in general he was much safer than he thought he was. We explored the various experiences of terror and paranoia in detail. Stephen gradually comprehended that he was indeed much safer within these situations than he had thought. I explained to him that his terror-filled, paranoid thoughts were an outward projection of his inner fear and self-doubt. In public places, he would often have thoughts such as 'they're talking about me. I can tell by the way they are laughing that they are laughing at me'. Now, he realised that what he was feeling was more accurately expressed as 'I feel extremely unsafe, insecure and unprotected right now. I feel terrified, and I'm scared that there could be threats to me here in this crowded place'.

This change in his understanding brought about a considerable shift. Previously, his thinking was preoccupied by the supposed threat that could lie around every corner. Now he was bringing his attention back to himself and what he was actually experiencing. Stephen was now aware of his own terror and inability to make himself feel safe, whereas previously he was not aware of this and instead was entirely focused on the dangers that lay waiting relentlessly for him everywhere.

As Stephen was now truly aware of the role he played in his paranoid thinking, we had something substantial to work on. I used every possible opportunity to discuss self-protection and self-generated security with him. We explored his experiences of paranoia in great detail as they occurred. Our work became firmly grounded on what had actually happened within himself and his personal space in a given situation, rather than focusing on his projections into, and his assumptions about, others and the outside world.

People experiencing paranoia also experience their thinking speeding up, reflecting their terror. Thoughts keep coming, in an ever-more-frantic cascading sequence. The person creates an entire scenario in their minds based on their initial first thoughts. The initial thought may be somewhat based on reality. For example, a person across the bar happens to look in their direction. The person runs with this, creating a complicated sequence of events in their minds, a fantasy created under the influence of immense terror and great lack of inner safety. In a matter of minutes, sometimes seconds, they become convinced that there is a sinister plot to harm them in some way.

I used these experiences to get Stephen thinking about the accuracy of his interpretations of these episodes. I explained the futility and the dangers of attempting to read people's minds, a habit that generally results in erroneous conclusions. He began to experiment with these ideas in areas where it really mattered, in the real world. In public places, Stephen would remember our conversations, notice how he was feeling, and whether or not he was attempting to read the minds of others. For example, when in a bar and a paranoid thought sequence was beginning to gather pace, he was able to stop for a minute, bring his attention back to himself. He could now connect with what was going on for him, look around him, and reassure himself that at this moment, he was not in any danger.

In contrast, like a rabbit caught in headlights, Stephen would previously have become increasingly transfixed by an unfolding scenario outside of himself, that he was actually creating through outward projection of his feeling unsafe. I had encouraged Stephen to see things as they were, to resist the temptation to read into people's actions and gestures and create his own fictional version of events. His previous pattern of projection had being going on constantly for him, but at an unaware level. He did not realise that he was doing this himself. For example, if a person looked at him and then looked left, he often concluded that this meant he was in trouble. If they turned their face to the right, it meant he would probably be okay, for now at least. Stephen believed that he was just tuning in to what was really out there in the world, but he was in fact creating this scenario himself.

I suggested to Stephen that he needed to separate out the other person's action from the meaning that he (and not the other person) was placing on this action. I explained that he was relinquishing his power over himself to other people, most of whom neither wanted this power nor were aware that they were being dragged into this situation. Stephen grasped these ideas and applied them in real-life situations, and in time he was able to extricate himself from his previous pattern of terror-based paranoid thinking.

We explored methods of raising his level of self-protection and self-generated security. These included repeatedly reminding himself that he lived within his personal space and boundary, that this was *his* space, that he was safe within this space, and that there was much he could do in any given situation to make himself safe. When feeling unsafe, he would appraise the situation, see things and people as they were and be aware that any meaning he attached to them was entirely his creation and had little or nothing to do with other people or the situation. He reassured himself repeatedly every day that he was safe, that he could make himself safe and protect himself in any situation. When he experienced an episode of extreme fear or paranoia, he practised what we had done together many times in my office. He separated what was really there from the story he had created, and then reassured himself several times that what he feared would happen had not actually come to pass.

This practise had the desired effect. His level of self-protection and self-generated security began to increase, slowly at first, then gathering pace. Stephen made considerable progress in raising his level of selfhood, of which, for him, self-protection and self-generated security were key factors. Because he was doing well, his psychiatrist agreed to reduce his medication slightly, and I subsequently continued the process of gradually reducing Stephen's medication. Stephen has been off all schizophrenia medication for over three years. He lives a full life, goes where he likes, thrives in social situations, and has a level of selfhood higher that at any previous time in his life.

CONCLUSION

Selfhood and relationships

Our need to relate and to create relationships of various kinds is an important aspect of being human, a key human need. Our ability to deal effectively with relationships directly parallels our level of selfhood. Few things test our level of selfhood more than relationships, because so much is at stake. Entering and maintaining relationships involves many potential risks. In order to relate effectively to others, we need to have a solid sense of selfhood, and relatively intact and functioning boundaries. Relating to others represents quite a challenge to our sense of selfhood, our boundaries, and how we manage our personal space.

Different types of relationships create different challenges. The more intimate the relationship, the more there is at stake. This is one reason why many people with a very low level of selfhood do not have intimate long-term relationships, or do so at considerable cost in terms of the distress they experience when in relationships. A person with a low level of selfhood may genuinely feel that they risk annihilation within relationships, and therefore steer clear of them. When they do risk entering close relationships, they may struggle greatly. Successfully navigating the complexities of relationships, of holding on to our sense of self within relationships can be quite a challenge. Meeting both our own needs and desires and those of others (which may not always coincide with ours) can seem a daunting task, especially when our sense of selfhood is very low. Being in relationships often involves experiencing considerable uncertainty, the risk of hurt, rejection and abandonment. It involves putting our heart on a plate for another with all the inherent risks. Conflict resolution can be very challenging and become extremely complicated when our level of selfhood is low. We may consequently be tempted to protect ourselves by ending the relationship, or by tolerating disrespect and abuse in a frantic attempt to maintain the relationship. A person with a very low sense of selfhood generally finds it extremely difficult to relate in a balanced fashion, experiencing this as too risky. Either their boundaries are too thick or too porous, or they swing between these opposites.

What we feel comfortable with in relationships and in contact with others is influenced by what we feel has worked for us previously. A person with a low sense of selfhood may struggle with one-to-one relating. Others are relatively comfortable relating one to one, as long as the relating feels relatively safe, with little risk of exposure, intimacy or commitment, but struggle in a group. In a one-to-one situation, they feel more in control, and can use various strategies to deflect attention away from themselves when they feel they need to. They experience being in groups as far more intimidating, feeling a much greater risk of exposure, as it is much more difficult to control a group situation. They fear that others in the group may be observing and judging them while they are interacting with one person. They worry that the observers might see through their defences and notice their fear, self-doubt, insecurity, anxiety and sadness.

Others may feel more comfortable in a group, where there is greater scope to act, to mask, to get attention while limiting or avoiding the risk of intimacy or self-revelation. The safer a person feels within their relationships, the more they may be prepared to gradually let down their guard and let more of themselves shine through. Real and important issues can then be discussed and worked through.

Boundaries and personal space play a key part in relationships. Rebecca's experience illustrates one aspect of this reality. The mother of a three-month-old baby girl, Rebecca and her husband found the months after childbirth to be very stressful. I knew both Rebecca and her husband quite well, and I knew them both to be caring and conscientious people. However, three months after the birth of their baby, they were not getting on. Their relating consisted of virtually constant bickering. It was clear to me that the personal space of each of them was full to bursting point of stress, tiredness, and unmet need. There was no room inside their own personal space for anything other than their current, intense stress, no space to fully hear, meet and honour the other's experience. Rebecca felt overwhelmed with the responsibilities of being a mother, the isolation of being away from work and friends, and deprivation of sleep and pleasure. Her husband felt that he was constantly under pressure. As soon as he came home after a long stressful day's work, he was handed the baby, and felt he had to look after the child until bedtime. We resolved this situation through more effective use of time and space. Each ensured that they got some time, for themselves individually, and as a couple. Gradually, they tended to their unmet needs, and within weeks, both felt much better about themselves, their relationship, and their new family.

Many people with a low sense of selfhood lose themselves when in contact with people who are aggressive, loud, or even quietly assertive. They become frightened, acquiescent, and they retreat. Their boundary is not sufficiently intact for them to feel safe enough to stay fully in the moment. Working to increase your level of selfhood will help you deal more effectively with the challenges inherent in being in relationships. Notice how you react in different situations within your various relationships. Consider the degree to which your needs around relationships are met by how you handle relating and relationships. You may feel that your relationship needs are being met, for example, by avoidance. You may have persuaded yourself that aloneness is really what you want. It may be, and there is nothing wrong with that. Where it gets tricky is when we convince ourselves of this, do not properly consider this issue, and let many years pass. We may be avoiding addressing our fears around relationships and relating, and in the end we could be the losers. Notice the good and the problematic aspects of your relationships. To what degree does your level of selfhood and your patterns of choice-making contribute to issues within your relationships? Answering this question honestly may give you much food for thought and possible areas to significantly improve your relationships by raising your level of selfhood.

The peace dividend
The growth of selfhood is always accompanied by the growth of inner peace, in addition to the growth of the components of selfhood, and an inner-felt sense of dealing more effectively with the world. The gradual growth of serenity and inner peace is one of the greatest gains from the

journey of recovery of selfhood, in contrast to the inner chaos and turmoil that characterises the loss of selfhood. If you have worked through the book as recommended, you may already have noticed many changes in yourself, evidence of definite progress and change, of growth in your sense of selfhood. Many people report experiencing some progress after just a few weeks.

Personal testimonies
Here are some personal testimonies, written by people who have worked to regain their sense of selfhood through working with me according to the principles outlined in this book. Here is the testimony of a young woman, who has made major progress on her journey of recovery of her sense of selfhood, with consequent enormous benefits for her emotional and mental health:

> There is no comparison to how I felt before I started working with Terry Lynch and what I feel about myself now. It is very difficult to look back and describe in words how anxious and hopeless I was feeling.
>
> I have always had low confidence and self-belief, but after going on medication for my skin, the side effects caused whatever little confidence I had to completely erode. I felt like I couldn't do anything, even simple things like going on a bus, walking to the shop, socialising, everyday things people take for granted caused me so much anxiety and panic. I was afraid of absolutely everything and there was no way I could live a normal life. I felt like there was no light or hope in my life, that everything was in darkness and negativity. I had so much self-doubt, I didn't believe in myself enough to do anything. I basically felt like my life was over at the age of twenty.
>
> The main difference between then and now is that now I have a proper life and am living it. I am risking much more than I had been in the past, and reaping the benefits. I have done and am doing things that I never thought possible such as moving to a new city on my own where I knew no one, going to college, doing presentations, volunteer work, learning to drive, being more social with others and being more assertive. I am doing

things that I never thought I would have the belief or confidence to do. The possibilities are endless and I am so much happier and content than I was before. I also have a far greater knowledge of who I am as a person, and other people have also commented on how much I have grown in confidence. This work has taught me that I am the most important person in my life, and that other people's opinions of me really do not matter.

The road to getting here was the hardest thing I have ever done. At times I was so terrified and anxious, I thought I was just going to completely crumble under the anxiety. It has taken two long years of hard work, constantly reading notes Terry Lynch gave me, and risking and doing things that terrified me. But I am so glad I did this, as I now have a proper life and am doing things I never would have thought possible. I do get days when I have a lot of self-doubt and anxiety, but the difference is that I now have the tools to help myself cope with it. I do not feel like I am restricted like I was before, as I am taking risks. I might feel anxious before I do something, but I now have the belief that I can do it and that builds my confidence to keep going. I am not hiding any more, I am here living my life.

The following testimony was written by a sixty-year-old man, who has had his challenges and struggles in life, but has emerged with a strong and solid sense of self:

In the life long process of becoming me, ever changing, ever different, within the home, family, education system, religious upbringing, in relationships, in jobs, within organisations (including voluntary groups and Alcoholics Anonymous), and many other hobbies, pastimes and distractions, I have struggled to have the courage to simply be me. I am not a by-product of the influences of anything really. I am me, within my unique thoughts, feelings and emotions, growing and sometimes in conflict with life, but free. I don't need at a personal level to conform in order to be. I stand alone.

Below is the testimony of a twenty-nine year-old man. He is virtually at the end of a process of full recovery from schizophrenia, a process that revolved around the gradual recovery of his sense of selfhood. As I said earlier, the loss of selfhood experienced by people who are diagnosed with schizophrenia is catastrophic, therefore their recovery of selfhood takes correspondingly longer. When he first attended me several years ago, he was taking fourteen tablets a day, stuck in a deep rut, constantly at home with his parents, with no external activities in his life and no prospect of any on the horizon. Our work together revolved around the principles set out in this book. Twelve weeks ago, having been taking just a quarter of one tablet for the preceding three months, having discussed his situation in detail with me, he ceased taking medication. Twelve weeks on, he continues to do and be well in his life. We will remain in regular and frequent contact, to ensure that he remains well. He has just completed an honours MA university course, having obtained his degree last year:

At the early stages of attending Terry, I was often in a very restless state. The fear and turmoil within me were causing anxiety and frustration routinely, and my life had become without direction or stability. I had lost self-belief and self-trust from feeling lost and unwell due to disconnection in society, feeling judged in the world around me, and consequently this led to a lot of apprehension and fear. My daily life was filled with these feelings, as well as with obstacles to finding personal development and peace of mind, including a quantity of medication. This meant that the weight of expectation, obstacles and anxiety led to a life where progress had halted and hopes had diminished.

Over the course of working with Terry, my inner belief and trust has grown, and now I feel much better about myself. Part of the process is that I have achieved well on my career path and have overcome the overwhelming feelings of instability that had prevented prospects for a fulfilling and rewarding life. It is regaining direction in life, giving a purpose to it and connecting better in the world around me, that increases my self-esteem. The possibilities that now exist for me, that did not previously exist, are due to the career achievements, and the stability provided by working with Terry's expert direction.

I feel better within myself for having realised my abilities through achieving career goals I thought would never happen. I also feel less anxious as the self-doubts have been replaced by greater self-confidence. The consequent self-acceptance, arising from the prospect of stability in career and life, means that I now feel much more peaceful from day to day.

Next, the testimony of a sixteen-year-old girl, who experienced a major loss of selfhood prior to attending me. When she began attending me, she was taking antidepressants and tranquillisers prescribed by her psychiatrist. This doctor also recommended Zyprexa at one stage, a drug prescribed for schizophrenia and bipolar disorder, one of whose most common effects is major tranquillisation. She has now been off all medication for two years, and has not attended a psychiatrist for over two years:

> I used to be controlled by what I thought other people might say, do and think. I couldn't be free to be myself around people, including my friends. The reason for this is that I knew my inner peace could be shaken by other people's actions, or by what they would say. This fear would completely take me over, and throw me off course for some time. There was no room in my mind for other thoughts. All I could think about was what this or that person said or did, completely breaking down my inner peace. Now, my inner peace is a constant. I am confident and comfortable to be myself. I no longer allow things to affect my inner peace and if I do, I can quickly centre myself. If my inner peace was a lake and a pebble was thrown in, there would no longer be a ripple effect, whereas before, those ripples regularly turned into waves. I also imagine my inner peace as a rubber band. If any obstacles come my way and my inner peace is disturbed, I can quickly snap back into place. My inner peace is now calm, still and generally undisturbed from outside interference.

The following is the personal testimony of a twenty-one-year old woman, whose sense of selfhood had been low for years, which was an instrumental factor in her becoming diagnosed with and treated for depression:

Before I met Terry, I felt lost within my own personal space. I had little or no sense of self. I was full of convoluted emotions, unable to decipher how I felt and why I did so. Terry helped me understand exactly what I needed to do to deal with the pain. It did take work, but with continuous mental exercises I managed to find inner peace. Before, my personal space was crowded, which made me feel as if I was suffocating. I experienced emotions such as deep intense anger, thoughts of hopelessness and anxiousness, and I was so sick of feeling like this. I did not even imagine that the problem was to do with my boundary, personal space and sense of self, and that it was so fixable.

I began the work almost immediately, and every day I struggled with what I can now easily recognise as boundary issues. Before, I had allowed things from the outside world to invade my personal space and therefore disrupt by inner peace. My boundary was too open. However, the assignments and exercises I was given helped me so much in how I view myself, the world around me and how I can manage things. My inner peace is now calm and still. I feel centred, with my feet firmly on the ground. I am now in charge of myself and my boundary. I can decide what I let in and what I keep out. It feels so great.

The sense of achievement gives me a power boost too. I feel that this accomplishment will make me strive to achieve more things in the future. I cannot remember the last time I felt this together, this in-charge, this peaceful. I have learned that your personal space is key to how you feel, and now that my boundary is intact and my personal space is peaceful, I feel wonderful.

In their writings, these individuals are describing their experience of growing inner peace, happiness and contentment. Happiness is not an aim in itself. It is a by-product of how we live, of the level of selfhood we live with, the degree to which our needs are met, and the sense of autonomy, fulfilment and purpose we have in our lives.

The benefits you reap from this book will generally parallel your persistence and your commitment to the work. I wrote earlier about mental fitness, and I mentioned that ongoing work to maintain mental fitness is as necessary as ongoing physical activity is for physical fitness. Do not forget about the contents of this book and the work once you have completed it, as you would then risk slipping back into old habits. Selfhood is for life, a lifetime commitment. Maintaining a solid sense of selfhood requires ongoing daily work, though in time it becomes increasingly effortless and second nature. Most things that are worthwhile take time to achieve. Raising your sense of selfhood may be one of the most important things you ever do. Be prepared to give it time, and to continue to nurture your sense of selfhood on an ongoing basis.

Now that you have completed the book, consider working through it a second time. It is often said that by reading a book a second time, we pick up ideas that we missed first time around, and the ideas we did initially pick up on become reinforced within us. There is a lot of material in this book, and continuing to use it on a daily basis will help you get the most out of it.

The intention is to integrate the information within you, so you come to live this way instinctively and intuitively. You also have the option of dipping in and out of the book if you wish. You could choose to keep practising the actions, the daily reflections and the affirmations, in addition to regularly reading portions of the book. Doing so will help to integrate and ground your sense of selfhood on a solid foundation.

I would like to express my thanks and my appreciation to the people with whom I have had the privilege to work. It has been humbling to have been welcomed into their private and very personal worlds, and a great honour to have accompanied them on their life journey.

APPENDIX ONE

Affirmations

'My boundary is intact, and I am in charge of it. I live within my boundary, in my own personal space as I go through the day. My personal space is peaceful and calm.'

'I am centred within myself in all of my interactions and activities.'

'I belong to and within myself, within my boundary, in my personal space – my home.'

'I practise balanced self-containment in my actions and interactions.'

'I balance living largely within my comfort zone with a willingness to go beyond my comfort zone when doing so is genuinely for my own good, my own growth'.

'I talk to myself with gentleness, respect and understanding, which I deserve. Every aspect of me is valid. I continually affirm myself. I approve of me.'

'I have free-flowing access to the entire rainbow of my emotions.'

'All of my feelings make sense. I accept whatever feelings I experience, and I work through them.'

'I am attuned to and mindful of myself, my feelings and my needs.'

'Every day, I come to know myself a little better.'

'I make good contact with myself, including the aspects of myself I might prefer to avoid.'

'I am connected to, aware of, and proud of my sexuality.'

'I take good care of myself in every situation and interaction.'

'My relationship with myself is the most important relationship in my life, and I relate to myself accordingly.'

'I love myself, and I am my own best friend.'

'I empathise with myself and others in a balanced fashion.'

'My needs matter. My needs are fundamentally my responsibility. I ensure that, as much as possible, my needs are met.'

'I support myself in everything that I do. I provide my own reassurance.'

'I regulate myself as necessary, to bring myself back into balance.'

'I comfort and soothe myself. I am gentle with myself. I am capable of soothing myself in times of crisis or distress. I sense when I need comforting and I take the time to do so.'

'I am me. I see myself as the capable, loving and lovable person that I am. My identity is not dependent on anything or anyone. I am a unique, priceless, worthy human being. I appreciate myself. I hold myself in high regard. I am the provider of my esteem for myself.'

'I respect myself at all times. I honour myself in my everyday life. I assert myself as necessary and appropriate.'

'I practise a gentle and consistent self-discipline in my life.'

'I own everything about myself and my actions. I take responsibility for myself.'

'It is safe to be honest with myself. I commit to self-honesty, knowing that this will help to foster my personal growth.'

'I reveal myself to myself, all of who I am, what I feel and experience. I reveal myself to others as feels appropriate for me.'

'I accept myself, my current reality, and all of my feelings and experiences.'

'I forgive myself for the mistakes I have made in the past. I now give myself permission to move forward with my life.'

'I am my own person, self-willed in my thoughts, feelings and interactions. I rely on myself. I refer everything primarily to myself, and in my everyday life I am directed from within myself.'

'I am safe. I can protect myself. I am the provider of my own protection, security and reassurance.'

'I have confidence in myself in several aspects of my life. I am working toward increasing my confidence in myself in the areas of life that I am less confident about.'

'I believe in myself. I trust myself.'

'I hold on to my power in every interaction and situation I encounter.'

'I express my own truth, as I know and experience it, to myself and to others.'

'I am working toward self-actualisation in my life. I have the capacity to realise my potential, one step at a time. I am moving gently toward a healthy balance between the four seasons of new growth, fruition, slowing down, and endings.'

'I am a creative being. I channel my creativity in ways that are positive and enhancing in my life.'

INDEX

Lightning Source UK Ltd.
Milton Keynes UK
UKOW042327040713

213234UK00006B/104/P